THE MAURYAN POLITY

THE MAURYAN POLITY

V. R. Ramachandra Dikshitar

MOTILAL BANARSIDASS PUBLISHERS
PRIVATE LIMITED • DELHI

First Edition: Madras, 1932
Reprint: Delhi, 1993

ISBN: 81-208-1023-6

Also available at:
MOTILAL BANARSIDASS
41 U.A. Bungalow Road, Jawahar Nagar, Delhi 110 007
120 Royapettah High Road, Mylapore, Madras 600 004
16 St. Mark's Road, Bangalore 560 001
Ashok Rajpath, Patna 800 004
Chowk, Varanasi 221 001

PRINTED IN INDIA

BY JAINENDRA PRAKASH JAIN AT SHRI JAINENDRA PRESS, A-45 NARAINA INDUSTRIAL AREA, PHASE I, NEW DELHI 110 028 AND PUBLISHED BY NARENDRA PRAKASH JAIN FOR MOTILAL BANARSIDASS PUBLISHERS PVT. LTD., BUNGALOW ROAD, JAWAHAR NAGAR, DELHI 110 007

CONTENTS

PREFATORY NOTE

THE accompanying pages are an amplification of five lectures delivered at the University in 1929-30. The main sources of information are the Kauṭalīya Arthaśāstra, the inscriptions of Aśoka and the fragments of Megasthenes. In the first chapter will be found a critical examination of their authenticity and their value as sources to the history of Mauryan India. I have come to the conclusion that the extant Arthaśāstra is the accredited work of the chancellor of Candragupta Maurya. The inscriptions of Aśoka follow, to a large extent, this all important treatise. Though the fragments of Megasthenes could not be credited with much trustworthiness, they are used as supplementing the primary sources.

One chapter is devoted to the character and extent of the Empire. Three chapters on the Central Administration, and one on the Provincial and Local Governments follow. A careful comparison between the Kauṭalīyan polity and the polity lying behind the inscriptions of Aśoka, confirms the view, as will be seen from these chapters, that the polity behind the Edicts is the Kauṭalīyan polity. The last chapter is on the religion of the Mauryas in general, and that of Candragupta and of Aśoka in particular. A critical study of the relevant inscriptions, not to speak of literary evidences, has led me to conclude that neither Aśoka was a Buddhist nor Candragupta a Jain.

The correspondences between the Arthaśāstra texts and the text of the inscriptions of Aśoka are so glaring that it would be far from the truth to postulate the theory that the dumb documents left to us as legacy by Aśoka are essentially religious in tone or in character. In the light of new interpretations suggested for different terms and passages of the edicts, it is found that the inscriptions contain much reliable data to re-construct the political history of Aśoka and his predecessors.

In this re-construction of institutions, religious and political, checked and verified wherever possible from the accounts of classical writers, an endeavour is made to establish a thesis as to the character of the Government of the time. The constitution was a benevolent form of monarchy with democratic institutions, almost modern in character.

My grateful acknowledgments are due to Professors S. Krishnaswami Aiyangar and K. A. Nilakanta Sastri for valuable suggestions and guidance in the whole work.

LIMBDI GARDENS,
MADRAS,
11*th July*, 1932.

V. R. RAMACHANDRA DIKSHITAR.

CHAPTER I

SOURCES OF INFORMATION

Sec. i. *THE EVIDENCE OF THE PURĀṆAS*

HISTORIANS of Ancient India generally classify the original authorities for the early history of India into four definite divisions: (1) tradition mainly based on literary records, (2) contemporary literature, (3) notes and accounts of foreigners who visited India, and (4) archæological evidence.[1] Let us take up these sources one by one and categorically examine their value in reconstructing the Mauryan epoch of Indian History, especially its administrative side. Though the ancient Hindus did not possess the so-called historical sense in that they had not left accounts of the different members of a dynasty with dates of their accession and succession together with their activities in chronological order, still they had an historical outlook and a geographical outlook as well. Much is spoken to-day of the value of geographical studies and their importance to the historian. A similar study of geography coupled with history was attempted with success by the composers of the Purāṇic literature. Each of the eighteen *Mahāpurāṇas,* called such because there were numbers of other smaller purāṇas (in later days even the *Sthalamāhātmyas* became included into this class), deals, though not systematically, with five main topics

[1] *See* V. A. Smith, *Early History of India,* 4th Ed., p. 9 ff.

(*pañcalakṣaṇa*), namely, primary creation (*sarga*), secondary creation (*pratisarga*), genealogies of gods and patriarchs (*vaṁśa*), reigns of various Manus (*manvantara*), and the history of the old dynasties of kings (*vaṁśānucarita*).[1] In a recent valuable work of Von Willibald Kirfel entitled "*Das Purāṇa Pañcalakṣaṇa*"[2] an attempt is made to group together the common texts of these purāṇas on the five main topics. An early endeavour in this direction was made by F. E. Pargiter who in his works "*Ancient Indian Historical Tradition*" and "*Purāṇa Text of the Dynasties of the Kali Age*" was concerned chiefly with the last of the five topics of this class. Reducing these five topics for the sake of convenience to two—creation of the universe and the genealogy of gods and kings—we find the principal aim of the purāṇas to be a comprehensive study of the geography and the history of the then known world. The first two out of the five deal with the earth and its surface, atmosphere, climate, land and water forms, geography of vegetation and animal life including the habitations of man. The last three topics are the history of gods, of Manu the first king and of the other later kings. From this the object of the Purāṇa literature is evident that it is to impart a knowledge of the geography and the history of the land. If we are permitted to make a conjecture, the ancient writers conceived that a study of geography, *i.e.*, the various phenomena of nature precedes any study of history. Having thrown open the study of these purāṇas to the members of all castes and creeds it seems that the Purāṇic writers of Ancient India expect-

[1] Macdonell, *History of Sanskrit Literature*, p. 301.

[2] Kurt Schroeder, Bonn 1927.

ed every citizen of the land first to acquaint himself or herself with a scientific knowledge of the historical geography of the land.

If this position be granted, the Purāṇas are to be treated as the most systematic records which transmit ancient Indian historical tradition. No doubt the accounts are in certain places embellished unduly and sometimes unnaturally. Omitting such embellishments, the fact remains that any scientific historian of India can have ample materials which, if properly investigated, would go a long way to fill in the gaps left here and there in the various epochs of ancient history. The researches of Bühler have led him to conclude that inasmuch as *Vāyu, Viṣṇu, Matsya,* and *Brahmāṇḍa Purāṇas* refer to royal dynasties including that of the Guptas, they may be styled as historical Purāṇas.[1] The *Bhāgavata Purāṇa* takes us a little further and deals with post-Gupta dynasties also. These purāṇas above mentioned are invaluable to our study, for they transmit the Kauṭalīyan tradition, namely, Kauṭalya helped Candragupta, the first Mauryan King in establishing his rule by defeating the reigning king of the Nanda dynasty. Further these purāṇas enable us to add much to the history of the pre-Mauryan India by way of information.

According to this source of information the Nandas reigned the earth only for one hundred years and were succeeded by the Mauryas. This change in dynasty was effected with the help of a Brahman Kauṭalya by name. The latter had Candragupta anointed as King. The Mauryan kings reigned for

[1] *Ind. Ant.* XXV, 1896, pp. 323-28.

137 years and then the Government passed into the hands of the Śuṅgas. Collating all the purāṇic materials available the following is the categorical list of the 13 kings of the Mauryan dynasty with respective periods of their rule:—

Candragupta	..	24 years.
Bindusāra (Bhadrasāra)	..	24 years.
Aśoka	..	36 years.
Kunāla (Aśoka's son)	..	8 years.
Bandhupālita	..	8 years.
Indrapālita	..	10 years.
Daśona	..	7 years.
Daśaratha	..	8 years.
Samprati	..	9 years.
Śaliśuka	..	13 years.
Devadharman (Devavarman)	..	7 years.
Śatadhara (Śata-dhanus)	..	8 years.
Bṛhadratha (Bṛhadaśva)	..	70 years.
		232 years.

But some purāṇas like the Matsya and the Vāyu[1] mention nine kings of the dynasty omitting four names Daśona, Daśaratha, Samprati, and Śaliśuka and bring

[1] uddhariṣyati tān sarvān Kauṭilyo vai dviraṣṭabhiḥ|
bhuktvā mahīm varṣaśatam nandenduḥ sa bhaviṣyati||
Candraguptam nṛpam rājye Kauṭilyaḥ sthāpayiṣyati|
caturviṁśat samā rājā Candragupto bhaviṣyati||
bhavitā Bhadrasārastu pañcaviṁśatsamā nṛpaḥ|
saḍviṁśattu samā rājā Aśoko bhavitā nṛṣu||
tasya putraḥ Kunālastu varṣānaṣṭau bhaviṣyati|
Kunālasūnuraṣṭau ca bhoktā vai Bandhupālitaḥ||
Bandhupālitadāyādo daśamānīndrapālitaḥ|
bhavitā saptavarṣāni Devavarmā narādhipaḥ||
rājā Śatadharaścāṣṭau tasya putro bhaviṣyati|
Bṛhadaśvaśca varṣāṇi sapta vai bhavitā nṛpaḥ||

the reigning time of the dynasty to 137 years though it is actually 133 years.

Though the extant purāṇas do not agree in certain details and however conflicting the accounts may be, they have done a distinct service by mentioning at least the names of the various kings of the dynasty. Pargiter has remarked rather doubtfully that the account of this dynasty suffered more than that of any other and that this was because its great fame in Buddhism disgraced it in Brahmanical eyes.[1] There is no warrant for this supposition. It is yet a problem whether the Mauryas won great fame in Buddhism as Pargiter would have it. Our investigation into the subject leads to a different view. It is a controversial point to which we shall revert in a later chapter. Granting for our present purpose that Aśoka was a Buddhist by conviction can we conclude on this account that all the Mauryan monarchs favoured Buddhism? Surely Aśoka cannot be taken to represent all the Mauryan dynasty. There are other monarchs equally great and equally tolerant and generally accepted to be non-Buddhists. Thus the argument of Pargiter is a mere assumption and lacks the support of tangible evidence. It is again unconvincing. A remarkable circumstance in this connection is that the successors of the Mauryan dynasty, namely, the Śuṅgas and Kaṇvas or Kaṇvayānas are generally believed to be Brahmanical in their outlook and policy. This view is also shared by Pargiter. Do we get any

ityete nava bhūpā ye bhokṣyanti ca vasundharām|
saptatrimśacchatam pūrṇam tebhya śuṅgān gamiṣyati||

—*Vāyu,* Ch. 99, st. 330-36.
cp. *Matsya,* Ch. 272, st. 22-26.

[1] *Purāṇa Text of Dynasties of Kali Age,* p. 26.

more detail of these dynasties than that of the Mauryan dynasty? The accounts here are nothing more nor anything less than those for the Mauryan dynasty. Therefore to characterise the account of this particular dynasty as having suffered in the hands of its writers is to strain possibilities far too much.

Sec. ii. CONTEMPORARY LITERATURE

From the accounts given in the Purāṇas one fact emerges, namely, that Kauṭalya was the moving spirit during the reign of the first emperor of the Mauryan dynasty, if not also of the second. Recently a notable work on ancient Indian polity entitled *Kauṭalya's Arthaśāstra* was discovered by Shāma Śāstri of Mysore who edited and then translated it. The editor of this remarkable treatise and other scholars, European and Indian, examined its antiquity and came to the only possible conclusion that this work must be the work of the famous Minister of Candragupta Maurya. But scholars like Professors Keith and Winternitz have questioned the authenticity of the work and they hold, in spite of a volume of opinion based on facts to the contrary, that it belongs to the School of Kauṭalya and that it must have been a composition of the second or third century after Christ. The following pages are based on the theory that *Kauṭalya's Arthaśāstra* is a work of the fourth century before Christ and it will not be out of place here to examine the arguments for, and against, the theory and arrive at some definite conclusion.

Identification of Cīna.

It is said that "The mention of Cīna (*cīnapaṭṭaśca cīnabhūmijaḥ*) is remarkable in 300 B.C. and impossible if the name is derived from the Thsin dynasty (247 B.C.)."[1]

The identification of Cīna with China is indeed incongruous. Many a country in the Himālayan tracts is mentioned among the flourishing Jānapadas in ancient Indian epic and Purāṇic literature. In the *Vāyu Purāṇa*[2] the Cīna country is located in the Himālayan regions. The suggestion[3] that the term refers to Shīna, the Gilgit tribe which still retains the word as well as the silk industry is probable. The reference, then, is possibly to the Shin race which must have been famous for silk manufacture in those days. Again in interpreting this term we must take into account the circumstances under which it is used by the author. The *Arthaśāstra* in its reference to the silk of the Shin country distinguishes it from other kinds by calling it the Cīnapaṭṭa and this shows that the ancient Cīnas spoke a language related to Sanskrit. It is stretching the argument too far to say that these words have any kind of affinity to the Chinese language. What is more reasonable is that these were Himālayan peoples and indigenous tribes perhaps of Kṣatriya origin. From the chapter in which the term occurs it can be gathered[4] that the empire had to import furs and skins from the neighbouring country called Bālhava. Bālhavi, according to the commentator Bhaṭṭaṣvāmin, is again Himālayan deśa.[5] Added to

[1] Keith in *J.R.A.S.*, 1916, p. 136. Cp. Nag, *Les Theories Diplomatiques*, p. 118.

[2] Chap. 58, 83.

[3] See K. P. Jayaswal, *Hindu Polity*, Part I, p. 212.

[4] *Arthaśāstra*, XI. 2.

[5] *Vide* Bhaṭṭaṣvāmin's Commentary, p. 42, published in *J.B.O.R.S.*, Vol. XI, Pt. II. Unfortunately we are not in possession of the whole

this is the fact that Ch and Sh (Shin, Chin) can be interchanged in Shin, *e.g.*, push—puch.[1] Thus this will be no argument for pushing down the date of the *Kauṭalīya*. Above all the derivation of the name Cīna from the Dynasty of Thsin rests on doubtful premises.[2]

The Philological Data.

The following is another argument. "The metre of the ślokas (300 in number) in the *Arthaśāstra* is far more classical in type than that of the *Rāmāyaṇa* itself, and it contains correct Triṣṭubh stanzas in regular metre which is clear proof of comparatively recent date. . . . This fact, coupled with the fact that the language is not markedly archaic, suggests that we cannot look for a very early date for the work."[3] This leads us to examine the philological data which find mention in the work.[4]

The data furnished in the *Arthaśāstra* do not seem at first sight to follow Pāṇini. The inference is that either the *Kauṭalīya* was a pre-Pāṇinīyan work or Kauṭalya rejected Pāṇini's classification and preferred the old Vedic philology. Pāṇini's date itself is a bone of contention among

of this commentary as is the case with the other commentary *Nayacandrika* published in the Punjab Sanskrit series. We are thankful to the late Gaṇapati Śāstri for his full and learned commentary on this all important book.

1 *Hindu Polity,* Part I, p. 212.

2 See *Ency. Brit.,* 9th ed., Vol. V, p. 626, on China.

3 See Jolly's edition of the *Arthaśāstra,* Intro., p. 5.

4 See K. V. Rangaswāmi Aiyangar's *Some Aspects of Indian Polity,* pp. 120-123.

scholars, the lowest limit being B.C. 350.[1] Considered from different points of view there is no warrant to place the work before Pāṇini. It would appear that Kauṭalya must have known the work but rejected, as Patañjali, the great commentator on Pāṇini, did in regard to some details, *e.g.*, classification of speech. The *Mahābhāṣya*[2] like the *Arthaśāstra* classifies the parts of speech as four while Pāṇini and his school lay down twofold classification of the parts of speech.[3]

On this account can one call Patañjali pre-Pāṇinīyan or can he be credited with ignorance of Pāṇini? Apparently there was one set of scholars, perhaps a conservative school, who still clung to Vedic philology in spite of the rich fruits of the Pāṇinīyan school. There is evidence to show that Kauṭalya was not ignorant of the Pāṇinīyan rules. In Bk. II, chap. 10, he shows himself familiar with *Aṣṭādhyāyī,* a book of eight chapters in sūtras. Kauṭalya mentions names of some *gaṇas* like *prādi* and *cādi* found in Pāṇini's *gaṇapāṭha*. Further there are found in the treatise some technical terms of Sanskrit grammar. There are, on the other hand, facts which bear out the statement that Kauṭalya follows the Vedic system of philology. First, mention is made of the fourfold classification of the parts of speech.[4] Secondly, Kauṭalya

1. See A. A. Macdonell, *India's Past,* pp. 36-37 (Oxford, 1927).

2. Vol. I, p. 3, Ed. Kielhorn.

3. *Suptiñantam Padam* I.4.14. The term used in the *Arthaśāstra* *Nāmākhyātopasarganipātāḥ,* II. 10.

4. *Varṇasaṃghātaḥ padam|*
Taccaturvidham Nāmākhyātopasarganipātāśceti|
Tatra nāma satvābhidhāyi|
Aviśiṣṭaliṅgam ākhyātam Kriyāvāci|

uses the term *avyaya* in the masculine gender. But the *Liṅgānuśāsana* traditionally ascribed to Pāṇini uses the word in both the masculine and neuter genders. Pāṇini distinctly classifies it under neuter gender.[1] It may be remembered in this connection that the *Liṅgānuśāsana* is an important work consisting of 183 sūtras. It prescribes rules for determining the gender of nouns. For "unlike modern languages Sanskrit has a gender for every noun not necessarily determined by the sex."[2] In the same way we come across a large number of *upasarga* and *nipāta*.[3] The *Arthaśāstra* enumerates letters of the alphabet as sixty-three: *akārādayo varṇāḥ Triṣaṣṭiḥ.* The Pāṇinīyan Śikṣa also says that the alphabet consists of 63 or 64 letters, these being divided into five classes. Whether it is a *bona fide* work of the great grammarian is seriously questioned in different quarters. The book commences with a salutation to Pāṇini, and Pāṇini is often repeated in the verses which are 59 in number dealing with a variety of metres. Here as in the *Kauṭalīya* the author speaks in the third person which is a feature of all ancient works. The *Vyākaraṇa,* which constitutes the teachings of Pāṇini,

Kriyāviśeṣakāḥ prādaya upasargāḥ|
Avyayāścādayo nipātāḥ|

—*Arthaśāstra,* II.10.

Cp. Kātyāyana *Prātiśākhya* otherwise known as Vājasaneyi *Prātiśākhya,* Ch. VIII, sūtra 47-50.

Yāska's *Nirukta,* I.1.1; I.1.4.

For *nipātaḥ,* see ibid. I.1.5 to I.3.6.
Nirukta, Vol. II (Bibliotheca Indica).
Pūrvāṣṭaka.

See also Weber, *Indische Studien,* Vol. IV, Part II.

[1] I.1.6; I.3.; I.1.37.

[2] H. P. Śāstri, *Magadhan Lit.,* p. 32 (1923) Patna.

[3] II.10. Cp. Macdonell, *Sans. Lit.,* p. 267.

furnishes us with 14 alphabetical sūtras, Māheśvara sūtras or Pratyāhāra sūtras, consisting of 42 letters of which nine are vowels and thirty-three are consonants. Notwithstanding these, there is justification for concluding that Pāṇini is distinctly older than Kauṭalya even though the lowest limit of 350 B.C. is to be finally established.

Again the argument that the work contains correct *triṣṭubh* stanzas in regular metre and the metre of the ślokas is far more classical than that of the *Rāmāyaṇa* is no proof of the later date of the *Arthaśāstra*, but is a proof positive as to the antiquity of the epic, the *Rāmāyaṇa*. India was familiar with classical metre and *triṣṭubh* ślokas in the sixth century B.C. if not earlier. We know that as many as 43 stanzas occur in the *Bṛhaddevata* whose approximate date is fixed as later than 500 B.C. and earlier than 400 B.C.[1] On this account, therefore, to bring down the age of the work is inconclusive.

In regard to the archaic style, the *Arthaśāstra* certainly cultivates the peculiar archaic style of the sūtras and this is itself an evidence for an early date. Dr. Keith is of opinion that the language is not markedly archaic.[2] It is difficult to accept this view. For a reference to Appendix III of Gaṇapati Śāstri's edition of the *Arthaśāstra* furnishes the following among other *ārṣa* words: *ādēyāt, mārgāyukaḥ, ākāṅkṣēta, paścānhaḥ, pārañcikam, varṣārātram, rajjunā, apakrāntavyam.* It is further interesting to note that

[1] See *The Bṛhaddevata*, edited by A. A. Macdonell, Part I, Intro., pp. xxii-xxiii.

[2] *J.R.A.S.*, 1916, p. 137.

Jolly accepts this fact. He says: "Such archaic style is peculiar to Vālmīki, Vyāsa, Bhāsa and Kauṭalya."

Again the classical style of the ślokas and the metre need not be reckoned as serious arguments. Their evidence is not of much value in determining the date of a piece of composition. Whatever that may be, the apparent non-conformity to Pāṇinīyan rules, the markedly archaic style, and the system of philology which is distinctly Vedic, show that the author of the extant *Arthaśāstra* must have been considerably ancient.

The evidence of the Mahābhāṣya.

Yet another argument is that the *Mahābhāṣya* nowhere mentions Kauṭalya or the *Arthaśāstra,* as also the Rājadharma sections of the *Mahābhārata.* In his introduction to the edition of the *Arthaśāstra* Jolly himself has pointed out the futility of an *argumentum ex silentium.*[1] Absence of notice of a certain person or book is no warrant to conclude the non-existence of the person or the book. Patañjali did not mention Kauṭalya because there was no occasion for him to do it. Has he mentioned the name of Aśoka? On that account could we relegate the ancient Emperor Aśoka to the realm of pure mythology? It has been well said that the author of the *Mahābhāṣya* was not writing a history of Sanskrit literature.[2]

The evidence of the Mahābhārata and the Purāṇas.

As regards the Rājadharma section of the *Mahābhārata* it is difficult to accept the theory that that

[1] Introduction, p. 25.

[2] *Hindu Polity,* I, p. 208.

section must have been introduced in much later times. The *Mahābhārata,* at least a very considerable portion of it, is an early work, earlier than the *Dharmaśāstras* and the *Jātakas.* From the manuscript of its commentary by Vimala Bodhācārya we can gather some astronomical data which give the clue to arrive at the date of the Mahābhārata War. From this the epoch of the War is presumed to be the same as that of the *Vedāṇga Jyotiṣa* (11th or 12th Century B.C.).[1] Examining the date of the composition of the *Mahābhārata* "the archaic style, words and metre of the so-called duṣkara or difficult verses of the *Mahābhārata* furnish an additional proof in support of such a remote antiquity claimed for the epic on astronomical grounds."[2] "From a reference to the solstitial colure in the Ardhāśleṣa and Śraviṣṭha, it can be concluded that the *Mahābhārata* proper is as old as the 10th century B.C."[3] If the *Mahābhārata* proper can be assigned to the 10th century B.C. the Rājadharma section cannot be an addition after a lapse of ten centuries and more. Again, the matter contained in the Rājadharma section is probably older than that in the extant *Arthaśāstra.* This section of the *Mahābhārata* like the *Arthaśāstra* aimed at collating the different views so as to give them a practical shape for use to the man at the apex of the State. Mention is here made of different authors on polity but no mention is made of Kauṭalya. Again that Kauṭalya is indebted to the *Mahābhārata* is seen from the several references[4] which he makes to it. Perhaps

[1] See Annual Report of Mysore Arch. Dept. for 1927, p. 8 ff. Cp. Pradhan's *Chronology of Ancient India,* Ch. XXIII.

[2] *Ibid.,* p. 14.

[3] *Ibid.,* p. 15.

[4] Bk. I.6: IV.8.

Kauṭalya found the Rājadharma section of the *Mahābhārata* loose in its presentation, discussing subjects off-hand, and with no pre-conceived plan. Hence he felt the necessity for a systematic and analytical and elaborate treatment of the whole subject, and there is no gainsaying that he has succeeded in it. In regard to the *Purāṇas* some of them are admittedly older works than the *Kauṭalīya* and this is revealed to us by the fact of Kauṭalya's acquaintance with the *Purāṇas*. The *Upaniṣads* like the *Chāndogya*[1] and the *Dharmasūtras* like that of Āpastamba[2] mention the Purāṇa.[3] Āpastamba refers distinctly to the *Bhaviṣya Purāṇa* also.[4] The opinion of Weber and Max Muller[5] that the extant *Purāṇas* are independent of the works designated by that title in Vedic literature is not shared by Bühler who is disposed to believe that the existing *Purāṇas* are not altogether independent of those mentioned in the Vedic works.[6] That the *Purāṇas* had attained celebrity and influence in the latter half of the Vedic period is obvious. And it is in no way incompatible that Kauṭalya was familiar with their contents.

Kauṭalya, a figure of mythology?

It is indeed a strange position taken by Jolly that after all Kauṭalya may be a figure of pure mythology.[7] His theory is based on three grounds. First,

[1] II.3.

[2] I.6.19.13; I.10.29.7.

[3] See Bühler's article, *Ind. Ant.*, Vol. 25, pp. 323-28.

[4] II.9.24.6.

[5] *Ans. Sans. Lit.*, pp. 40-42.

[6] *S.B.E.*, Vol. II, Intro., pp. xxviii and xxix, especially the footnote.

[7] Introduction, p. 34.

Greek reports do not mention him. Secondly, Hemacandra relates marvellous stories about Kauṭalya. Thirdly, the minister Rākṣasa in the *Mudrārākṣasa* is probably a myth, why should not Kauṭalya be mythical as well? The first is an *argumentum ex silentium* which Jolly himself has decried. There is nothing surprising about the fact that legends have grown round the person of Kauṭalya. Every hero and heroine of note is raised aloft by mythological and legendary stories invented by the fertile brains of the writers. It is one of their accepted ways of glorification of the hero or heroine as the case may be. Apart from the legends which have grown around the epic heroes and heroines we can point to a number of such legends regarding others, for example, Aśoka. There are some Buddhist books like the *Divyāvadāna* where several legendary stories are narrated about that great monarch, some of them incredible and verging on the border of absurdity. On the strength of these legends could we portray the character of Aśoka in a light different from the established one? We cannot seriously attach any importance to the legends and begin to build a theory on them. As regards Rākṣasa in the *Mudrārākṣasa* it has not been proved on any evidence that the character of Rākṣasa is a myth, though Professor Jolly speaks of it as probable. It has been well said that from unknown to unknown is not a logical step.[1] Such straining and twisting cannot carry us very far. On the other hand, they leave us at the original place whence we started. The attempt made by Prof. Jolly to make out Kauṭalya to be a legendary figure cannot

[1] *Hindu Polity*, Vol. I, p. 210.

be treated more seriously than Bishop Whately's similar effort in regard to Napoleon I in his book entitled "*"Historical Doubts concerning Napoleon.*"[1]

Greek and other foreign influence?

Kauṭalya refers to a scientific treatise on Metallurgy called *Śulbadhātu Śāstra* (Copper), and mentions alchemy which was a late growth on the tree of Indian science, besides making a reference to *suruṅgā* which is from the Greek word syrinx.[2] These statements only reflect a tendency among some scholars to characterise all technical treatises as post-Alexandrian. It is wrong to think of a history of ancient India to commence with Alexander's march to India. India has a much older history and a more hoary civilisation and culture, the beginnings of which are still a puzzle to specialists in archæology, anthropology, biology, geology, and scientific history. We cannot fix with any satisfaction the actual origins of science and scientific knowledge in this country or any country whatsoever. From Alberuni[3] it is seen that India knew alchemy before Christ and now the theory of its Arabian origin falls to the ground. Vyāḍi to whom is attributed a knowledge of alchemy may be identified with ācārya Vyāḍi, the author of the *Saṅgraha,* a work on Pāṇini's School of *Vyākaraṇā* to which Patañjali was indebted.[4] As regards the argument that *suruṅgā* is from the Greek word syrinx

[1] Referred to by J. J. Meyer in his Introduction (pp. liii-iv) *Das Altindische Buch Vom Weltund Staatsleben* (Leipzig).

[2] Jolly, Intro., pp. 33-34. *Z.I.I.,* Vol. III.2. 1925. O. Stein's essays, pp. 280-318; M. Winternitz *Suruṅgā and the Kauṭalīya Arthaśāstra, I.H.Q.,* Vol. I, p. 429 f.

[3] Ch. XVII, *Alberuni's India* by Sachau (Trübner's Orient: Series, London).

[4] See Bhartṛhari's *Vākyapadīya,* Kāṇḍa, II, 483-5 (Benares Sans. Series, 1887).

it is obvious that the terms *śulba* and *suṛuṅgā* are words borrowed from the Dravidian languages. While the term *suṛuṅgā* is seen almost in the same form in the chief Dravidian languages Tamil,[1] Kannaḍa, and Telugu, the word *śulba* has its proto-type in the Dravidian *śeppu* or *śembu.*[2] Thus the term *suṛuṅgā* need not necessarily be from the Greek expression *syrinx.* Syrinx has been frequently employed in siege warfare of Ancient India. It was in use in India when Alexander invaded it Granting the word *suṛuṅgā* is derived from the Greek term it cannot be denied that the use of syrinx was known to India before Alexander's invasion. For in much earlier times the Greeks were living on the western borders of India on the Kabul river and also under the Persians in the Punjab as is evidenced by the use of Greek letters on Persian coins of that time.[3] There is again not much force in the argument advanced with reference to Indian alchemy. Jolly and Schmidt basing their authority on later texts on Indian alchemy believe that between the two possible hypotheses of a Greco-Syriac or of an Arabian source, the former derivation is more probable. They conclude that alchemy might have been imported into India at the commencement of the Christian era. But Dr. P. C. Roy has proved that its origin and growth are 'the outcome of purely indigenous traits'.[4] Thus these arguments lose their value in the light of more positive evidence to the contrary.

[1] See *Śilappadikāram,* Canto XIV, l. 65; *Maṇimēkalai,* Canto XII, l. 79.

[2] *Q.J.M. Society,* Vol. XVI, pp. 40-41, A. R. Sarasvati's article.

[3] See *Hindu Polity,* Part I, pp. 147-148 and 210.

[4] See *History of Hindu Chemistry,* Vol. II, ch. i and v (1909).

Priority of Bhāsa.

Again the contention that Kauṭalya was indebted to the dramatist Bhāsa from whose *Pratijñāyaugandharāyaṇa* he has quoted a verse is true. Kauṭalya makes no pretension that the verse in question is his own. He clearly makes us understand that it is a quotation from his statement *apīha ślokau bhavataḥ.* It is difficult to accept the theory that Bhāsa was a later writer and Kauṭalya must have therefore lived after him. The date of Bhāsa has been as much a vexed question as that of Pāṇini or even Kauṭalya. A number of dates ranging from the 6th century B.C. to the 7th century A.D. has been assigned by scholars mostly from imaginative reasoning. The discoverer and the learned editor of Bhāsa's plays M. M. Gaṇapati Śāstri has, thoroughly and in detail, examined the views of all critics and has come to the conclusion that Bhāsa is pre-Kauṭalīyan. He assigns 5th or 6th century B.C. to Bhāsa basing his arguments on indisputable evidence.[1] This learned view of one Mahāmahōpādhyāya is confirmed by the equally learned view of another Mahāmahōpādhyāya Haraprasāda Ṣāstri who accepts without any reserve the priority of Bhāsa to Kauṭalya on different grounds of which two may be cited here. (1) The king of the country mentioned in the *bharatavākya* of every one of Bhāsa's plays is one of the Nanda dynasty which preceded the Mauryas. (2) Bhāsa belongs to one of the older schools of Dramaturgy, and is unacquainted with the rules laid down in the *Bharata Nāṭya Śāstra* (now published in the Kāvyamāla series. H. P. Śāstri

[1] *Bhāsa's Plays—A Criticism,* pp. 74-75.

continues: "I have got a curious confirmation of the existence of the dramaturgy in Ancient India in the fact that Kauṭalya has classed *Kuśīlavas* or actors with the Śūdras. *Nāṭyaśāstra* says that the original *Kuśīlavas* were all Brahmans or better still of divine origin but they ridiculed the Ṛṣis and therefore they were cursed to become Śūdras. So their Śūdra-hood is later than the origin of the drama. As in Cāṇakya's time they were classed to be Śūdras, we are to infer that at that time drama was an old institution."[1]

Fortified then by the consolidated opinions of two Mahāmahōpādhyāyas of no mean repute we are inclined to assign Bhāsa to a period of antiquity not earlier than the 6th century B.C. It would not be therefore unreasonable to assign to the *Kauṭalīya* 4th century B.C.

Yājñavalkyasmṛti and Arthaśāstra.

Equally inconclusive is the effort of some scholars to fix the date of *Yājñavalkyasmṛti* in the 3rd century A.D.[2] and to bring down the *Arthaśāstra* to a later date on the evidence of several parallel passages. The close affinity of both the *Arthaśāstra* and the *Dharmaśāstra* of Yājñavalkya lands us in the difficulty to determine which was the earlier. There are three schools of thought. One holds the view that Yājñavalkya

[1] See *Bhāsa's Plays,* p. 54, footnote.

[2] The law-book of Yājñavalkya has been recently the subject of critical study by two German scholars. J. J. Meyer argues that individual authors were at the bottom of the law-books of ancient India in his learned work *Uber das Wesen der altindischen Rechtsschriften* (Leipzig, 1927). This assumption is questioned by Hans Losch in his new book *Die Yājñavalkya Smṛti* (Otto Harrassowitz, Leipzig, 1927). This provoked a reply from Meyer, in his *Gesetzbuch und Purāṇa* (Breslau, 1929). Here Meyer reaffirms the position which he has originally taken, in regard to the authorship of *Yājñavalkyasmṛti.*

was a pre-Kauṭalīyan writer. The second view is that whatever be the date of Yājñavalkya he drew his materials from Kauṭalya. The third school maintains that Kauṭalya lived in or about the third century A.D. (one date for the *Yājñavalkyasmṛti*), and the composition of the *Arthaśāstra* must have been about that date. Though arguments advanced by each school of thought are supported by evidence of some kind or other, the substantive weight of the argument is cast on the side of the first school of thought whose staunch supporter is the late Gaṇapati Śāstri. In the introduction to his edition of the *Arthaśāstra* the learned Indologist has examined this question in a scholarly spirit and his conclusion must appeal to every impartial student of Sanskrit literature. It would not be out of place to refer to some of his arguments as they are of much consequence.

(*a*) Viśvarūpācārya *alias* Sureśvarācārya in his commentary *Bālakrīdā* on the *Yājñavalkya Smṛti*[1] gives quotations from the *Arthaśāstra* of Bṛhaspati and Viśālākṣa, the predecessors of Kauṭalya Gaṇapati Śāstri says: "It is the proper practice of a commentator that he should supply deficiencies in the statements of an author advisedly left out to be learnt from other sources by having recourse to those writers who are known either as ancient or contemporary authority to the author himself, but not to those that are posterior to the author." He did not quote Kauṭalya because the latter was posterior to Yājñavalkya.[2]

(*b*) Yājñavalkya, the author of the Smṛti, who studied his Yajurveda under Vaiśampāyana, was a

[1] *T. S. S.*, No. 74.
[2] P. 6, Intro., Vol. I.

contemporary of Sūta of Purāṇic celebrity referred to in the *Arthaśāstra.*[1] In dealing with *Pratiloma* marriages Kauṭalya defines Sūta as a son begotten of a Brahman woman by a Kṣatriya and Māgadha as a son begotten of a Kṣatriya woman by a Vaiśya. At the same time he takes care to restrict the application of his definition in the case of Sūta-Paurāṇika and Māgadha, the panegyrist, both sprung up from the holy sacrificial ground of king Pṛthu.[2] "It is certain that centuries must have intervened between Sūta and Kauṭalya before the latter could have believed in the works of Sūta as Purāṇas of archaic celebrity.[3]"

(*c*) Shāma Śāstri's contention is that Yājñavalkya and not Kauṭalya would have to be regarded as the borrower, for there are certain technical terms which Kauṭalya appears to have used in a more original and appropriate sense. For example, *śapathavākyānuyoga* of the *Kauṭalīya* means 'trial of a criminal on oath' whereas Yājñavalkya's *ayuktam śapatham* means 'an improper oath'. The term *ayukta* in the *Kauṭalīya* means 'an official' while *ayogya* of Yājñavalkya means 'improper'. Gaṇapati Śāstri has pointed out against this, that *śapatha* of the *Smṛti* is in the opinion of Kauṭalya an unauthorised demand for statements on oath.[4] Similarly *yoga* and *niyoga* mean a 'privilege'. One having *yoga* is *yukta* and one deserving of *yoga* is *yogya.* Thus the difference between *yogya* and *yukta* is but nominal, and both really mean the same thing. It is then evident, as the learned scholar concludes, that Kauṭalya was

[1] Bk. III, ch. 7.
[2] Bk. III, ch. 12.
[3] Vol. I, Intro., pp. 6-7.
[4] *Ibid.*, p. 9: Jolly's Intro., p. 18.

indebted to the *smṛtis* and his position in respect of the *smṛtis* was that of a commentator. It therefore follows that the contention that Yājñavalkya is posterior to Kauṭalya is untenable.[1]

Evidence of the Pañcatantra.

A number of passages can be quoted from the *Pañcatantra* where explicit references are made to Kauṭalya and his Śāstra.[2] In a recent Annual Report (1927) of the Mysore Archæological Department the question of the date of the *Kauṭalīya Arthaśāstra* has been re-opened and an endeavour is made to reaffirm the generally accepted date of the work 350 to 300 B.C.[3] It is generally agreed that the stories in the *Pañcatantra*[4] are based upon the political maxims propounded in the *Kauṭalīya.* The Report referred to above says: "The titles, such as separation of friends, winning of friends, war and peace, the loss of one's acquisition and hasty action, given to the five books of the *Pañcatantra* are political ideas explained in no work earlier than the *Arthaśāstra.*" Again there is reason to believe that the author of the *Pañcatantra* is indebted to the *Arthaśāstra* for the use of the word *prakṛti* in the technical sense of sovereigns to be considered in time of war.[5] The interpretation of the term in this sense is Kauṭalya's own coining (*svasaṁjñā*).

[1] See Introduction, Trivandrum ed., Vol. I, p. 9; cp. Jolly, Intro., p. 18; Shāma Śāstri (1919) Ed. Intro., p. vii f; see also *Yāj. Smṛti* with Viśvarūpa Commentary T.S.S., 74, Intro., p. iv-viii.

[2] Arthaśāstrāṇi cāṇakyādīni|

—Bk. I.1.

sa auśanasabārhaspatya cāṇakyamatavittadanuṣṭhātā|

[3] See p. 15 ff.

[4] Ed. by J. Hertel and Dr. F. Edgerton.

[5] *mitraprakṛti* and *ariprakṛti* (*Ar. Śās.*, Bk. VIII, ch. 2; *Tantrayukti*, Bk. XV, Ch. I.

The author of the *Pañcatantra* uses again the very words of Kauṭalya when dealing with the objects of *lokayātrā.*[1]

This is not all. Some more passages are borrowed from different portions of the *Arthaśāstra.* According to Hertel the Kashṃirian recension of the *Pañcatantra* which bears the title *Tantrākhyāyikā* dates from about 200 B.C. It can be presumed that the *Arthaśāstra* which is repeatedly quoted must have been very familiar for a good number of years before the *Pañcatantra.* At the least an interval of a century would not be too high. Even Prof. Keith concedes that "it is however perfectly possible that the *Arthaśāstra* is an early work and that it may be assigned to the first century B.C. while its matter very probably is older by a good deal than that."[2]

Religious Data.

An examination *in extenso* of the religious data[3] afforded by the *Arthaśāstra* shows that it belongs to a period when the Vedic religious practices and rituals were in vogue. Great significance is indeed attached to the performance of *yajñas* or sacrifices[4] and there is an unreasoned belief in the efficacy and fruitfulness of such sacrifices. Whenever the kingdom or king was visited by *vyasana* or dangers, providential or otherwise, prayers were offered to the Vedic deities[5] like Indra, Varuṇa, Agni, Aśvins, Jayanta and others.

1 P. 1.1.

2 *J.R.A.S.*, 1916, p. 137.

3 See author's article on the *Religious Data in the Arthaśāstra*, *Zeitschrift für Indologie*, Vol. VII.2 (1929).

4 Bk. iii, ch. 14.

5 Bk. iv, ch. 3; Bk. xiii, ch. 1-2; Bk. ii, ch. 4.

Belief was then current that by propitiating these Gods calamities of all sorts could be averted, or at least modified to a considerable extent. Even the worship of nature and nature deities like the rivers and mountains is seriously recommended. Worship of snakes, rats, and other similar creatures is not unknown. A recommendation is also made for achieving objects desired through spells, incantations, and mystical rites prescribed in the *Atharvaveda Saṁhitā.* The sacred books recommended for regal and other studies[1] are the three Vedas and their six Aṅgas besides the Ithihāsa which is also mentioned under the category of the Vedic literature. Hindu social polity of *varṇadharma* and *āśramadharma* is explained and too much insistence is made on the principle of *svadharma* the fundamental basis of all *varṇāśramadharma* system. A high place is given to the *śrotriya*—the ideal Brahman—who is the veritable master of all sacred literature and who puts into practice the ideals contained in those books. The Purohita is glorified and he occupies a social status, equal, if not higher than the reigning chieftain of the land.[2]

There is little or no trace of Buddhism or Jainism. There is indeed a mention of heretical sects especially monastic. Though Kauṭalya was not against *sannyāsa* still he did not allow people to indiscriminately don the robes of a Sannyāsin[3] on one day and give them up on the morrow if it did not suit their purpose. Absence of direct reference to Buddhism or Jainism leaves one with the impression that these religious movements had not gained sufficient currency

[1] Bk. I, ch. iii.
[2] See author's *Hindu Administrative Institutions,* p. 123 ff.
[3] Bk. II, ch. 1.

or enough influence in the country. These and other details which are scattered all through the pages of the work lead us on to the conclusive observation that the work belongs to an earlier epoch of Hinduism when the Vedic religion held firm sway in the minds of the people. The religious data furnished may possibly go to support an early date for the composition of the work probably not later than 300 B.C.

Astronomical Data.

In fixing the date of the composition of the *Arthaśāstra* the astronomical evidence comes in very handy. Two Indian scholars have independently examined this question and the results of their investigations have been curiously identical. These are the late Rājarāja Varma of Trivandrum and L. D. Swamikannu Pillai.[1]

The Chapter 20 of Book II of the *Arthaśāstra* gives us enough details to arrive at a satisfactory calculation. The term *yuga* is used in the sense of a period of five years which is, in other words, the Vedic quinquennial cycle.[2] That Kauṭalya is indebted to the *Vedāṅga Jyotiṣa* is evident. Among the regal studies mentioned are the four Vedas and six Aṅgas of which Jyotiṣa or astronomy is one.[3] Kauṭalya says that the equinox is in the months of *caitra* and *āśvayuja*[4] (vernal and autumnal equinox), and it increases or diminishes

[1] See *Some Aspects of An. Ind. Polity,* pp. 123-127; 153-154. See also Jacobi's observations in *Indian Antiquary,* Vol. 47, pp. 157-161 and pp. 187-195.

[2] Cp. *Vāyu Purāṇa,* ch. 31.28: 50.183, etc. I have discussed this at some length in my forthcoming paper on *Some Aspects of Vāyu Purāṇa.*

[3] Bk. I, ch. iii.

[4] Bk. II, ch. xx.

by three *muhūrtas* once in every six months. This means that the length of the day and night (*ahorātra*) may vary to the maximum extent of three *muhūrtas* or one and a half *muhūrtas* (72 minutes) before 6 A.M. and one and a half *muhūrtas* after 6 P.M. (local time). Says Swamikannu Pillai: "It will be seen from Table XIII appended to my Indian Chronology that this condition will be satisfied only above the thirtieth parallel of latitude where a maximum variation of about 70 minutes is attained in the moment of sunrise."[1]

Another statement that 'no shadow is cast at noon in the month of Āṣāḍha'[2] affords a positive clue that the author is a native of the tropics.

Again according to the *Arthaśāstra* the solar month consists of 30½ days whereas the lunar month consists of 29½ days. Thus the lunar year is said to consist of 354 days and the solar year 366 days. In the five-year cycle the difference between the solar, and the lunar, years is sixty days. These are characterised as *adhimāsas*.[3] Thus "the position of the solstices as well as the occurrence of intercalary months and other items of lunisolar calendar in the *Arthaśāstra*, are in agreement with the conclusions of the *Vedāṅga Jyotiṣa*".[4]

The *Arthaśāstra* knows of the sexagesimal system when it says two *nāḻikas* equal one *muhūrta*[5]

15 *muhūrtas* equal a day, or a night and

1 *Some Aspects of An. Ind. Polity*, p. 124.
2 Bk. II, ch. xx.
3 *Ibid.*
4 *Some Aspects of An. Ind. Polity*, p. 123.
5 Bk. II, ch. xx.

30 *muhūrtas* equal one day and a night or 60 *nāḻikās.*

According to Dr. Burgess the sexagesimal system of Hindu astronomy was borrowed from the Greeks.[1] This implies that the *Jyotiṣa Vedāṅga* which has become a popular work in pre-Kauṭalīyan days (4th century B.C.) must have been written after India's contact with the Greeks. It is an untenable position. *Jyotiṣa Vedāṅga* is an ancient production belonging at least to the later half of the Vedic Period. It holds the field as a valuable piece of scientific composition. If Greece could develop in the direction of sexagesimal system, could not India develop also in that line? Further that the sexagesimal system is exclusively Greek in origin has not been proved. It is just possible that India developed this system on independent lines.

Sec. iii. EVIDENCE OF CLASSICAL WRITERS

So much has been written both on points of similarity and points of dissimilarity between Megasthenes' Fragments and the *Kauṭalīya Arthaśāstra.* Every scholar who has had to deal with the Mauryan period or with the *Arthaśāstra* has not failed to refer to the fragments of Megasthenes. A notable endeavour in this direction is by Otto Stein who has examined the whole question in his book *Megasthenes und Kauṭalya* and has essayed not with much success to establish the thesis that Kauṭalya the author of the *Arthaśāstra* could not have been a contemporary of Megasthenes. In the introduction Stein writes: "The aim of this work

[1] *J.R.A.S.*, 1893, p. 753.

is as far as possible to give all the corresponding items between the two and compare them in details. It is however difficult to find out an objective view-point for the order of the passages which have been compared, because we are concerned with works of different nature. In the one we have a collection of geographical and ethnographical fragments. In the other we have a text-book about administration including home and foreign policy. Besides one cannot include topographical, mythological, and even pseudo-historical statements. A comparison in the order of fragments would lead an an external view-point which is unpractical for our present purpose."[1]

The remarks of Otto Stein in the above passage demonstrate how on a feeble foundation a theory is being built by him. No theory can stand by mere comparison or contrast of two sets of documents, one foreign and the other indigenous, which treat, in Stein's own words, of different subject-matter. The following reasons could be adduced in favour of the theory that Megasthenes' Fragments could not be taken seriously as a source of evidence for reconstructing the history of Mauryan India.

First, about the personality of the Greek writer, Megasthenes, ancient literary records offer only scanty

[1] "Zweck der vorliegenden Arbeit ist es, eine in einzelnan durchgeführte Vergleichung möglichst aller vergleichbaren Punkte zu geben. Schwer ist es, einen objektiven Gesichtspunkt für die Anardnung der verglichenen Stellen zu finden, da es sich doch um in ihrer Natur verschiedene Werke—hier eine geographisch-ethnigraphische Fragmentsammlung, dort ein Lehrbuch über Verwaltung, innere and äusere Politik—handelt. Ferner musten geographische, mythologische, (pseudo-) historische Nachrichten auser Betracht bleiben; eine Vergleichung der Fragmente ihrer Reihenfolge nach-wäre ein äuselicher, zudem für die Darstellung unpraktischer Gesichtspunkt gewesen." *Megasthenes und Kauṭalya,* p. 16.

information. It has not been conclusively shown which his native home was and in what dialect he left his accounts. It is obvious that he was a Greek. Anything more than this is a supposition with no evidence to support.[1]

Secondly, we are not in possession of all the documents which Megasthenes is said to have left concerning India.[2] It is generally believed that Megasthenes' *Indika* consisted of four books. But what we have to-day is a fragment culled out from his books of *Indika* here and there by other interested writers. It is highly regrettable that not even one full book of the *Indika* is available. And what is available, though fragmentary, is not even the original document but quotations made by his contemporaries and successors from such original documents. How far the quotations are faithful to the original is of course a matter of opinion. Granting them to be faithful only such statements as particularly interest the writer would have been quoted leaving out of account the context or the chain of circumstances under which they were made by the author. It is, therefore, difficult to attach full significance to these fragments.

Thirdly, the value of the statements expressed therein is not quite appreciable.[3] We cannot take every one of the statements at its face value and implicitly believe it to be a true picture of the times. Regarding the veracity of Megasthenes and the value of his writings, Schwanbeck, who has done signal

[1] *Megasthenes und Kauṭalya,* p. 1. Cp. B. Breloer, *Kauṭalīya Studien* (1927), I, p. 48.

[2] Breloer op. cit., p. 47.

[3] See *Vedic Index,* Vol. II, p. 214; N. N. Law, *Studies in Ind. History and Culture,* p. 230 ff.

service for the cause of Indian history by collecting together the Fragments of the *Indika* of Megasthenes in one volume, writes: "The ancient writers, whenever they judge of those who have written on Indian matters, are without doubt wont to reckon Megasthenes among those writers who are given to lying and least worthy of credit and to rank him almost on a par with Ktesias."[1] It has been already said that the *Indika* was largely used by subsequent writers. Among them figure Strabo, Arrian, Diodorus, and Plinius. How these writers handled the *Indika* is given to us by the same authority Schwanbeck. It is said that both Strabo and Arrian did not take the very original but abridged the descriptions given by Megasthenes and presented them in an agreeable and pleasant style. Consequently the writers omitted '"whatever would be out of place in an entertaining narrative". Such particulars which have been left unmentioned or partially mentioned would have enriched our knowledge of India in the 4th century B.C. Diodorus, on the other hand, did not attempt in the style in which Strabo wanted it. The object of Diodorus seems to have been to use the *Indika* for imparting instruction to others. Diodorus then had an express view and with this view he made extracts from the *Indika* at random. The result was that he had to omit not only fiction but also fact. Again Strabo and others narrate to us practically the same things and no fresh material is made available. This evidently shows that the major and perhaps the more valuable portion of the *Indika* has been lost beyond any probability of recovery.[2]

1 *Ancient India as described by Megasthenes and Arrian,* Tr. McCrindle, p. 18.

2 *Ibid.,* pp. 18 and 19.

Among the writers who are indebted to the *Indika* for the knowledge of India, Strabo's name was mentioned. Let us hear what he has to say about Megasthenes' writings. Strabo says: "Generally speaking the men who have hitherto written on the affairs of India were a set of liars. Deimachos holds the first place in the list, Megasthenes comes next; while Onesikritos and Nearchos with others of same class, manage to stammer out a few words of truth."[1] That is then the tribute paid to Megasthenes by one of his own countrymen who lived not very long after Megasthenes.

Fourthly, there is the fact of the idealising tendency which is deeply marked in every page of his writings. In this strain says Jolly, Megasthenes "was anxious to present the life and manners of the Indians in a very favourable light, much as at a later period Tacitus in his *Germania* held out the Germans of his time as a model to his own countrymen".[2] Influenced perhaps by the stoic philosophy of his times, Megasthenes carried too far the tendency of idealising things so much so that his statements are open to question. Continues Jolly: "In some Megasthenes may have arbitrarily assigned the institutions of other countries to India. Thus his seven classes of population may be an imitation of the seven classes of the Egyptian people, according to Herodotus, though the details differ. The milestones may be a Persian institution. The Philosopher Plato in his idealistic work on the state might have furnished or influenced some of the political theories of Megasthenes. The sensational

[1] *Ancient India as described by Megasthenes*, Tr. McCrindle, p. 20.

[2] *Punjab Sanskrit Series*: *Kauṭalīya Arthaśāstra*, Intro., p. 38.

element is represented by winged serpents, one-horned horses and long-lived elephants of Megasthenes as also by his assertions about the enormous size of the continent of India and the gigantic dimensions of the ditch surrounding the capital of Pāṭaliputra."[1] This view of the learned German scholar, if true, must relegate to the background the Fragments of *Indika*. If the tendency to idealise things is prominent it would be rather difficult to get at the fact. As regards the sensational element at least one explanation may be offered. It is that Megasthenes confused folklore with historical facts. Even to-day such folk-tales of winged serpents and horned horses are commonplace in India. Megasthenes might have heard of such stories and without inquiring into the truth muddled up facts with fiction. If we again agree that some institutions of other countries have been arbitrarily assigned to India then any institution may be foreign. There will, therefore, be no necessity for us to compare coincidences or otherwise with a native contemporary work in India. For it is building a theory on doubtful issues.

There is again another point which must be seriously considered. Is the information contained in the *Indika* an outcome of the first-hand knowledge? In other words, did Megasthenes personally visit, study, and note down his own observations? Were his impressions the consequence of a personal and intimate knowledge of men and things which he observed during his sojourn to this ancient land? It is not very difficult to answer these questions. How many times Megasthenes came to India and how long he stayed

[1] Jolly's edition, p. 41.

each time are still matters of dispute among scholars. Though there is a view that he visited India more than once[1] some scholars are of decided opinion that he must have visited the country only once and would not have stayed long enough to get into touch with the whole of the machinery of administration including social, political, and economic organisations of the land. Schwanbeck is of opinion that he visited India only on one occasion and that he did not see more of India than the parts including Kabul and the Punjab leading to Pāṭaliputra through the royal road. Schwanbeck adds that Megasthenes acknowledges that he knew of the lower part of the country traversed by the Ganges only from hearsay and report.[2] It is reasonable to presume that Megasthenes could not have had a first-hand knowledge of things excepting the administration of the Capital city where he must have stayed for some time as a state guest. The major portion of the *Indika* must have hence been drawn from mere hearsay and report. Even here he was confronted by a serious handicap which was his ignorance of the language or languages of India. Unacquainted with the languages and literature of the India which he visited Megasthenes could not have correctly portrayed the story of his India however reliable may be the source from which he had his report. We can attach importance and value to a work which is the result of vast travel, long stay, and a good acquaintance with the languages of the country. These three are hardly applicable in the case of Megasthenes. His travel seems to have

1. Max Müller, *A History of Ancient Sanskrit Literature*, (1859) p. 277.

2 Quoted in the Intro., M'Crindle, *Ancient India*, pp. 15-16 (ed. Cal. 1926).

been limited to a straight road leading to the Capital. As an ambassador we cannot expect him to stay for a long time. After he had delivered the message of his chief he should have left the place. Thirdly he was not familiar with the Indian languages. In these circumstances peculiar in themselves Jolly's remarks can be taken as true: "His (Megasthenes) work, though earlier in date, is far inferior in intrinsic value to the Itineraries of the Chinese Pilgrims and to the great Arabian work of Alberuni on India."[1]

Date of the visit.

Equally important is the fixing of the date of the visit. Megasthenes was the representative of Seleukos at the Court of Sibyrtius, Satrap of Arachosia. He was sent to Pāṭaliputra, Candragupta's Court, as King's ambassador. Seleukos Nikator defeated Demetrios, son of Antigonus, in B.C. 312 and got possession of Babylon. He continued to extend his successful march until he reached India in B.C. 305. Perhaps a war broke out which ultimately dwindled into petty skirmishes. Seleukos felt the weight of the strong arm of Candragupta and preferred the path of negotiations to the actual field-operations. By entering into a treaty with Candragupta, Seleukos got a free hand for settling the affairs of the West. In connection with this Megasthenes was sent to the court of Candragupta.

Hence Megasthenes must have visited the Indian Capital some time between 302 and 288 B.C. We cannot with any certainty fix exactly the year when he visited Candragupta. There is a version,

[1] Intro., p. 41 to his edition of the *Arthaśāstra.*

as has already been pointed out, that Megasthenes' visits to the Indian continent were often and frequent. This view is apparently based on the statement made by Arrian in his *Exped. Alex.* V, (vi), 2. Here he refers— according to Schwanbeck's interpretation of the passage—to *frequent interviews* with the kings and *not frequent* visits as rendered by other writers.[1] In the same way in his *Indika*[2] Arrian says: "Megasthenes, so far as appears, did not travel over much of India, though no doubt he saw more of it than those who came with Alexander, the son of Philip, for as he tells us, he resided at the Court of Sandrokottos, the greatest king in India, and also at the Court of Poros, who was still greater than he". This would imply that Megasthenes visited king Poros who was dead in B.C. 317. Lassen regarded this hardly credible and thought 'the mention of Poros a careless addition of a chance transcriber'.[3] Schwanbeck would retain the phrase and translate the original "and who was even greater than Poros".[4] Thus the theory that Megasthenes visited India more than once was due to the misunderstanding of Arrian's statement. Excepting these uncertain passages, there is no other evidence to confirm the theory of frequent visits. On the other hand there is the evidence of Strabo[5] and of Pliny where mention is made of only one embassy. The passage of Pliny as translated runs thus: "Megasthenes remained for some time with the Indian kings and wrote a history of Indian affairs, that he might hand down to posterity

[1] The Italics are mine.

[2] V, p. 220.

[3] See Intro., p. 14.

[4] *Ibid.*

[5] XV, p. 702 (Frag. 25); II, p. 70 (Frag. 29).

a faithful account of all that he had witnessed."[1] It is therefore difficult to credit Megasthenes with frequent visits to the Indian Empire. It is reasonable to believe that he saw Candragupta in connection with the treaty and left his impressions of a people whose culture and civilisation evoked enthusiasm and wonderment in his mind.

If then Megasthenes visited India between the years 302 and 298 B.C.,[2] he must have noticed the administration of the land in its fully developed state. It was more than two decades since Candragupta ascended the Magadha throne and consolidated his newly acquired empire. And so, his visit should have been during the closing years of the reign of that remarkable emperor. We could be really and fully indebted to Megasthenes if he had taken pains to give us a fuller account like Fa-Hien and Yuan Chwang of later days. The administrative edifice had been erected and it was almost nearing completion. A trustworthy and true representation of that edifice would have been invaluable. But as it is, the whole account is vitiated by discrepancies of a glaring character and this has considerably reduced its intrinsic worth as a source of information for an important period of Hindu India. The evidence of Megasthenes could not be looked upon as something positive and conclusive. The same view has to be pronounced more or less on the evidence of other Greek writers who have written on India. Some of the classical writers who come under this category are Justin, Arrian, Diodorus Siculus, Strabo, Quintus Cur-

[1] Quoted in Intro., p. 13 (Cal. ed.).
[2] See Smith, *Early History of India*, p. 126.

tius and Ktesias. Justin narrates legends as historical facts when he says: "Having offended Alexander by his impertinent language he was ordered to be put to death and escaped only by flight. Fatigued with his journey he lay down to rest, when a lion of large size came and licked off the sweat that poured from him with his tongue, and retired without doing him any harm. The prodigy inspired him with ambitious hopes and collecting bands of robbers he roused the Indians to rebellion. When he prepared for war against the captains of Alexander, a wild elephant of enormous size approached him and received him on his back as if he had been tamed."[1] This admixture of history with fable in the account of Justin detracts the value of his documents as a source for reliable history. In regard to Arrian's account, again the same uncertainty prevails. It must be said to his credit that he himself confesses that most of his statements are not original but based on other reports. He says: "Now if any-one wishes to state a reason to account for the number and magnitude of the Indian rivers let him state it. As for myself I have written on this point, as on others, from hearsay."[2] Though no further proof is required to show that the material contained in his *Indika* is secondhand, still it may be remarked that the *Indika* of Arrian can admit of a three-fold division—the general description of India, the voyage of Nearchos and a description of the southern parts of the world. Of these the first part is based on the accounts of Megasthenes and Eratosthenes and the second on the account left by Nearchos himself. The next set of

[1] Justini *Hist. Philipp. Lib.*, XV, ch. iv, quoted in Müller's *History of Ancient Sanskrit Literature*.

[2] *Indika*, p. 200 (Cal. ed.).

Greek writers are Diodorus Siculus and Quintus Curtius. Lack of space forbids us to examine their records in detail. How their accounts are inconsistent and conflicting can be seen from their statements regarding Xandrames. The quotations speak for themselves. Diodorus says of him, "that the king was but of mean and obscure extraction, accounted to be a barber's son; that the queen, however, had fallen in love with the barber, had murdered her husband, and that the kingdom had thus devolved upon Xandrames."[1]

According to Curtius[2] "the father of Xandrames had murdered the king, and under pretence of acting as guardian to his sons, got them into his power and put them to death; that after their extermination he begot the son who was then king, and who, more worthy of his father's condition than his own, was odious and contemptible to his subjects."[3] Strabo like Arrian based his writings on those of Megasthenes, and his account is generally regarded as much less careful than others. Schwanbeck remarks: "Nay, Strabo in his eagerness to be interesting, has gone so far that the topography of India is almost entirely a blank in his pages."[4] Suffice it to say that Ktesias is also liable to make inaccurate statements. In regard to the value of the records of these classical writers the estimate of Pliny seems to approach nearer the truth. He says[5]: "India was opened up to our knowledge . . . . even by other Greek writers, who, having resided with Indian kings—as for instance Megasthenes and Dionysius—

[1] XVII, 93

[2] IX, 2.

[3] Quoted in Müller's *History of Ancient Sanskrit Literature*, p. 277.

[4] Intro., pp. 17-18*n* (Cal. ed.).

[5] *His. Nat.*, VI, XXI, 3, quoted in Intro.; p. 20 (Cal. ed.).

made known the strength of the races which peopled the country. It is not, however, worth while to study their accounts with care, so conflicting are they, and incredible." On this account these records are not to be discarded as entirely valueless and thus relegated to oblivion. They are useful as supplementing the knowledge which we gather from other sources of evidence, literary and otherwise. Some unintelligible details and facts presented meagrely in contemporary literature would be made intelligible if the writings could in any way help us. The classical writings are, therefore, useful in that they are supplementary. Such being the case any endeavour to find coincidences and differentiations with an accredited work of the period is bound to prove futile. Still we are compelled to do this[1] because scholars have attempted it rightly or wrongly and have drawn conclusions mostly of an untenable character.

Sec. iv. INSCRIPTIONS OF AŚOKA

Thanks to the energy and enthusiasm as well as transparent earnestness of scholars in the field of Aśokan script, we have to-day the history of Aśokan studies. The discovery, decipherment and interpretation of the *Inscriptions of Piyadasi*, as the late Senart styled them, cover a long and fruitful period of nearly two centuries commencing roughly from the middle of the eighteenth century. It would be interesting to know that Aśokan scholarship had an ancient history as well. In the everflowing and nay, overflowing stream of foreign travellers and visitors to this ancient land from very early times for some reason or other,

[1] See **Appendix.**

one could reckon two celebrated names Fa-Hien and Yuan Chwang. These were two Chinese travellers who came to India at long intervals, the first visiting it in the fourth century after Christ and the second in the seventh century. Our thanks are due to these two savants, who have left behind them the invaluable legacy of their writings which has considerably contributed to enrich our knowledge of Indian History. These travellers endeavoured to get a true interpretation of Aśokan inscriptions though not with much success. When Fa-Hien visited this land in the fourth century A.D. hardly six centuries have passed after Aśoka and it is indeed a wonder that this traveller was not able to get at experts who would rightly and correctly interpret the script contained on the rocks and pillars where Aśoka had caused his ordinances to be inscribed. This mainly explains that the knowledge of the script had decayed so much that these inscriptions became sealed to an ordinary Indian of the fourth century A.D. According to a recent writer these travellers "have recorded wrong readings of those inscriptions, the results of mere guess work or hearsay information of local people not confessing to their own ignorance of the scripts."[1] This reminds us of the accounts left by Megasthenes some centuries earlier, some of which is treated as either drawn from imagination or from hearsay information. We do not know of any other attempt made afterwards in the direction of deciphering the script. As a matter of fact these accounts were forgotten by the sons of India, and the inscriptions stood dumb and silent for centuries together.

[1] R. K. Mookerji's *Asoka,* Prefatory Note, pp. vii and viii.

The first honour of discovery of these records so important to the study of Indian History goes to Padre Tieffenthaler who found a few fragments of the Delhi Pillar at the city of Delhi as early as 1750 or thereabout. In the year 1785 the Barābar and Nagarjuni Hill caves were visited for the first time by J. H. Harington. The next stage was when Captain Polier had the privilege of discovering the Delhi-Topra Pillar Inscription. Some of these discoveries were published in the *Asiatic Researches* in 1801.

The next stage was when Colonel James Tod discovered in 1822 the Girnār Rock Inscription and M. A. Court the Shāhbāzgarhī Rock Edict in 1836. The next year witnessed the discovery by Lieutenant Kittoe of the Dhauli Rock Edict. In 1840 Captain Burt discovered the Bairāt Rock Inscription otherwise known as the Bhābrā Edict. Other discoveries then followed: the Jaugaḍa Rock Inscription in 1850, the Kālsī Rock Inscription in 1860, and the Bairāt Minor Rock Edict in 1872, by Sir Walter Elliot, Forrest and Carlleyle respectively. The latter made also another important discovery in the Rāmpūrvā Pillar Edict. The Rūpnāth Minor Rock Edict was the other discovery of this time, and needless to say, that these discoveries enriched the Aśokan scholarship by attracting many a savant in this direction. A detailed study is bound to swell the section. Other important discoveries were the three Mysore Minor Rock Edicts found by Lewis Rice in 1891, the Niglīva Pillar Edicts and the Rummindēī in 1895 and 1896 respectively. Far more important than these was C. Beadon's discovery of the Maski Rock Inscription in 1915 in the Raichur District of the Nizam's Dominions.[1] The very first line of this remarkable inscription records *Devānaṁpiyasa Aśokasa.*[2] This is the key which opened to us the new knowledge that after all Piyadarśi of the Inscriptions is no one other than Aśoka. Last in the list but not least in importance is the new discovery made in 1928 of a set of Rock Edicts near Gooty in the Kurnool District.

But what is more important and perhaps valuable is the study of decipherment, in which direction much energy and time have been spent not without profit to the scholarly world. The publication of drawing lithographs, impressions, and full copies of the inscriptions discovered next occupied the attention of Indoogists. In 1834 in the *Journal of the Asiatic Society of Bengal* (Vol. III) James Prinsep, the father of the interpretation of these dumb Edicts, essayed to read and understand the Aśokan alphabet by the classification of vowels, consonants, etc. His attempt produced vast and fruitful results. For Prinsep was able to read the Delhi-Topra Pillar Edicts fully and successfully and published it with his translation in the *Journal of the Asiatic Society of Bengal* (Vol. VI). He pursued his studies with that critical and inquiring zeal characteristic of a born researcher. In 1838 he began a comparative study of the two inscriptions at Dhauli and Girnār and he found to his surprise that both of them were identical in every respect, whether it be in script, contents or otherwise. He translated them and had

[1] See *J. R. A. S.*, 1916, pp. 838-39. Also *Hyderabad Arch. Ser.* No. I (1915).

[2] *Corpus*, p. 174.

the whole published in the VII Volume of the *Journal of the Asiatic Society of Bengal.*[1] The year 1879 is memorable in the long and interesting story of Aśokan scholarship from a variety of standpoints. Then was published the first volume of the *Corpus Inscriptionum Indicarum* by Cunningham on the Inscriptions of Aśoka. The *Corpus* embodied the Rock Edicts, the Pillar Edicts, and the Cave Inscriptions so far discovered. A quick succession of publications with different interpretations followed. Prominent among these early works were Senart's *Les Inscriptions de Piyadasi* (1881) and Bühlers' contributions to the *Z. D. M. G.* and *Epigraphia Indica* (Vols. I and II). The momentous publication of all is the new edition of the *Corpus* by the late Hultzsch in 1925 whose life-work for the cause of Indian History is too well known to need mention here. It is a monumental publication, very valuable to students of India's Ancient History.

In addition to these various publications in all the learned journals throughout the world, we have four biographical sketches on the life and career of that unique personality who satisfies the qualities and qualifications of a Rājasattama as described in the Epic literature. These are by V. A. Smith, D. R. Bhandarkar, J. M. Macphail and R. K. Mookerji. When Senart and Bühler tried to interpret these records, they had neither the facility nor the opportunity of a scholar of to-day in the shape of numerous Pāli publications, and above all the discovery and publication of the *Kauṭalīya Arthaśāstra* which has very much modified the interpretation of these inscriptions. A comparative study

[1] See Sylvain Levi's remarks in the *Journal of Department of Letters,* (Cal.) IX, p. 11.

of the different terms[1] and even of contents of both Aśoka's Inscriptions and the *Arthaśāstra* has been attempted by many a scholar, sometimes leading to a thorough revision and a radical change in the original interpretation. In spite of the ever-growing voluminous studies in this particular direction, a vast field still exists for a critical student of comparative studies. In interpreting these records, one must be very familiar not only with the tradition handed down from earliest times, but also contemporary history, and the history and policy of Aśoka's immediate predecessors. In the light of this study a new outlook and a new interpretation of the Edicts seems to be called for, with all due respect to scholars whose sincere endeavours in this direction no one can dispute. The next question to ask is whether the Edicts have materially helped the historian of Ancient India and if so, in what respects. A bird's eye-view of the whole indicates that the Edicts enable us to construct a true history of the great Mauryan Emperor Aśoka. Before the discovery of all these inscriptions we had simply to depend on the legendary accounts of the Pāli texts and Buddhist literature which claim the Emperor to be a Buddhist. Such evidence could only be one view of his life and career and cannot be the unquestioned view. The inscriptions[2] have thrown welcome light especially with regard to his relations with his kith and kin though the legends make him out to be a blood-thirsty tyrant who killed his near and dear for the sake of the Magadha throne. This is only one instance among the many which go to show that

[1] See the last two pages at the end of the chapter.

[2] *Corpus*, Intro., p. xlviii.

fundamental differences exist between the accredited authority of the inscriptions and the Buddhist legends. The inscriptions again prove that Aśoka's Dharma was not merely the Buddhist, as is repeatedly made out,[1] but was non-sectarian in character. Its aim was to bring satisfaction to all sects—orthodox as well as heterodox—of the Empire. Aśoka felt it the duty of the State to afford protection and peace to any faith or creed so long as that creed or faith did not interfere with the neighbouring faith, and so long as there was no misunderstanding among them. Aśoka promulgated a policy which helped the different religious sects to move on friendly terms, with no spirit of rivalry or rancour.

The inscriptions of Aśoka are important from political and economic points of view also. It is the narrow view of the writer in the *Encyclopaedia Brittanica* (11th edition) who remarks[2]: "The inscriptions, which contain altogether about 5,000 words, are entirely of religious import, and their references to worldly affairs are incidental." Perhaps the same view is held by another authority, E. Hultzsch, who says: "His Edicts are not concerned with public affairs, but are of an almost purely religious character."[3] This is due to the want of correct understanding of the ancient Hindu ideal of politics and religion. To the ancient Hindus politics and religion were intertwined, and neither could exist by itself. In fact secular affairs, as we understand to-day, were largely governed by religious and ethical ideas and ideals.[4] It was the *dharma*

[1] *Corpus,* Intro., ch. v.

[2] Vol. II, p. 764.

[3] *C. I. I.,* Vol. I, Intro., XXXVI.

[4] See Author's paper *Is Arthaśāstra secular?* See *Proceedings of the Third Oriental Conference,* 1924, pp. 614-631.

of the State, without which any function of the State would be ineffective and perfectly useless. Much of political and economic history could be gleaned from these inscriptions as could be seen from the following pages. Suffice it to say here that the inscriptions have enabled us to reconstruct an account of the central and provincial administration of the Mauryan empire. Aśoka's interest in live-stock, their improvement and efficiency, in agriculture, in the census for taxation and other purposes bears the testimony to prove that the Emperor was much concerned with the material welfare of the State.[1] This is the *trivarga* conception of the ancient political philosophers. A statesman like Aśoka must have known that both material welfare and moral welfare depended for their progressive realization on the political machinery of the land. Hence Aśoka took so much pains to carry on the administration of the land. In these respects the author of these inscriptions did not materially differ from the author of the *Arthaśāstra* and, on the other hand, the latter was the model for Aśoka to follow. Thus the inscriptions of Aśoka have a many-sided interest. They are in every way concerned with public affairs, the latter consisting mainly of the propagation and preservation of *dharma* in the wide sense of the term. In the absence of these records of incalculable value, there could be no authoritative history of Mauryan India. It is the discovery of the *Arthaśāstra* and the more important discovery of these Edicts that have enabled us to speak of Mauryan empire and Mauryan history. These have enriched the history of this epoch for which we had to

[1] *Corpus*, p. xlix (Introduction).

depend till very recently only on the writings of Megasthenes and other classical writers. We are to-day in possession of different and independent sources of information, a comparative study of which bears the test that the Mauryan India was socially, economically, and politically in an advanced state, its institutions largely anticipating those of modern times.

The following are, among others, the terms whose interpretations have been arrived at by their identification with the Kauṭalīyan expressions:—

	Inscriptions of Aśoka.	*Arthaśāstra.*
1.	Yuta (R.E. III)	Yukta (Bk. II, ch. 5 and 9).
2.	Prādeśika (R.E. III)	Pradeṣṭṛ (Bk. IV, ch. 1).
3.	Pariśa (R.E. I, VII)	Pariṣad (Bk. IV, ch. 1).
4.	Pulisa (Pillar E. IV)	Puruṣa (Bk. II, ch. 5).
5.	Gaṇanāyam (R.E. III)	Gaṇanāyam (Bk. II, ch. 6).
6.	tadatvāye āyatiye ca (R.E. X; Jaugaḍa version)	tadātve ca āyatyāṁ ca (Bk. V, ch. 1 and 4).
7.	Vraca (II, R.E.; VI, R.E.)	Vraja (Bk. II, sec. 1).
8.	Nagala-viyohālaka (I Sep. R. E., Dhauli)	Paura-vyāvahārika (Bk. I, ch. 12).
9.	Palikileśa (Do.)	Parikleśa (Bk. IV, ch. 9).
10.	Dharmavijaya (R. E. XIII).	Dharmavijaya (Bk. XII, ch. 1).
11.	Aṭhabhagiya (Rummindeī Pillar).	Aṣṭabhāga (Bk. II, ch. 24).
12.	Vivūtha (Shāsram R.I.)	Vyuṣṭam (Bk. II, ch. 6).
13.	Simāle (V P.E.)	Śrīmāra (Bk. II, ch. 17).
14.	Vracabhūmika (Shāh. and Māns. Edicts)	Vivītādhyakṣa (Bk. II, ch. 34).

	Original meaning.	*Interpretation in the light of the Arthaśāstra.*
1.	Officer.	Subordinate Government servant.
2.	Provincial chief or officer.	Officer in charge of criminal administration.
3.	School, Committee.	Council.
4.	Agents.	Assistants to Yuktas.
5.	For registering these rules, for purposes of accounts.	Department of accounts.
6.	Immediate and long time to come.	Present and future.
7.	Cow, cattle.	Pasture.
8.	Officer in charge of administration of city.	City Magistrate.
9.	Trouble, torture, harsh treatment.	Punishment amounting to torture.
10.	'Conquest by morality.'	Righteous war.
11.	Partaking of riches.	An eighth share.
12.	A civil day spent in travelling.	A night and a day.
13.	Some eatable animal.	Stag.
14.	Officer in charge of high roads, etc.	Superintendent of pastures.

NOTE.—Since this was written I found a contribution on the subject of *Parallelism between Aśoka's Edicts and Kauṭalya's Arthaśāstra* by Dr. Radhakumud Mookerji in the *Proceedings of the Fifth Oriental Conference* (Lahore), pp. 329-347.

CHAPTER II

THE EXTENT AND CHARACTER OF THE EMPIRE

Sec. i. THE EXTENT OF THE EMPIRE

Elsewhere[1] has been shown how from early Vedic times the king of the ancient Hindu State was the mainspring of the polity, and this state of affairs continued to exist down to the period of the *Kauṭalīya Arthaśāstra,* if not, still later. Before we go to examine the position of the monarch in the polity of the Mauryas, and the nature and extent of authority exercised by him in this period, it will be well to survey briefly the events and circumstances, which in the epoch immediately preceding that of the Mauryas, had tended largely to contribute to the consolidation of regal power.

That the royal dynasty which immediately preceded the Mauryan was that of the great Nandas who exercised their sway for well-nigh a century, is quite clear. But the materials available at present are too meagre to enable us to ascertain and describe the exact limits of their empire. But this much is certain that it included a good portion of the south of India in addition to their vast territory in the north. An inscription of the twelfth century after Christ records a tradition that one of the provinces subject to the rule of the

[1] Author's *Hindu Administrative Institutions, (Madras University,* 1929).

Nandas was Kuntala which comprised the Western Dekhan and the North of Mysore. And this derives very strong support from another fact, namely, that the Kadamba kings of South India trace their descent from a certain Nanda, undoubtedly a member of this ancient royal family.[1] The above inscription therefore shows that the Nanda empire embraced also a good portion of the South. That being so, it may be safely assumed and it is not an improbable assumption that when Candragupta Maurya ascended the throne he was in possession of the whole of this empire left intact by his Nanda predecessors. It has been contended, however, that in the revolution effected by Candragupta with the help of his minister Cāṇakya, several States which had been loosely attached to the Empire under the strong hand of the Nandas cut themselves off the Empire and declared their independence. Among these were, perhaps, the South Indian provinces as they were far away from the Capital. That this was a possibility can be seen from the history of the Mauryas. Mention may be made of four factors in the light of which one may conclude that the Empire of the Nandas slowly expanded itself under the first rulers of the Mauryas.

The Jaina Tradition

First, there is the tradition transmitted by the sacred books of the Jains that Candragupta Maurya was a Jaina by religion, and that in the evening of his life he abdicated his throne in favour of his son Bindusāra who succeeded him in 298 B.C., and that after the abdication Candragupta placed himself under the

[1] See Rice, *Mysore and Coorg from the Inscriptions,* (1909), p. 3; Smith, *Early History of India,* 4th Ed., p. 158; G. M. Moraes, *Kadamba Kula,* p. 9 (Bombay, 1931).

spiritual guidance of Bhadrabāhu, the last in the category of the Jaina saints well known as the Śrutakevalins. Both appear to have gone so far south as Śravaṇa Belgola in the Mysore State where Candragupta embraced asceticism, and finally gave up his life in that very place by starvation, so highly meritorious in the eyes of the Jainas. Consequently Śravaṇa Belgola is even to-day held in great veneration by the members of the Jaina sect. If this story is not 'imaginative history' as V. A. Smith remarked in the first edition of his *Early History of India,* but 'has a solid foundation on fact' according to the revised opinion of the same historian, then it is quite reasonable to assume that the southern province of the Nandas remained an integral part of the empire and did not show any signs of revolt during the change of dynasty. The possible alternative supposition that Candragupta might have conquered the southern province will not stand to reason, since Candragupta was the first monarch of a new line of kings who came to the throne after overthrowing the reigning Nanda dynasty. To effect this in his own Capital and to make the Empire rest on an unshakable foundation would have required and absorbed all the energy and effort of a life-time. Thus busy at home, Candragupta could have hardly directed his attention or diverted his activity to the Dekhan also. If again the tradition that Candragupta chose the far south, Śravaṇa Belgola, for his retirement and death is trustworthy,[1] Mysore must have been to him quite

[1] For Jaina tradition, see Rice, *Mysore and Coorg,* pp. 3-9; *Q.J.M.S.,* Bangalore, October, 1922; *E. I.,* Vol. XIII, pp. 430-47; Rice, *Inscriptions* at *Śravaṇa Belgola* (1889), Intro., pp. 1-15. *Contra* J. F. Fleet, *Ind. Ant.,* Vol. XXI (1892), pp. 156-60; *Ep. Indica,* Vol. III, p. 171, *note.*

a home, which a recently conquered province could never be. It may then appear, that Candragupta must have succeeded to the Nanda empire including the Dekhan province.

Lewis Rice draws our attention to a number of inscriptions at Śravaṇa Belgola discovered by him in 1874 where Bhadrabāhu and Candragupta Munīndra are frequently and jointly mentioned,[1] adding that Candragupta attained such spiritual eminence as he was for a long time served by the forest deities. This, Mr. Rice, substantiates from literature. The *Bṛhatkathākośa* of Hariṣeṇa (10th century) refers to King Candragupta as a disciple of Bhadrabāhu. There is, besides, another work, *Bhadrabāhucarita,* attributed to Ratnānandi of the 15th century, where a similar account occurs. The same is found in another modern work *Rājāvali-kathā* by Devacandra, perhaps belonging to the earlier part of the 19th century. The migration was, according to the *Bṛhatkathākośa,* to the Punnāṭa, a province in the south-west of Mysore[2] famous for its beryl even in the second century A.D. according to Ptolemy who calls it Pounnāṭa.

The evidence of Tāranātha

Secondly, there is the evidence of the Tibetan historian Tāranātha,[3] according to whom, Bindusāra assisted by the glorious Cāṇakya, who was responsible to a great extent for Candragupta's accession to the

[1] *Mysore and Coorg from the Inscriptions,* pp. 3 and 4.

[2] saṁghopi samasta guruvākyataḥ dakṣiṇā pathadeśastha punnāṭaviṣayam yayuḥ|

[3] Schiefner p. 89, Tāranātha's *Geschichte Des Buddhismus,* (1869).

Magadha throne, is said to have made extensive conquests in the country south of the Vindhyas. "Afterwards there ruled the son of Candragupta, by name Bindusāra who was born in the country of Gaura, for 35 years. The Minister and Brahman Cāṇakya conjured up the jealous Yamāntaka. After he had seen his face the power of his *mantra* became very great. By means of magic, he killed the kings and ministers of about 16 towns. And when in consequence of this, the king began a war, he brought the country which was situated between East and West Oceans into his power.[1] Then this Brahman killed, by different methods, 3,000 people and by different uses of *narkoṭa* he fooled nearly 10,000 people. Further he expelled several people, disunited them, made them immovable, dumb, etc. As a result of all these sins, he died of a loathsome disease and was confined to Hell. During the time of this king, in the town of Kusumapura a vihāra named Kusumālaṅkāra was erected in which the great Ācārya Mātṛceta lived and propagated the law of the Mahāyāna and Hīnayāna. Towards the end of the life of the Ācārya Mātṛceta there ruled Bindusāra's brother's son, King Śrīcandra. He built a temple to the Ārya Avalokiteśvara, and supported 2,000 Bhikṣus who taught the Mahāyāna. When Rāhulabhadrā was teaching in Nālanda he built there fourteen beautiful halls and fourteen incomparable religious schools. After King Śrīcandra had ended his rule many years had passed by, when in the west in the kingdoms of Ṭili and Mālva a young king Kaṇika was elected ruler. At that time 28 mines with pre-

[1] This means that Bindusāra enlarged the territory already in possession under his father.

cious stones were discovered and the king became rich. In all parts of the world he built big temples and entertained 20,000 Bhikṣus of great and small vehicles. Therefore one must know that the kings Kaniṣka and Kaṇika are not one and the same person."[1] Though the above statement is open to question inasmuch as it refers, to the time of Bindusāra, the Mahāyāna and the Hīnayāna systems which were the products of much later times, yet it clearly demonstrates that Bindusāra of whom we have unfortunately no documents, literary or epigraphical, was busy extending the empire in the south of India in addition to that left by his father. That Bindusāra must have been a great soldier and conqueror is corroborated by the testimony of the Greek writers who refer to him as Amitrochates (Sans.: Amitraghāta), a terror to the enemies. It is not a name but a surname which indicates his great prowess in war and his extensive conquests.[2] Bindusāra could not have earned this title for nothing. There was no necessity for his conquest of the North India as the whole territory was under his father's suzerainty. Nor is there any possibility of Bindusāra carrying his arms beyond the borders of the Indian continent. It is, therefore, obvious that his conquests of the Dekhan must have been so difficult and arduous as to merit this hard-earned title. In conclusion Candragupta succeeded to the Kuntala province left to him by the Nandas. His son Bindusāra acquired further territories so much so that the empire of Aśoka comprised the whole of the Peninsular India roughly

[1] Tr. from Schiefner, pp. 89-90.

[2] That it is but a mere title is proved by the *Rāmāyaṇa* where Vālmīki describes the bold warrior Kumbhakarṇa as amitraghāta (VI, 60-97).

down to the latitude of Nellore. If it is conceded that Aśoka conquered the province of Kaliṅga, then Bindusāra either in the capacity of the Viceroy under his father at the provincial capital, Vidiśa, or in his own personal capacity as king, must have been busy in conquering and acquiring the southern parts other than that of the Kuntala.

Conquest of Kaliṅga?

It has been suggested that even the conquest of Kaliṅga was not the conquest of an independent province but only a suppression of a rebellion.[1] There is of course the evidence of the Purāṇas that the empire of the Nandas was as large and as extensive as that of the Mauryan empire at the commencement. We have already shown how the Kuntala province must have been a part of the empire of Magadha under the Nandas. There is again inscriptional evidence to show that Kaliṅga was also one of these provinces. In the course of a learned note on the Hathi-gumpha Inscriptions of Khāravela, R. D. Banerjea remarks: "Three centuries before Khāravela and two hundred years before Aśoka, Kaliṅga was conquered by Nanda I or Nandivardhana, the founder of the Nanda dynasty of Magadha. This invasion was not a mere raid and Kaliṅga continued under the Nanda kings at least for some time. This is proved by the mention of public works undertaken during the reign of Nanda I, who excavated a canal in this country."[2]

We are not in possession of facts or figures which would definitely mark out the period when Kaliṅga

[1] *Vide* P. T. S., *History of Tamils,* p. 140. Prof. E. J. Rapson seems to think that this was possible from his alternative statement 'or that it had revolted and was reconquered by Aśoka' (*C.H.I.,* p. 315).

[2] *See* line 6 of the inscription. Also *J.B.O.R.S.*, III, pp. 502-3.

threw off the yoke of the empire of Magadha, and whether it effected its independence even during the epoch of the Nandas or in the revolution effected by Candragupta Maurya or even later. If the Mauryan invasion of South India is an historical fact, and if Bindusāra's conquests were mainly beyond the Vindhyas, then it is plausible to postulate a theory that Kaliṅga continued to be a part of the Magadha empire under the two first Mauryan emperors. But soon after Aśoka's succession, the sturdy Kaliṅgas declared independence. The emperor, though actuated by the principle of *dharmavijaya,* had no other option than to engage himself in *asuravijaya* by conquering them with sword and bloodshed. There is of course a view that Aśoka's eclectic ethics were the consequence of Kaliṅga war, its horrors and atrocities. Though we do not hear of any other incident which made it necessary on the part of the Emperor to take arms it could not by itself be the starting point of enunciating the policy of peace and good-will. Aśoka must have possessed divine temperament from his early life, which enabled him to turn even sour things sweet. The peculiar character in him, viz., to girdle all around with music, the music of the heart, must have been an inborn characteristic and not the mere outcome of a particular incident or even a series of incidents.[1] Until it is proved on reliable evidence that Kaliṅga was an independent country at the accession of Aśoka, and that the latter pursued at the outset a policy of aggression and self-aggrandisement for en-

[1] This seems to be also the view of Edmund Hardy. See *Konig Asoka,* p. 21 (last para.), published by Von Kirchheim & Co., Mains, 1913.

larging the territorial limits of his empire, it is reasonable to presume that Kaliṅga continued to be a part of the empire of Magadha from Nanda I to Aśoka, and asserted its autonomy under Aśoka. This he put down with a strong hand, as befits the duty of an emperor of even of the Rājasattama type.

The evidence of the Edicts

The next remarkable circumstance in this connection is the fact that the Rock Edicts of Aśoka have been discovered in a number of places in South India such as Siddhapura, Brahmagiri, Jaṭinga Rāmeśvara hill in Mysore in 1892, in Maski in the Nizam's dominions[1] and lastly in a place near Gooty in the Kurnool District discovered by Anu Ghose, the well-known geologist of Calcutta, while directing mining operations in that district. The discovery of the Aśokan Edicts in these places is in itself a sufficient testimony to the extent of the empire during the time of Aśoka. In addition to this there is again evidence of rare value in the inscriptions themselves. Three inscriptions of Aśoka, Rock Edicts II, V and XIII make specific mention of the southern provinces describing them at the same time as either dependent on, or independent of, the Mauryan empire. In the Second Edict, mention is made of the neighbouring countries such as the Colas, the Pāṇḍyas, the Satyaputra, the Keralaputra and the Tāmbapanni. In the V Rock Edict the neighbours mentioned are the Yonas, Kambojas, Gāndhāras, Riṣṭikas, Pitinikas, etc. In the thirteenth Rock Edict the Colas, the Pāṇḍyas and the Tāmbapanni are mentioned in addition to the statement "likewise where the king

[1] For details, see *Hyderabad Arch. Series,* No. 1, 1915.

dwells among the Viśas, Vajris, the Āndhras and Pulidas."[1] From these it is quite safe to infer that the Mauryan empire must have had its southern limits extended up to the Tamil kingdoms before Aśoka's time, or at any rate in Bindusāra's reign.

The evidence of Tamil Literature

The fourth and last is the evidence to be found on this point in early Tamil literature. There are four clear references to the Southern invasion of the Mauryas, three in the *Ahanāṉūṟu* and one in the *Puṟanāṉūṟu*. The following is the literal translation of the passages in question:

1. "The rock of the sky-kissing high mountain which the Moriyar had cut down for the free passage of their golden chariot-wheels."[2]

2. "If he should hear of our unbearable anguish and grief here he would not, even for the sake of the *immense riches of the Nandas,* tarry there amidst the mountain rocks which the new Moriyar had cut down for the smooth passage of their well-adorned chariot-wheels when they came down upon the south with an army of horses and elephants because the king of Mohūr had refused to submit when the Kośar with chariots, swift-flying like the winds, routed the enemies' forces on the field of battle with their drums vociferously sounding on the high hoary Podiyil hill."[3]

[1] Bühler, *Ep. Ind.*, II, p. 471 and S. K. Aiyangar, *Beginnings of South Indian History,* pp. 69-70.

[2] Viṇporu neḍuvarai iyaltēr mōriyar
Poṉpuṉai tikiri tiritarak kuṟaitta
aṟai . . .
—*Aham,* 69, by Paraṅkoṟṟaṉār.

[3] Nāmpaṭar kūṟum-arutuyar kētpin
Nandaṉ veṟukkai eaitiṉum maṟṟavaṭ-

a circle of states consists of eighteen elements, the fifteen of the three states, and their kings.[1]

Śakti and Siddhi

While the conqueror's circle of states is the primary circle, three other circles are also mentioned. They are the potential enemy's circle, the Madhyama king's circle of states, and the Udāsīna king's circle of states. Thus the total number of kings constituting the *maṇḍala* are twelve and each possessing five elements of sovereignty, the aggregate of elements in the big circle of twelve kings is sixty. The chieftains of these twelve states constitute themselves twelve sovereign elements. The *dvādaśarājamaṇḍala* then contained altogether seventy-two elements of sovereignty. Every one of the states possessed besides the elements of sovereignty two chief factors all contributing to defining the active or inactive policy of every state. The two factors are the consummation (*siddhi*) and power consisting of strength of wisdom, strength of treasury and army, and strength of energy and enthusiasm (*śakti*). In other words these were the means to the end in view, namely happiness. This end was three-fold, the consequence of the three-fold *śakti* or strength. That monarch who possessed of these elements and the means above mentioned became the overlord of not only his *maṇḍala* but

[1] vijigīṣurmitram mitramitram vā asya prakṛtayastisraḥ|
tāḥ pañcabhiramātyajanapadadurga
kośadaṇḍaprakṛtibhirekaikaśaḥ samyuktā maṇḍalamaṣṭādaśakam bhavati|
anena maṇḍalapṛthaktvam vyākhyātam arimadhyamōdāsīnānām|
evam caturmaṇḍalasaṁkṣepaḥ| dvādaśa rājaprakṛtayah; ṣaṣṭirdravyaprakṛtayah; saṁkṣepeṇa dvisaptatihi|

—*Arthaśāstra,* Bk. VI, ch. ii.

of the whole of the *maṇḍala* through further exertion of his power (*śakti*). By augmenting his own power and behaving righteously towards his neighbours the power of the inferior is thrown into the shade, and these have no option but to accept the overlordship of the Vijigīṣu or the conquering monarch. After giving such details and more, the *Kauṭalīya* ends the section with the very instructive and informing verse which says : "Throwing the circumference of the circle of states beyond his friend's territory, and making the kings of those states as the spokes of that circle, the conqueror shall make himself as the nave of that circle."[1]

Primary kings and subsidiary states

From this we are not to conclude that the whole of the then known world was divided into twelve states and their relations were consequently defined. These twelve kings were primary kings, heads of the primary states. It can be, therefore, affirmed with reasonable confidence that these chief states were in their turn the overlords of several small subsidiary states, each enjoying internal autonomy and responsible to his superior so far as external policy of that kingdom was concerned. Thus there was a number of small states, all in a subordinate capacity to the superior who must have been one among the twelve kings comprising the *maṇḍala* group. When one of these twelve kings augmented his power and means, he became superior to other kings and his suzerain power was acknowledged by one and all. He was then the *emperor* of the land and his kingdom was *empire* and his policy was that of

[1] Trans., Bk. VI, ch. ii; cp. Bk. VII, ch. xviii.

the *imperialist*. This is the idea of an empire set forth in the *Arthaśāstra*, and any other construction is to misunderstand the true conception that lies behind this significant notion. It has been remarked that the policy enunciated by the author of the *Arthaśāstra* is not imperial in outlook but narrowed down to a small state. But let it be noted that the policy enunciated is applicable to a small state as well as to a large state which we call an empire.

The views of Dr. S. K. Aiyangar

In this connection Dr. S. K. Aiyangar's remarks seem apposite: "Empires in India under the Hindus attempted to be no more than kingdoms, of a small compass comparatively, which gathered together under the ægis of the leading state, which went by the name of imperial state for the time being, other kingdoms constituting merely an expanding *maṇḍala* in political dependence. The administration that had to be carried on by the imperial state was a comparatively simple one, as by a well established principle of devolution, most of the actual administration was carried on by local bodies for comparatively small states. . . . . . If that is granted there is no difficulty in understanding that what seems to be laid down for a congeries of smaller states cannot be far different from what was necessary for a really imperial state. Examined in this light it will be found that even the *Arthaśāstra* polity provides the machinery for carrying on the imperial administration as well as the administration of a comparatively small state."[1]

[1] Author's *Hindu Administrative Institutions*, Intro., pp. xiii-xiv.

State, federal not unitary

From this we are to understand that the state in Ancient India, at least so far as the Mauryan India was concerned, was not unitary in type but federal in character, speaking in the language of modern political science. It was roughly a composite of federal states. It is indeed difficult to determine the nature of the ancient Indian state in general, and the Mauryan state in particular. It is again an intricate task to set forth the substantial relations which existed between the imperial Government and each of the provinces or states now united in the Empire as its member. Every student of modern Political Science knows that federation which has its roots in the remote past 'varies in form from place to place, and from time to time'.[1] One view of a federal state is that when a central authority exercises limited jurisdiction over authorities beneath it, then that authority is a federal authority. Viewed in this light the Mauryan state was a federal state. For it cannot be claimed to have exercised unlimited jurisdiction over states beneath it, a mark of a unitary state. But its was not a rigid federal constitution. It was a loose form of confederation made up of congeries of states.[2]

Vassal provinces

If it, then, be accepted that the Mauryan state was of a confederate type or rather federal in character, then it may be asked how could such elaborate

[1] C. F. Strong, *Modern Political Constitutions,* (1930, London), p. 98.

[2] *Ibid.*, p. 82.

provincial system of administration be in vogue as is evident from the Edicts of Aśoka, not to speak of other evidences. This topic then requires a new and independent examination. It would seem that these provinces would come under the name of vassal provinces, one form of the sub-division of what Bluntschli calls the compound states (*Zusammen gesetzte Statsform*).

Relation of the central states to provinces

A province can be likened to a colony which is "at the outset no state. It is a local Government with perhaps more or less of local autonomy."[1] The separate organisation is only a form of Government, and not a state, for if we subject this case to a rigid scientific test, the moment a province becomes a state it ceases to be a part of the empire. The constitution was, therefore, a confederation of a number of states effected not necessarily by a treaty but with the express consent of the parties themselves. It was a sort of inter-state agreement by which the Imperial Government or the Emperor representing that Government, introduced a sort of governmental organisation which consisted of a Viceroy and his Council of Ministers. The provinces which were in the nature of different states agreed to abide by the recommendations of this body. This agreement, it is reasonable to infer, must have been "for the accomplishment of certain limited and restricted purposes". This system may, perhaps, roughly answer to what Burgess conceives to be a simple state of wider organisation.[2] Viewed in terms

[1] Burgess, *Political Science and Constitutional Law,* Vol. I, pp. 77-78.

[2] *Ibid.,* p. 79.

of modern political science it may not be right to style these provinces as states though in fact some continued as subordinate states. It is true that imperial officers were stationed at the provincial headquarters. But our contention is that these imperial officers at the provincial capitals were there to suppress any political rising against the Imperial Power and to see that these states did not wilfully evade the payment of tribute or presents to be paid to the emperor according to the original agreement with him. Nothing more was executed by this body. But it can be asserted with reasonable confidence that these imperial officers at the provincial headquarters aided the provincial or state authorities in the conduct of their government, without any interference in the details of internal administration. They seem to have occupied a position that can be compared to that of the representatives of the central government in the Native States of Modern India. The states, loosely called provinces, continued to be precisely the same from the standpoint of law and custom.

Sec. iv. THE ENDS OF THE MAURYAN STATE

Mauryan administration not a military rule

To understand correctly the Mauryan administrative system and its achievements and failure, it is necessary that we must first examine the aims and ends of the Mauryan state. What is true of the Mauryan state is largely true of Hindu states in general; for the Mauryan state was not a departure from the established tradition of the land. When we speak of the ends of the state, there is the implication that the ends of state were both proximate and ultimate. The ultimate end was spiritual in character and religious in scope. It perhaps approached the doctrine inculcated by Hegel that morality (*sittlicheit*) is the end of the state. By its nature the Mauryan administration was not a military rule and consequently the state was not a centralised despotism. As has been stated elsewhere, the end of the state, namely the moral and material welfare of the citizens at large, could not be realised in a polity which made militarism its essential feature. No doubt wars were fought and territories conquered. The object was to bring the whole country under one sceptre. The laws of war are only a code of honour very skilfully incorporated into the body of the civil law, so that militarism may not show itself in all its nakedness.[1] The other aspect, which is, that the Mauryan state was not a centralised despotism, will be examined in the next chapter.

Purpose of the State

We may point out *en passant* that the Aśokan inscriptions betray a scheme of decentralisation, the signs of which are already visible in the *Arthaśāstra*. The insistence on the principle of *svadharma* in the *Kauṭalīya*,[2] and the inculcation of the laws of dharma or practice of morality by Aśoka have no other end in view than the attainment of heavenly bliss. If this was the chief purpose of the state, what were then the proximate ends which contributed to the realization of this ultimate end?

[1] *Hindu Adm. Inst.*, p. 382.

[2] See Winternitz, *Dharmaśāstra and Arthaśāstra* in the *Sir Asutosh Memorial Volume*, Patna.

The triple end

From a study of the literature and epigraphical records concerned, it appears that the triple end advocated by Von Holtzendorff, approximately answers to the proximate ends of the Mauryan state.

The first is *der nationale Machtzweck.* This is claiming a position of overlordship over other states in addition to its own subjects by proper exercise of true power.

The second is *der individuelle Rechtszweck.* This is to let every citizen of the state enjoy liberty according to his station and purpose in life, but of course with due regard to the conventions of society.

The third and last purpose of the state is *der gezellschaftliche culturzweck,* general happiness. Towards this end, the state recognizes the existence of institutions, social and religious, within its territorial limits, and keeps a vigilant watch over these organisations lest they should undermine the power of the state. Other duties of the state under this category are mentioned as follows: "It must prevent the rivalries between different associations from coming to a breach of the peace. It must protect the rights of the individual member of any association against the tyranny of the association. It must hold all associations to their primary purpose, if such they have, and aid them, if strictly necessary, in its accomplishment. Finally, it must direct education of its subjects."[1]

Immediate ends of the State

Though there is a confusion here of an admixture of functions of government and functions of state as

[1] Burgess, *Political Science and Constitutional Law,* Vol. I, p. 84.

Burgess holds, still they are important since they clearly show the immediate ends of the state as realised in ancient Hindu polity. Attention has been already drawn to the Kauṭalīyan recommendation of the two aspects of government, power (*śakti*) and consummation (*siddhi*), and the different elements constituted by each. The *Arthaśāstra,* if it teaches anything, teaches the king to concentrate all his power so as to ensure the *lokayātrā* to his subjects and retain that power through an elaborate official machinery. The social organization with its principle of *svadharma* so much insisted in the *Arthaśāstra* is conceived to be the body politic composed of individuals in various states of evolution discharging their respective duties and yet enjoying freedom. This freedom of the individual is not of the type aimed at by the political philosophers of the 19th century. The individual of Hindu social polity aimed not at asserting his rights and privileges but aimed at the far more important thing, namely, the liberation of his soul by faithfully discharging his obligations and by means of supreme knowledge (*jñāna*). This opens to him the royal path which ultimately leads him to the *mokṣa,* the final release from the bondage of birth and death (*saṁsāra*). Not the least interesting is the fact that the chief proximate end of the state as proclaimed in the *Kauṭalīya* and vociferously reiterated in the Edicts of Aśoka, (which no political philosopher of modern times could ignore) is summed up in two pregnant lines:

"In the happiness of the subjects lies the happiness of the king: it is no happiness or welfare to the king which is not the happiness or welfare of the people at large."[1]

[1] Bk. I, ch. 19; R. E. VI, First Separate Edict at Jaugada, and Pillar Edict VI.

Towards this end Aśoka directed all his energy and effort. He protected the rights of individual associations in the land whether it be Brahmanical, Buddhist, Jaina, Ājīvaka or any other. He strove to promote brotherly feeling among these sects of various denominations and character. He allowed them to have their own ways of religious worship and philosophical speculation. He aided these associations in their functioning and in their accomplishment. He promulgated regulations and ordinances to prevent a breach of the peace among these sects. Aśoka felt these to be the primary duties of the state and executed them to the best of his abilities. Why these things were zealously pursued is explained by him and by the author of the *Arthaśāstra*. These are towards realising the ultimate end, which, according to the belief of the times, was to find an honoured place in Heaven.

CHAPTER III.

THE CENTRAL ADMINISTRATION

Sec. i. *THE CHARACTER OF MAURYAN MONARCHY*

Introductory

At the helm of this vast Empire girt by the seas in the east and the west were, one after another, Candragupta, Bindusāra, Aśokavardhana and other great kings for nearly a century and a half. It was Puṣyamitra Śuṅga who extinguished the line and started the Śuṅga dynasty. The evidence of the *Arthaśāstra,* of classical writers like Megasthenes, of Buddhist literature, and of inscriptions like those of Aśoka supply us with a wealth of material which helps us to frame an accurate picture of the polity in vogue in these early days of Hindu India. From all the pieces of evidence literary or epigraphical, we come upon one clear fact, that the king was an important limb of the body politic. In fact, he is one among the seven constituents constituting a state (the *saptāṅga* of the Hindu literature). The *Arthaśāstra,* as has been already said, is one of the sources of information for this period. There is a view that the *Arthaśāstra* is merely a theoretical treatise on polity in general and does not treat of the conditions of the time. But a significant circumstance in this connection is that there is an express statement by the author in unequivocal terms that the treatise was composed for the use of Narendra. In this term there has been no difficulty in recognising

Candragupta Maurya.[1] Besides the fact that the Purāṇas give a second name of Candragupta as Narendra, Jayaswal draws out attention to the term *narendrāṇka,* being the monogram or mark to be put on arms.[2]

Succession generally hereditary

Proceeding then on the assumption that the *Artha-śāstra* formed the manual or the code on which the Mauryas including Aśoka and Daśaratha based their administration we find the king hereditary, constitutional, and limited by a system of checks and balances. That it was hereditary no one will dispute. According to Strabo son succeeded father.[3] Every one knows Bindusāra as the son of Candragupta and Aśoka, the grandson. The mere fact that a prince happened to be the son of his father did not procure him the throne. Pliny states that the king was chosen by people with thirty councillors.[4] Besides the officials of the state, the commonalty of the people were also present on this great occasion, as well as the representatives of the Paura, Jānapada and other corporate institutions. This choice of the king by the people is an important democratic factor which one cannot easily argue away. The principle of common will was thus a factor reckoned with in the constitution of ancient Indian polity. Generally the eldest son succeeded, while other sons were sent out as provincial

[1] Bk. II, ch. 10.

sarvaśāstrāṇyanukramya prayogamupalabhya ca|
Kauṭalyena narendrārthe śāsanasya vidhiḥ kṛtaḥ||

[2] See *In. Ant.*, 1918, p. 55, and *Hindu Polity*, Pt. I, p. 214.

[3] *Ancient India as described in Classical Literature*, p. 55.

[4] *Ancient India in Classical Literature*, Sec. V.

viceroys or posted in other superior stations. The legend contained in the *Pāṁsupradāna* section popularly known as *Aśokavadāna*[1] to the effect that Aśoka had to kill his near and dear including his brothers to get at the throne has been justly discredited. That the story extant in the Buddhist work is an imagination of the writer rather than an historical fact has been proved from one of the inscriptions where Aśoka is said to have bestowed special care and attention to the habitations of his brothers and sisters, to the harem, etc.[2] It is impossible to think of Aśoka devoid of family affection and brotherly goodwill.

Though the succession was generally hereditary, one could not style himself Rāja or Mahārāja until he went through the time-honoured ceremony of *Abhiṣecanīya.* This was the anointing of the prince by the Purohita and other higher officers of the state. This institution is an ancient Vedic institution and is described in detail in the *Aitareya Brāhmaṇa.* It was an important occasion of feast and festivity. There was an age limit to this anointing ceremony[3] and if the tradition that Aśoka was crowned four years after his accession to the throne has any meaning, it is that Aśoka had only a formal vesting of regal powers at his father's death and that he had the legal *abhiṣeka* in his twenty-fifth year.[4]

[1] See *Divyāvādāna,* XXVI.

[2] *Corpus,* p. 155; Pillar Edict VI.

[3] See Jayaswal, *Hindu Polity,* II, pp. 52-3. According to the inscription of Khāravela the completion of the 24th year is the age for coronation.

[4] See *J.B.O.R.S.,* Vol. I, p. 93, and Vol. III, p. 438.

Abdication

There was also the practice of relinquishing the throne and the numerous honours pertaining to it by the sitting king in favour of his son and the Yuvarāja. Such abdication was voluntary, dictated by honest and well-meaning motives. It has been a tradition, both Vedic and epic, that in ancient India when the king attained a certain age fit for the third *āśrama,* the *vānaprastha,* he abdicated his throne in favour of his son and retired to the forest to lead a godly life of penance and prayer. If we are to believe the Jaina tradition, Candragupta must have felt that his son had come of sufficient age to take up the responsibilities of ruling the empire, and that it was high time he retired from the din and bustle of political administration to one of peaceful meditation. Whether he was attracted by the Jaina doctrines on the eve of his life and whether he stuck to them, it is not possible to show in any conclusive manner from the materials available. V. A. Smith did not attach any value to this tradition in his first edition of the *Early History of India.* In subsequent editions, however, he has changed his opinion and thinks that it may be possible that Candragupta died as a Jaina.[1] Whatever be the truth underlying this tradition the fact remains that Candragupta after a reign of 24 years abdicated in favour of his son Bindusāra who ruled the empire equally well for 25 years according to the Purāṇas and 28 years according to the Ceylon chronicles.[2]

[1] See above, p. 51.

[2] It is an intricate attempt to find a safe shore from the troublous sea of Mauryan chronology. The date of accession of Candragupta to the throne is still far from being settled. The latest writer on the

Abdication of Aśoka

There is a similar tradition with regard to the abdication of Aśoka in the evening of his life. Of the three Edicts in the Mysore territory—Brahmagiri, Siddhāpura and Jaṭinga Rameśvara Hill[1]—Fleet would attach special interest to the version of the Brahmagiri text which discloses the fact that it was framed on the anniversary of Aśoka's abdication, while he was living in religious retirement on the hill Suvarṇagiri.[2]

subject is Otto Stein, who in an article entitled the *Coronation of Candragupta Maurya* in the *Journal of Czecho-slovakia Oriental Institute,* Prague, Vol. I, 3, argues on the strength of the classical sources that the accession could not be earlier than B.C. 318. Hultzsch agrees with Fleet in fixing B.C. 320. (*C.I.I.*, Vol. I, Intro., p. xxxv.) V. A. Smith is inclined to B.C. 322 (*Early History of India,* p. 45). The writer in the *Cambridge History of India* makes out a case for B.C. 321, while J. Carpentier brings it down to B.C. 313 (*Ibid.,* pp. 156-64). Prof. Kern pleads for B.C. 322 (*Ind. Ant.,* Vol. III, p. 79), while J. Sen for 325 B.C. (*Ind. His. Quar.,* Vol. V, pp. 6-14). K. G. Sankara assigns 321 B.C. (*Ind. Ant.,* 1920, 49f). L. D. Barnett also suggests this date (*Antiquities of India,* p. 39). I am rather inclined to take the date furnished by Jayaswal cir. 326|25 B.C. (*J.B.O.R.S.*, Vol. I, Pt. 1, p. 116). The same difficulty is met with in the case of Bindusāra and Aśoka. The date of Bindusāra's coronation ranges from 296 to 298 B.C. That the reign of Candragupta extended for 24 years seems to be generally adopted. But Bindusāra's rule was 25 years according to the *Purāṇas* and 28 years according to the Ceylon chronicles. The same confusion awaits us when we come to Aśoka. Professor Kern is inclined towards 270 B.C. when Aśoka became emperor (*Int. Ant.,* Vol. III, p. 79). According to Barnett Aśoka succeeded his father about 268 B.C. and his coronation was in 264 B.C. (*Antiquities of India,* p. 39). H. C. Ray Chaudry in his *Political History of Ancient India* pleads for 273 B.C. It is said that Aśoka died in 232 B.C. after a reign of about forty years. Barnett assigns 226 B.C. as the year of Aśoka's death (*Antiquities,* p. 40). Aśoka's reign was for 36 years according to the *Vāyu Purāṇa* and 37 according to the *Mahāv śa.* Kern places his death in 234 or 233 B.C. (*Ind. Ant.,* Vol. III, p 79).

[1] *Corpus,* pp. 175-79.

[2] *J.R.A.S.*, 1905, p. 304. Here Fleet identifies Suvarṇagiri with Songir, one of the hills round the city of Girivraja in Magadha. I think the identification with Kanakagiri Hill is more probable.

But what we can gather from this is that Aśoka also abdicated his throne and led a life of penance and prayer. This may perhaps explain the tradition contained in the *Kalpanāmaṇḍiṭikā* of *Kumāralāta*[1]:

tyāgaśūro narendro sāvaśoko maurya-kuñjaraḥ|
jambūdvīpeśvaro bhūtvā jāto ardhāmalakeśvaraḥ||
bhṛtyaiḥ sa bhūmipatiḥ adya hṛtādhikāro
dānam prayacchati kilāmalakārdham etat|
śrībhoga vistaramadair atigarvitānām
pratyādiśann iva manāṁsi pṛthagjanānām||

"Aśoka, the great Maurya, noted for his liberality, became the lord of half of the *āmalaka* fruit after ruling over Jampūdvīpa.

"Having now been deprived of his kingdom by his servants (entrusted his kingdom to his servants?) he gives away in charity half of the *āmalaka* he has on hand as if to direct the minds of ordinary men elated with extensive riches (to do charitable deeds)."

A Constitutional Monarchy

The Mauryan king was again a constitutional monarch, law-abiding in the sense that he obeyed the law of the land. Almost every writer on the subject has uniformly characterised the Mauryan monarchy as autocratic. Unfortunately the statement seems to have been made without any warrant for it.[2] If by autocracy is meant absolute government wherein the ruler was all in all, and above whom there was no authority to control and influence his acts and deeds, then it does not admit of application in the case of

[1] H. Lüders, *Bruchstücke Der Kalpanāmaṇḍiṭikā Des Kumāralāta*, p. 150 (Leipzig, 1926).

[2] *Early History*, p. 145; *Early History of Bengal*, p. 35; D. R. Bhandarkar, *Aśoka*, p. 98; *R. K. Mookerji*; *Aśoka*; pp. 47-49; Smith, Aśoka, p. 92, 3rd ed.

Mauryan monarchs. The question has been to some extent discussed elsewhere[1] but still we cannot refrain from referring to it once again here. It is a question of moment and it must be settled once for all.

King, not a law-maker

Before we enter into the detailed examination of checks and balances which considerably limited the power and extent of the king's authority, there is the great conception of the ancient Hindus that the king could not be, and was not, a law-maker. The law is eternal (*sanātana*) and is contained in the law-codes or the *Dharmaśāstras* of the different *smṛti-kartas,* which were based on the *śṛuti.* The king of the land was to act according to the laws prescribed by these law-givers and he could not override them. To override the laws already established was considered sacrilege. If he did act contrary to the principles of the established law, people disowned him, rose in rebellion against him, removed him from the throne and set up another in his stead. Therefore, the law of the law-books was the real sovereign of the land. The king's orders amounted to proclamations explaining existing laws or reviving those which had fallen into disuse. He could not, and did not, make any legislation for the state.[2]

[1] See author's *Hindu Ad. Inst.,* pp. 72-76.

[2] The observations of E. B. Havell may be quoted here: "The student of Indian History may also be led to consider whether the Imperial Parliament of Great Britain constituted as it is now is on more or less empirical lines, is really more efficient as political machinery than was the philosophic scheme of Indo-Aryan polity, in which the common law of the land, formulated by the chosen representatives of the people, had a religious as well as a legal sanction, and represented the highest power of the state to which even the king and his ministers must bow. It will be a surprise to many readers to discover that the Mother of Western Parliaments had an Aryan relative in India, show-

Aśoka, no legislator

It is sometimes claimed with no justification whatever that Aśoka's Edicts were laws promulgated by the Emperor Aśoka in utter disregard of this sacred tradition.[1] It is an erroneous position taken by the historian. Aśoka has nowhere claimed that he made any departure in the legislation of the land. He simply enforced the regulations which had fallen into disuse by long and continual neglect. If Aśoka did anything, he revived old practices and put them in working order. The idea that the Hindu king was a law-maker is not countenanced in Indian jurisprudence at all. To regard therefore the *śāsana* contained in the Edicts of Aśoka as amounting to legislation by the king is, to say the least, uncritical. What Aśoka did was the re-affirmation of old laws which had gone out of practice. Therefore the term *śāsana* (rendered 'ordinance' by V. A. Smith) occurring in the Sārnāth Pillar Edict[2] and continued in the pillar Edicts of Sāṁchī and Kauśāmbī (Allahabad), does not mean promulgation of a new law, but does mean a declaration of the old law without prejudice to the customary law or the *samaya* of the *Arthaśāstra*[3] and *Dharmaśāstras*.[4] In this sense the *Kauṭalīya* uses the term *śāsana* as can be seen from the chapter *śāsanādhikāraḥ*.[5] One punishment for infringing the

ing a strong family likeness, before the sixth century B.C., and that her descendants were a great power in the state at the time of the Norman conquest!" (Intro. xiii-xiv, *History of Aryan Rule in India*.)

[1] *See* Smith, *Asoka*, p. 92.

[2] See *Corpus*, pp. 161-3.

[3] *Ar. Śās.*, Bk. III, ch. 10.

[4] Manu, VIII, 218-21.

[5] *Ar. Śās.*, Bk. II, ch. 10.

monastic code was deportation of these monks to non-monastic places (*anāvāsa*), with a further penalty of replacing their yellow by white robes.[1] This is only a counterpart of the penalty of banishment to the misbehaved according to the *Dharmaśāstras.* That such cases of departure from monastic life were common is seen from the *Arthaśāstra* where stringent regulations are prescribed for donning the robes of a *sannyāsin.*[2] It is said that those who left the order of the monks for the world were entertained by the state for various purposes and especially as special intelligent officials who were let loose on the country so as to ascertain the honesty or otherwise of its officers.[3]

Like the term *śāsana* the expression *samaya* occurring in the First and Second Separate Edicts of Dhauli and the First Separate Edict of Jaugaḍa[4] has been used in the technical sense of resolution or decision especially of corporate bodies or of judges. The expression is preceded in all these cases by the word *sasvatam* and Hultzsch in rendering the phrase *sasvatam samayam* 'at all times' follows Kern[5] and Lüders.[6] The full sentence in the context as appears in the First Separate Rock Edict, Dhauli, is *nagala viyohālakā sasvataṁ samayaṁ yūjevuti.* Hultzsch interprets 'in order that the judicial officers of the city may strive at all times'. If the rendering 'at all times' is to be

1. *Corpus,* pp. 160-61; Cp. S.B.E., Vol. 17, p. 388, n. 1.
2. *Arthaśāstra,* Bk. II, ch. I.
3. *Ibid.,* Bk. I, ch. XI.
4. *Corpus,* pp. 92-94 and 98 and 99 and 112-113.
5. *J.R.A.S.,* 1880, p. 391.
6. *S.P.A.W.,* 1914, p. 864.

adopted the reading must be *sasvat*. A plausible reading is *śāśvataṁ* meaning eternal or immemorial and hence customary. Besides *śaśvat* means 'at all times,' and therefore no significance is attached to the expression *samayaṁ*. The translation suggested is 'in order that the judicial officers of the city may be bound by the customary law of the land'. Thus *śāsana* and the *samaya* of the Edicts as well as the punishments mentioned correspond to those of the *Arthaśāstra* to which Aśoka was of course indebted. In the light of the peculiar judicial concept of law as eternal, and *samaya* an important factor of the law, it is misreading the history of Ancient India if we style any monarch as a law-maker. In the nature of things and in the circumstances in which he accepts the crown the king is bound to be non-autocratic and non-absolute. In fact there is no place for an autocrat in the polity of ancient Hindus.

Checks and balances

This was not all. There were the chambers of the council and of the assembly where the representatives of the groups and communities sat and discussed the affairs of the state. One was the *mantri-pariṣad* of which the important official was the Purohita who was the king's conscience-keeper, or in plain language, confidential adviser to the crown in matters spiritual and secular. In addition to other duties these ministers with the Purohita were to guide the king in the right path lest he should fall into pitfalls due to carelessness.[1] That these ministers of the Maurya kings discharged their duties properly is

[1] *Ar. Śās.*, Bk. I, ch. vii.

evident from the peaceful administration of the land during this epoch. A vast empire like that of the Mauryas could not be sustained for a long time if it were simply crushed down by the heavy weight of the iron hands of the king. The kingdom endured for a long time because the people willingly acquiesced in the administration of the land. They acquiesced because the kings ruled them justly and in a perfectly constitutional manner. In this connection it may be remembered that the empire depended on the dominant personality of the emperor. Whence once that personality disappeared from the arena of the empire, the latter collapsed. In other words, the empire arose under strong rulers and broke under weak ones.[1] There was, then, an institution, a council or assembly, the *pariṣad* of Aśoka inscriptions[2] which proved an effective check on the monarch by going astray from the ordained path.[3]

The *mantripariṣad* of the *Kauṭalīya* was the Council of Ministers whose chief functions are categorically stated: to undertake a new work, to complete the work already begun, to develop other possibilities, and to enforce discipline in the administration. The king usually consulted his counsellors and the assembly of ministers as well, before he finally set his seal of approval or rejection of a certain decision. If an

[1] See above, p. 74.

[2] R. E. III and VI; *Corpus*, pp. 73: 52; 57-58 and 576.

[3] Two Indian scholars among others, K. P. Jayaswal and Dr. Bhandarkar, have identified not without reason the *Pariṣad* of the inscriptions with the *Mantripariṣad* of the *Arthaśāstra* of Kauṭalīya. (Bk. I, 14.) The interpretation suggested to the term by Lassen 'Assembly of the Doctors,' Senart as 'Clergy,' and Bühler 'Teachers and Ascetics of Schools,' falls to the ground in the light of the *Arthaśāstra*.

emergency presented itself the king summoned his counsellors and ministers and generally adopted the course of action suggested by them.[1]

There are what we may call administrative Edicts[2] and from them we gather four facts among others: (1) The *pariṣad* enforced the execution of the king's orders by the officials; (2) it was summoned by the king whenever necessary for consultation and advice; (3) the king interfered with its work whenever differences of opinion arose amongst its members; and (4) it had a controlling influence over the officials of the state. After a close examination of these details, K. P. Jayaswal conclusively shows that the Council of Ministers was so powerful that the Emperor was virtually deprived of his sovereign authority.[3]

The evidence of Mudrārākṣasa

The *Mudrārākṣasa* of Viśākhadatta which can be counted as one of the source-books for the Mauryan epoch[4] speaks in so many words of the delegation of the authority to such an extent that the king resents that he is nothing if he is simply to carry out the proposal of the chief minister and his council. It has been suggested that the passages in question refer to the fact that the minister was all powerful but not the council of ministers.[5] We shall examine in the sequel how weak the argument advanced for this assumption is.

1 *Ar. Śās.*, Bk. I, ch. xv.

2 Bhandarkar, *Aśoka*, pp. 59-62.

3 *J.B.O.R.S.*, IV, 43; *I.H.Q.*, Vol. I, Radha Govinda Basak: *Ministers in Ancient India.*

4 See *Cambridge History of India*, Vol. I, p. 467.

5 *Glories of Magadha*, pp. 93-94*n*.

The evidence of the Divyāvadāna

Added to this is the significant statement of the *Divyāvadāna,* namely, 'the king to-day has been deprived of authority by his servants'[1]:

> bhṛtyaiḥ sa bhūmipatiradya hṛtādhikāro
> dānam prayachati kilāmalakārdham etat||

This passage only corroborates our view that the *pariṣad* (Council) exercised real executive powers and the king was only the nominal sovereign authority. This reminds us of the present Parliamentary system of Government in Great Britain where the real sovereign authority is the Parliament though the formal assent of the King is necessary to every administrative measure, including the appointment of higher officials. Nothing more or anything less is implied in the polity of the ancient Mauryas.

The evidence of Arrian

In addition to the Buddhist tradition contained in the *Divyāvadāna* there is the valuable testimony of the Greek writer Arrian.[2] "The seventh caste consists of the councillors and assessors who deliberate on public affairs." This fits in with the observation of Kauṭalya that all kinds of administrative measures were to be preceded by deliberations in a well-formed council.[3] Thus every independent evidence goes to show that executive powers were exercised by the Mauryan

[1] Cowell Ed., p. 432.

[2] For the reliability of Arrian's accounts see Prof. Freeman, *Historical Essays,* quoted by K. G. Sankara in his paper on *Some Problems in Indian Chronology*: *Annals of Bh. Or. R. Institute,* Vol. XII, Pt. VI.

[3] *Ar. Śās.* Bk. I, Ch. 14.

Council. In the light of such unanimous testimony can we still seriously believe that the Mauryan monarchs were absolute or autocratic?

The paternal conception

A significant circumstance in this connection is the paternal conception of the government so eloquently proclaimed by the inscriptions left to us as an invaluable legacy by Aśoka. Even to this concept Aśoka was indebted to the *Arthaśāstra*. This is evident from the fact that the *Arthaśāstra* pleads for such a healthy form of government. It is unfortunate that an indologist of the standing of Dr. D. R. Bhandarkar has fallen into an error in examining the real force that underlies the paternal conception of administration. He remarks[1]: "Just as children are solely dependent upon their parents who can do to them just what they like, the subjects were at the mercy of the king who was thus no better than a despot." The statement of Bhandarkar amounts to the fact that every father is a despot. If the feelings of a father towards his children are to be despotic it is impossible to cultivate homely virtues of peace and goodwill which were as much the crowning fruits of India's culture as those of other cultures. Nay, the notion of a father being despotic lays an axe at the root of all human relationships, and is contrary to all religious creeds. When we speak of parental feelings we mean undoubtedly genuine affection, transparent sincerity, and religious devotion to duty which consists in the upkeep of the children until they come of age and stand on their own legs. This and this alone is meant

[1] *Asoka*, p. 63.

by Kauṭalya in his *Arthaśāstra* and Aśoka in his inscriptions.[1]

Aśoka's aim was to win the affection of his people. Just as a father would do his best to his children, so that they may enjoy life thoroughly and well by pursuing a righteous path leading them ultimately to the heaven of bliss, so Aśoka wished to do to his people. He wanted to see that every one of his subjects was happy and contented. In a word, Aśoka liked to follow the *Rājadharma* in such a manner that it would tend to the *Yogakṣema* of the state comprised of different communities of people. Welfare and happiness (*hitasukham*) correspond to the happy phrase of the *Kauṭalīya Yogakṣema.* It was then the ambition of Aśoka to discharge his duty, namely protection of his subjects, in a way calculated to promote their best interests

[1] According to Kauṭalya 'happy is the king whose subjects are happy.'

prajā sukhe sukhaṁ rājñaḥ prajānām ca hite hitam
nātmapriyam hitam rājñaḥ prajānām tu priyaṁ hitam|
—*Ar. Śās.*, Bk. I, 19.

This was the paternal conception of the ancient Indian monarchy. Kauṭalya refers to this theory in more than one place where he advocates the remission of taxes whenever need arose for such a step. (Bk. II, 1; Bk. IV, 3.) In the chapter on *Janapadaniveśa* (Bk. II, 1) the king is asked to treat the newly settled people as his children (nivṛttaparihārān pitevānugṛhṇīyāt. Again in the chapter on *Upanipātapratīkāra* (Bk. IV, 3) the king is instructed to protect his subjects as his own children:

tān pitevānugṛhṇīyāt|

This is exactly what Aśoka advocates. (First Separate R. E. Dhauli, *Corpus,* p. 95.)

"All men are my children. As on behalf of (my. own) children I desire that they may be provided with complete welfare and happiness in this world and in the other world, the same I desire also on behalf of (all) men."

save munise pajā mamā| ath(ā)pajāye ichhāmi
h(a)ka(ṁ) kiṁti sa(ve)na hi ta-sukhena hidalo(kika)-
pālalokike(na) y(ūjev)ū (t)i [tathā . . muni]sesu
pi (i)chhāmi (ha)ka(ṁ).

Ibid., p. 93.

possible. Aśoka's was not mere lip sympathy. He in fact did his level best to advance the comforts of his subjects. His administration undertook such kinds of public works as were acceptable to the common will and tended towards public utility. These were hospitals for beast and man, rest-houses, roads with medicinal herbs and plants, wells, irrigation works, prohibition of the eating of flesh as far as possible, avoiding war and consequently bloodshed, endowments for religious purposes and propaganda for moral and material uplift.

The king, no despot

The above observations will then lead to the irresistible conclusion that the king was no despot who harassed the people at his will and pleasure, but a constitutionalist who promoted their welfare at all times, in all places, and at all costs. The king therefore felt that he was only the servant of the state. No pleasure was greater to him than to discharge the duties and responsibilities which he owed to the people and which he regarded as something sacred and religious. Any amount of reading through the several Edicts of Aśoka does not bring home to us the claim of royal prerogatives, privileges and rights. Aśoka tells us clearly and plainly that he would be available to his people at all times, and at all places, even when he dines and even when he bathes.[1] This is surely a lofty conception of the responsibility he feels to discharge, and not a privilege which he desires to abuse. Speaking on the

[1] s(a)ve kāle bhuṁj(a) mānasa me orodhanamhi gabhāgāramhi vachamhi va vīnītamhi cha uyāneṣu cha sarvatra paṭivedakā sṭitā athe me (ja)nasa paṭivedetha iti| sarvatra cha janasa athe karomi||

VI. R. E. *Corpus,* p. 11.

special tone of the Edicts, L. Rice remarks: "Solicitude for the welfare here and hereafter of all his subjects, high and low, is manifest throughout and it extended even to peoples beyond his boundaries in an all-embracing humanity."[1] A king who feels or is made to feel that he is only a superior servant of the state could hardly be termed an absolute ruler. In the light of the above observations there is no justification for the remark that the Mauryan kings were autocrats or absolutists.

Sec. ii. EDUCATION AND DISCIPLINE OF PRINCES

To be actuated by such high ideals, the king must have been well disciplined both in body and mind from his boyhood. The fruit of discipline is the result of proper educational training. We may regard Kauṭalya's prescription in regard to the education of a prince as the type in ancient states under Hindu monarchies. Discipline (*vinaya*), says Kauṭalya, is of two kinds, artificial (*kṛtaka*) and natural (*svābhāvika*).[2] Instruction proper disciplines the naturally good man possessing great and noble virtues of obedience, restraint, discrimination and other qualities. With the ceremony of tonsure which was usually at the age of three the prince learnt the alphabet (*lipi*) and arithmetic (*saṅkhyānam*).[3] Two stages could be distinguished in the matter of education. The first stage was between the years three and eleven. In

[1] *Mysore and Coorg from Inscriptions,* p. 14.

[2] Bk. I, ch. 5.

[3] *Ibid.*

this period what we call secondary education was completed. The first rudimentary principles of arts and sciences were learnt. From the age of eleven, the age for investiture ceremony, extending to sixteen, he was initiated into higher studies. Thus the educational training and practice were complete before the age of sixteen when the prince could enter the life of a householder. The higher education consisted in the study of the three Vedas, *ānvīkṣakī* (philosophy), *vārttā* (economics) and *daṇḍanīti* (politics). Different teachers were engaged to teach these sciences. The *trayī* and *ānvīkṣakī* were learnt from persons who were learned in the respective sciences (*adhyakṣa*), while *vārttā* and *daṇḍanīti* from expounders and administrators of law (*vaktṛprayoktṛbhyaḥ*).[1]

A perusal of the daily time-table of princes shows the heavy programme of work before them. The forenoons were devoted to the hearing of *itihāsas* or stories of ancient kings, who had led great and glorious lives.[2] Listening to chivalrous tales about far-famed ancestors from competent Purāṇa tellers would make a much greater impression on the mind of the young prince than simply reading them for himself. This was to infuse in him the fire of enthusiasm without which no noble work could be undertaken by any person. How it adds to the efficiency of learning is observed thus: "Knowledge arises out of hearing and produces steady application (*yoga*), which ultimately leads on to self-possession (*ātmavattā*)."[3] During the rest of the day and the

[1] *Ar. Śās.*, Bk. I, ch. 5.

[2] *Ibid.*

[3] śrutāddhi prajāñopajāyate| prajñāyā yogo yogādātmavatteti vidyāsāmarthyam||—*Ibid.*

night the prince not only learnt new lessons in other branches but revised the old lessons lest they should be forgotten. If he came across passages which were not clear and intelligible to him then he would enter into a discussion with the teachers and elders and thus free himself from doubts of any kind. Last but not least the prince was instructed to court the awe-inspiring company of the aged professors, the living example of great learning and healthy discipline.[1]

Kauṭalya raises a question why such attention should be bestowed on education and himself answers it excellently well. A prince with a disciplined mind and body could carry on administration on sound lines.[2] He alone would be able to control the organs of his senses properly and use them in the right direction. No learning, no discipline; then arise all troubles for all men and specially so for kings. An unlettered person is not able to discriminate between vice and virtue, nor to appreciate the evils of such vices. Vices are due primarily to anger (*kopa*) and desire (*kāma*). The triad of evils due to anger is abuse of decorum, abuse of money, and abuse of proper justice. The evils of *kāma* or desire are said to be fourfold, hunting, gambling, women, and drinking.[3] This does not mean that the king was prohibited from hunting, or in any way enjoying life. Only excess was condemned. They could be indulged in but within certain limitations. Excessive indulgence will be an abuse and a vice. We know from Megas-

[1] Bk. I, ch. v; Bk. VIII, ch. iii.

[2] prajānām vinaye rataḥ|—Bk. I, ch. 5.

[3] Bk. VIII, ch. 3.

thenes[1] that the king actually went out a hunt on certain occasions. Ktesias informs us that in India the king is not allowed to make himself drunk but that the Persian king is allowed to do so on one particular day, that on which sacrifice is offered to Mitras.[2] Though one need not give full support to such an ideal statement it is reasonable to assume that the king was expected to cultivate temperate habits and lead a temperate life which would enable him to bring his sense-organs under control. For it is said[3] that the vices of anger would generate people's fury against him, and the vices of *Kāma* would lead to negligence of the government and consequently to the discontent of the subjects. In both the cases the king would alienate the sympathies of his peoples with the result that the administration would seriously suffer. The fruits of discipline are then said to be freedom from lust, anger, avariciousness, pride, indolence, and extreme joy. These six are said to be the inveterate enemies of the king, and he who does not get over them cannot be in a position to control the whole kingdom.[4]

Having had the full course of study and having subjugated the sense-organs the king should endeavour to improve his general faculties. He should cultivate wisdom by association with the aged, the sense of sight through the *cāras* or Intelligence Officers, the means for general welfare and happiness by activity, the establishment of *svadharma* (doing

1 Fg. 27.

2 Fg. 32.

3 *Ar. Śās.*, Bk. VIII, ch. 3.

4 *Ibid.* Bk. I, ch. 6.

one's duty) by the exercise of his authority, discipline by learning, healthy relations with the people by proper administrative measures, and a proper course of conduct by wholesome methods of action and movement.[1]

utthāna or exertion of the king

In the chapter entitled the *prakṛtisampat*[2], among the varied virtues expected of a good monarch is mentioned that of *utthāna* or active exertion on the part of the king. It is in fact the result of transparent enthusiasm (*mahotsāho adīrghasūtraḥ*). The fruits of the practice of *utthāna* are then mentioned. Ever exerting, the king must exercise his authority. Exertion is the root of all *artha* (wealth and territory). Absence of exertion leads to the reverse. Lethargy leads on to the destruction of acquisitions, old and new. Exertion produces fruitful results and tends to increase the wealth.

That such instructions of the *Kauṭalīya* were followed by Aśoka in detail is evident from his inscriptions.[4]

[1] vṛddhasaṁyogena prajñām, cāreṇa cakṣuḥ, utthānena yogakṣemasādhanam, kāryānuśāsanena svadharmasthāpanam, vinayam vidyopadeśena, lokapriyatvam arthasaṁyogena, hitena vṛttim|
—*Ar. Śās.*, Bk. I, ch. 7.

[2] Bk. VI, ch. 1.

[3] tasmān nityotthito rājā kuryād arthānuśāsanaṁ|
arthasya mūlamutthānam anarthasya viparyayaḥ||
anutthāne dhruvo nāśaḥ prāptsyanāgadasya ca|
prāpyate phalam utthānāllabhate cārthasampadam||
—Bk. I, ch. 19.

[4] nāsti hi me to(s)o
usṭānaṁhi atha-saṁtīraṇāya va| katavya-mate
hi me sa(rva)-lokahitaṁ| tasca cha puna esa mūle
usṭānaṁ cha atha-saṁtīraṇā cha|
—R. E. VI (Girnār), *Corpus*, p. 12.

By the course of his conduct, and by administrative measures to promote the welfare of his subjects, Aśoka endeared himself to the people at large. The importance of the quality of *utthāna* was also realised to a full measure, for, every action and movement of his depended on his powers of exertion to which he set a special value above everything else.

Daily time-table

The Mauryan kings who set before themselves high ideals of royalty and were imbued with solicitude for the welfare of an all-embracing humanity could not have piloted the ship of administration if the daily life allocated to sovereigns in general in the *Arthaśāstra* was not normal. Days and nights were divided into eight periods respectively and a fixed time-table was drawn up. The king went to bed at 9 P.M., and got up at 3 A.M. accompanied by music on both occasions. From 3 to 4-30 A.M. he pondered over miscellaneous state business especially concerning the business of the day. At 4-30 A.M. came to his chamber *ṛtviks, ācāryas, purohita,* and showered on him choice blessings. Consultations were then held with the Physician, the Master of the Kitchen, and the Soothsayer respectively, and the king entered the Hall of Audience after the ceremony of circumambulating a cow with her calf, and a bull. We need not mention that even to this day it is reckoned to be auspicious to see a cow as first in the morning. Having entered the public hall of audience the king was engaged first in supervising and examining the balance-sheet comprising the receipts and expenditure, perhaps, of the previous day. From 7-30 to 9 A.M. ordinary citizens were allowed to have an audience with His Majesty and ventilate their grievances, if any, in person, so that immediate attention might be given to such affairs as would seem urgent. Exactly at 9 A.M. he left the hall for morning bath, prayers and breakfast all of which he used to finish in an hour and a half. For from 10-30 to 12 noon he looked to the affairs of the officers of the state to whom perhaps interviews were given and when a free expression of their views was heard. At 12 noon he entered the council chamber to confer with his counsellors and ministers on important affairs of state which required their mature deliberation and sound advice so as to pursue an effective policy. The period between 1-30 and 3 P.M. was devoted to rest by way of some amusement. The pastime being over, he took a general supervision of the whole army and devoted the evening to matters relating to diplomatic relations with other states including military operations and undertakings. Between 6 and 7-30 P.M. the king gave audience to special Intelligence Officers and other confidential agents of the realm. Then he went to supper after his evening bath and prayers.[1]

Some of the facts are corroborated by the testimony of classical writers. According to Strabo[2] the king did not sleep during day time. Megasthenes remarks that the king remained in the Court for the whole day.[3] It was shown above that excepting for a brief interval for both, breakfast and rest, the king was practically engaged with the business of the state from morning to evening. The programme of work

[1] *Ar. Śās.* Bk. I, Ch. 19.

[2] McCrindle: *Ancient India as described in Classical Literature, p.* 55.

[3] Fg. 27.

was indeed heavy and it required a strenuous and active man to follow. Need it be said that the first Mauryan kings were full of these characteristics.

Sec. iii. PERSONAL SAFETY OF THE MONARCH

It is but natural that any man at the helm of public affairs and especially with power in regard to the distribution of patronage would have a number of enemies from discontent, prejudice, and envy. Men at the head of the state are no exception to this. Stories were known of unfaithful wives, unfaithful sons, and disloyal officials and servants. Hence it was necessary to protect the royal person from these undesirables. From the prescription of the *Kauṭalīya* in this particular,[1] one cannot draw the inference that in those days despotic kings ruled the land, and to ensure their personal safety regulations were laid down. The *Kauṭalīya* is a manual on statecraft and the rules therein are intended for every possible contingency that may arise in the state at some time or other. It is a wrong interpretation of the *Arthaśāstra* to say that such dangers were the norm and that precautions to be actually taken were laid down in every detail. For example, there are prescriptions regarding precautions against fire, lightning, and snakes. Are we to take it that fire broke out every day, lightning devastated the land continuously, or that the fear of snakes was common? The fact is that they are possible dangers, to avert which Kauṭalya has prescribed means and methods.

[1] Bk. I, ch. 21.

The evidence of classical writers

From the writings of the classical writers it is seen that some general precautions were indeed adopted to protect the royal person from possible dangers. The king generally lived in a well-built palace with gates well defended by guards and the rest of the soldiery. The dimensions of the towers and castles of Pāṭaliputra[1] given in classical books approximately correspond to those mentioned in the three chapters of the *Arthaśāstra.*[2]

It is said that the royal palace was adorned with gilded pillars clasped all round by a vine embossed in gold while silver images of birds were a charm to the eye.[3] "In the parks tame peacocks are kept, and pheasants which have been domesticated; and among cultivated plants there are some to which the king's servants attend with special care, for there are shady groves and pasture-grounds planted with trees, and branches of trees which the art of the woodsman has deftly interwoven . . . . Parrots are natives of the country, and keep hovering about the king and wheeling round him, and vast though their numbers be, no Indian ever eats a parrot."[4] Again with regard to medicinal plants Aelian says that the country produces harmful and poisonous snakes. "But the same country produces plants which serve as antidotes to their bite, and of these the natives have so much knowledge and

[1] Fg. 26 and 27.

[2] bhūmicchidravidhānam, durgavidhānam, and durganiveśa (Bk. II, ch. 2-4).

[3] McCrindle, *Ancient India—Its invasion by Alexander,* p. 189.

[4] Aelian, Bk. XIII, c. xviii, *Ancient India in Classical Literature.*

skill that they can apply the remedy suitable for the wound inflicted by any kind of snake."[1]

It is interesting to give here a categorical list of pot herbs and plants as well as birds reared in the palace according to the *Arthaśāstra*. Jīvanti (Fæderia Fœtida), śevta (Aconitum Feron), mūṣkaka-puṣpa, vandāka (Epidendrum Tesselatum), pijāta, aśvattha (Ficus Religiosa) are the plants and trees. Cats peacocks, mongoose, spotted deer, parrots, *maināś,* and Malabar birds (*bhṛṅgarāja*), the heron, the pheasant, cuckoo, and partridge are the birds which could perceive and detect the smell of snake and other poisons.[2]

From the *Arthaśāstra* we gather that there were four compartments leading from the harem to the public hall. In the first compartment where there was the harem, were stationed women armed with bows; the second aged persons and attendants including the *kañcukin* and *uṣṇīṣin* (special servants who attended to the dress of the king), while the third was attended by the hunch-back and the dwarf, and the fourth by kinsmen and armed door-keepers. Most of these servants were hereditary and well-behaved.[3] Why such elaborate precautions were taken is answered by Kauṭalya himself that these are conducive to the happi-

[1] *Ibid.*, Bk. XII, ch. xxxii.

[2] Bk. I, ch. 22.

[3] śayanādutthitaḥ strīgaṇairdhanvībhiḥ parigṛhyeta|
dvitīyasyām kakṣyāyām kañjukoṣṇīṣibhirvarṣavarābhyāgārikaihi|
tṛtīyasyām kubjavāmanakirātaihi|
caturthyāṁ maṇtribhissambandhibhi dauvārikaiśca prāsapāṇibhihi|
pitṛpaitāmahaṁ mahāsambandhānubandhaṁ
śikṣitamanuraktaṁ kṛtakarmāṇam janamāsannam kurvīta|
—Bk. I, ch. 21.

ness of the king. If the king was worried by these trifles in the household, he could not properly attend to the affairs of the state, and hence these safeguards were taken.

Sec. iv. SOME HABITS OF THE KING

[1] "When the king condescends to show himself in public his attendants carry in their hands silver censers, and perfume with incense all the road by which it is his pleasure to be conveyed. He lolls in a golden palanquin, garnished with pearls, which dangle all round it, and he is robed in fine muslin embroidered with purple and gold. Behind his palanquin follow men-at-arms and his body-guards, of whom some carry boughs of trees, on which birds are perched, trained to interrupt business with their cries . . The palace is open to all comers even when the king is having his hair combed and dressed. It is then that he gives audience to ambassadors, and administers justice to his subjects. His slippers being after this taken off, his feet are rubbed with scented ointments. His principal exercise is hunting; amid the vows and songs of his courtesans he shoots the game enclosed within the royal park. . . . He rides on horseback when making short journeys, but when bound on a distant expedition he rides in a chariot (howdah) mounted on elephants, and, huge as these animals are, their bodies are covered completely over with trappings of gold. That no form of shameless profligacy may be wanting, he is accompanied by a long train of courtesans carried in golden

[1] McCrindle, *Ancient India, its Invasion by Alexander the Great* pp. 188-190.

palanquins, and this troop holds a separate place in the procession from the queen's retinue, and is as sumptuously appointed. His food is prepared by women, who also serve him with wine, which is much used by all the Indians. When the king falls into a drunken sleep his courtesans carry him away to his bed-chamber invoking the gods of the night in their native hymns." The last sentence of this long extract from the classical writer is quite a contrast to that of another classical writer Ktesias who says that the king of the Indians does not take wine.[1] This only shows that we cannot rely too much on their testimony. Theirs seems to be mostly hearsay and hence may be right or wrong. Generally the king appeared in public to receive petitions from his subjects, and dispose of their cases, to offer sacrifice in conformity with the religious practices of the time, and to go on hunting tours in the king's forest, and on military expeditions against recalcitrant kings and chiefs.[2]

Hunting expeditions

When he goes out for the chase he is said to depart in Bacchanalian fashion. Says Megasthenes: "Crowds of women surround him, and outside of this circle, spearmen are ranged. The road is marked off with ropes, and it is death, for man and woman alike, to pass within the ropes. Men with drums and gongs lead the procession. The king hunts in the enclosures and shoots arrows from a platform. At his side stand

[1] See above, p. 104.

[2] Strabo, 55; Meg. 27; see *Early History of India*, p. 130.

two or three armed women. If he hunts in the open grounds he shoots from the back of an elephant."[1]

The custom of massage

It would appear that massage or friction of limbs with ebony rollers was a custom and luxury indulged in by the monarch. The Greek writers inform us that the attendant went on massaging the king while he was in the court hearing causes. This may answer to the office of the *saṁvāhaka* mentioned in the *Kauṭalīya.*[2] It may be noted in passing that it was not the privilege of the monarch alone but a custom observed in India even to-day.

Ceremonial washing of the hair

Another peculiar custom of the Mauryan monarch was the ceremonial washing of the hair of the king on his birthday accompanied by festivities and festivals when the king was the recipient of many a rich present at the hands of his courtiers and the nobles of the land. It is not peculiarly a Persian custom as some would aver, but a common custom of all the Hindus, high and low.[3]

Ox races, etc.

One other royal amusement was the visiting by the king of the combats of animals, gladiatorial contests, and ox-races. The race grounds extended to 30 stadia or 6,000 yards, and betting was indulged in such races.

[1] Meg. 27, *cp. Ar. śās.*, Bk. I, ch. 21. *Cp. Śakuntalā*: King Duṣyanta going out for the chase is accompanied by Yavana women wearing garlands of different flowers and armed with bows and arrows.

[2] Bk. VII, ch. 17. *Cp. Mṛcchakaṭikā.*

[3] *Contra*: *Persian Influence on Mauryan India, Ind. Ant.*, 1905.

This reminds us of horse races which have become so very popular in India to-day.[1]

But it would appear from the prescriptions of the *Arthaśāstra* that such sports as involved the loss of life to the animals were discouraged by Candragupta, as also by Aśoka.[2] If we read the chapter entitled *sūnādhyakṣa* with the relevant text in the First Rock Edict, and the second Pillar Edict, we see that Aśoka enforces the laws of the *Arthaśāstra* even with regard to the animal kingdom. Aśoka was not against healthy sports where there was no slaughter of the animal. What he did was to abolish cruel and unhealthy sports; but he provided edifying shows.[3] On this topic it may be proved that Aśoka did not go far from the prescription of the *Arthaśāstra* so far as the killing of animals was concerned. Kauṭalya prohibits their killing for 15 days during *cāturmāsya* and four days of the full moon.[4] These are accepted Hindu fast-days. In the same way Aśoka who[5] did not discontinue their killing for his kitchen, forbade their killing on fast days (*anuposatham*). A remarkable circumstance in this connection is the common use of the term *cāturmāsya* both in the *Arthaśāstra* and the inscriptions. This coincidence demonstrates beyond doubt that Aśoka was not preaching Buddhism but was pursuing the *dharma* established in the state.

[1] Cp. Smith, *Aśoka,* p. 90.

[2] *vatsovṛṣo dhenuścaiṣāmavadhyāḥ,* Bk. II, Ch. 26.

[3] See *Corpus, Intro.* p. 51.

[4] *Ar. śās.,* Bk. XIV, Ch. 1.

[5] See Fifth Pillar Edict.

Sec. v. DUTIES OF THE KING

"In ancient India Government never signified mere police work. . . The Hindu conceived of the Government's function as comprising in its entirety the whole of protective and disciplinary measures, in addition to active duties necessary for ensuring the subject a proper realisation of his material ideals in human existence."[1] Besides the general routine of duties in the daily life of the king there were more onerous and more responsible duties which the monarch was expected to execute and fulfil.

The enforcing of svadharma

First among them was the enforcing of *svadharma* on the subjects of the state by regulations in regard to the practices, laws of castes and orders, according to the rules laid down in the Vedic literature.[2] The king was to see that people of different denominations pursued their own avocations without in any way interfering with the professions of others and thus not transgressing the established laws of the realm. The object of the maintenance of this social polity was the general welfare of the citizens at large. Need it be told that the insistence of the healthy principle of *svadharma* (doing one's own duty) avoided competitive impulses, and ensured the existence of the weak, side by side with the

[1] N. C. Bandyopādhyāya, *Kauṭilya,* p. 107.

[2] tasmāt svadharmaṁ bhūtānām rājā na vyabhicārayet|
svadharmair saṁdhadhāno hi pretya cātra ca nandati||
vyavasthitāryamaryādaḥ kṛtavarṇāśramastithiḥ|
trayyā hi rakṣito lokaḥ prasīdati na sīdati||

—Bk. I, ch. iii.

caturvarṇāśrmo loko rājñā daṇḍena pālitaḥ|
svadharmakarmābhirato vartate sveṣu vartmasu||

Bk. I, ch. iv.

strong. In other words, the struggle for existence and the survival of the fittest were unknown to that system of Hindu social polity.

Protection of life and property

Secondly, the state aimed at the *yogakṣema* of its citizens. This is protection of life and property as we understand it to-day. Hence the king is entitled as the *lokayātrārthi.* Progress of the world largely depends on the administration of the land by the king.[1] This is by the proper exercise of *daṇḍa* which is punishing the wicked and the wrong-doer, thus enabling the individual citizens to pursue their avocations in peace, undisturbed. In the conduct of his administration the king looked upon all people, of whatever caste or community, equally and impartially.[2]

Promotion of trade and commerce

Thirdly, promotion of agriculture and commerce was a function that devolved on the king. If the king and his council felt that a certain part of the empire was harassed by the enemy chieftains, and was subject to intermittent epidemics and famines, then the people were asked to emigrate to some other fertile region and there to settle in comfortable lodgings specially built. Much attention was bestowed on the development of agriculture. Arrangements were made to see that the livestock was free from cattle-lifters, wild animals and diseases peculiar to them. The king was to guarantee safety and security of commercial and trade routes, for the latter are liable to disturbance

[1] *Ar. śās.* Bk. I, Ch. 4.

[2] sarvabhūta hite rataḥ|—*Ibid.,* I, Ch. 5. See N. C. Bandyopadhyāya, *Development of Hindu Polity and Political Theories,* Pt. I (Cal. 1927), p. 295-ff.

from chief herdsmen, labourers, thieves, and boundary guards. In this way the king was to protect timber-forests, elephant-forests, dams, and embankments.[1]

Proper administration of justice

It was again his duty to see that justice was properly administered so that there would be no violation of the rules and laws established. Hence the king is called *dharma-pravartaka.*[2] Proper protection and impartial justice, it is said, find to the king the abode of heaven. In meting out justice, a king should make no distinction between his son and an enemy.[3] In a word, punishment was to be regulated according to the gravity of the offence.[4]

State and sannyāsins

Yet another function of the king was to watch the conduct as well as the movements of the ascetics as a class. Though Kauṭalya mentions in several places that due regard must be shown to ascetics, and preference must be given to cases touching them, yet unrighteous proceedings by them were not to be tolerated. Because they were Sannyāsins and consequently honoured by the state, they could not abuse their privilege. Any such abuse, wilful or improper, was dealt with. Fines were the usual form of punishment. It was realised that such improper conduct on the part of the Sannyāsin would be not only a negation of righteousness but the pre-

[1] *Ar. śās.* Bk. II, Ch. 1 and 34.
[2] *Ibid.,* Bk. III, Ch. 1.
[3] *Ibid.*
[4] *Ibid.,* Bk. IV, Ch. 4 and 10.

dominance of vice which, according to the author of the *Arthaśāstra,* would tend in the long run to be a source of harm to the king.[1]

Protection from calamities

The king was further to protect the land from national calamities including providential visitations. The latter are mentioned to be fire, floods, epidemics, famines, rats, wild animals, serpents, and demons. In these cases the king was expected to take precautionary measures and try to avert the visitations of such calamities. For prevention is better than cure. But if such untoward things happened it was for the monarch to rectify them with proper remedial measures. These measures included the propitiation of supernatural forces, and the performance of magical and religious rites. The belief was that such prayers would tend to minimise the evil effects of such an outbreak. In conclusion it is said that the king should ever protect the afflicted among his subjects as a father would his sons.[2]

Foreign policy

Another important function of the king was the conduct of foreign policy. The king who was generally a member in the circle of sovereign states, consisting of enemies, allies, and neutrals, should endeavour to attain the state of stagnation from that of deterioration, and in the end to the state of progress. This stage was to be reached by pursuing six different forms of state policy of which the primary forms, according

[1] Bk. III, Ch. 16. Cp. *Kauśāmbi Pillar-Edict*: *Allahabad-Kośam and Sāṁchi Pillar* where Aśoka refers to the nature of punishment to monks and nuns. *Corpus,* pp. 159-160.

[2] Bk. IV, ch. 3; Bk. VIII, ch. 4; Bk. IX, ch. 7.

to Vātavyādhi, are peace and war. It is thus prescribed: "A wise king shall pursue that form of policy which according to his knowledge will enable him to construct fortresses and other buildings, lay out trade-routes, open possibilities of colonisation, exploit mines and timber and elephant forests, and at the same time create disturbance to the similar works of his enemy."[1] It is also laid down that "enemies from enemies, subjects from subjects, should ever be guarded, and both from his subjects and enemies a learned man should ever guard his own person."[2]

Promotion of arts, education, etc

The king as the chief representative of the state attended also to the social and socialistic functions, such as promotion of arts and education, health and sanitation, medical aid and poor relief, and other charitable acts and deeds.[3] Hospitals, rest-houses, donations, grants to learning and learned men, and maintenance of the widow, the orphan and the helpless were some of the institutions which came under this category.[4]

[1] *Ar. śās.,* Bk. III, Ch. 1.

[2] pare parebhyassve svebhyaḥ sve parebhyassvataḥ pare|
rakṣyāssvebhyaḥ parebhyaśca nityamātmā vipaścitā||
—Bk. IX, ch. 3.

[3] See for details the chapter entitled *nāgarakapraṇidhi* in the *Arthaśāstra* bālavṛddhavyādhitavyasanyanāthāmśca rājā bibhṛyāt Bk. II, Ch. I ācāryāvidyāvantaśca pūjavetanāni yathārham labheran, pañcaśatāvaram sahasraparam|

[4] See *Second Rock Edict, Corpus, Girnār,* p. 3.

Sec. vi. *PRIVILEGES OF THE KING*

King owner of no-man's property

Apart from these responsibilities the Mauryan monarch enjoyed certain rights and privileges consistent with the dignity and status assigned to him by the law of the land. It is contended that the Mauryan king added the no-man's property such as forests, mines, and waste lands to his dominions with the result that the Mauryas became financially sound, and secured even financial independence.[1] History teaches us that financial independence of the king marks the beginning of despotic and irresponsible rule. Was this the case with the Mauryas? The answer is simple. There is no evidence to show that the Mauryas were financially independent in spite of the fact that the above property came to be reckoned as state property; for does not Kauṭalya prescribe many means to get the coffers of the state filled?

Public works undertaken

Granting that the Mauryas had a large and guaranteed money supply, there is nothing to show that they misused it in an irresponsible fashion sacrificing the public interests of the state at the altar of self-advancement. For the Mauryan state patronised many arts and crafts including architecture and sculpture whose excavations and discoveries are a surprise and puzzle to archæologists.[3] Money was lavishly spent on public works which tended to the common good, such

[1] See N.C. Bandyopādhyāya, *Kauṭilya,* pp. 87-89.

[2] *Ar. Śās.,* Bk. V, Ch. 2.

[3] On the *Art of the Maurya period* see, Monahan, *Early History of Bengal,* Ch. XIX.

as laying out grand trunk roads, constructing reservoirs and embankments for agricultural purposes, founding hospitals, rest-houses and store-houses on public roads and other prominent places.[1]

A Categorical list of Privileges

This then explains that the Mauryan king enjoyed prerogatives which went to him as a matter of right, accepted and approved by the common law of the land. But there was no assertion of such prerogatives and rights so as to nullify the will of the people. Some of the privileges enjoyed by him were the following:—

(1) Society conferred on him the headship of the kingdom, and all regard and honour due to that position were publicly shown.

(2) He became the owner of all the finds and treasure-troves valued 1,00,000 *paṇas* or above. For the less valued ones, the discoverer was entitled to one-sixth of the value. But no claim was made on such treasure-troves as a man of honesty could prove them to be his ancestral property.[2]

(3) All property where there was no legal heir to succeed, became the king's property. Even here, there were certain exceptions. For example, the king had not the right of escheat to the property of the *śrotriyas*. This was generally presented to other *śrotriyas* in the state.[3]

(4) All unclaimed property, whether lost or stolen, lapsed to the king. But when people would prove their title to such articles, they would be handed over to the

[1] *Ar. Śās.*, Bk. I, Ch. 1.
[2] *Ar. Śās.*, Bk. IV, Ch. 1.
[3] *Ibid.*, Bk. III, Ch. 5.

owners. As against this it may be pointed out there is a prescription in the same chapter that the king should compensate the loss accruing to his citizens by theft.[1]

(5) His social position is something more than that of an ordinary citizen. He could not be taken as a witness in the law-court. Perhaps the idea underlying this principle was that as the king of the realm he should be impartial and must not take one side or the other. To him all the subjects were equal.[2]

(6) The royal person was protected by special laws as the Law of Treason,[3] and this reminds us of the Law of Treason which was promulgated in the mediæval period of English History.

The following are treasons according to Kauṭalya:—[4]

(1) Endeavouring to subvert the authority in power.

(2) Violating the chastity of the members of the harem.

(3) Instigating forest tribes or enemies against the reigning monarch.

(4) Inciting fortresses, rural parts and the army against the king.

(5) Tampering with seals and forging of documents.[5]

(6) Insult offered to the king.

(7) Publishing state secrets.[6]

[1] *Ar. śās.*, Bk. III, Ch. 16.
[2] *Ibid.*, Bk. III, Ch. 11.
[3] *Ibid.*, Bk. IV, Ch. 11.
[4] See *Kautilya*, p. 232.
[5] *Ibid.*, Bk. IV, Ch. 9.
[6] *Ibid.*, Bk. IV, Ch. 10.

These rights and privileges which are nothing compared with the duties and responsibilities expected of the monarch have elicited the unwarranted opinion that the *Kauṭalīya* is a secular treatise, the politics of which are immoral. Against this it may be pointed out that the prescriptions of the *Arthaśāstra* always coincide with those of the *Dharmasūtras* and the *Dharmaśāstras,* and it is indeed difficult to mark out any deviations in that treatise from the ordained and accepted path of the land.[1] The privileges enjoyed by the monarch are after all not in any way striking as to arrest our special notice.

1. See author's paper *Is the Arthaśāstra secular?* in the *Proceedings of the Third Oriental Conference, Madras.*

CHAPTER IV

THE CENTRAL ADMINISTRATION—(*Contd.*)

Sec. i. *THE COUNCIL AND THE ASSEMBLY*

The council, an ancient institution

The chapter entitled *mantrādhikāraḥ* in the *Artha-śāstra* helps us much to understand the details connected with the *mantripariṣad* or the royal council of the Mauryas.[1] The learned discussion as regards the number of councillors to form the council enables us to infer rightly that an institution of the kind was not an innovation of the Mauryan genius but an institution of much earlier times. In the discussion Kauṭalya incorporates the views of other political philosophers such as Viśālākṣa, Piśuna and Parāśara who were his predecessors, and who lived long prior to the inauguration of the Mauryan epoch.

The council chamber

There was a council chamber. It was to be well guarded. It was a secret hall not easily accessible to man and beast. It was so constructed that any endeavour to overhear the proceedings would prove futile. Kauṭalya knows of cases where birds and beasts had disclosed the secrets of the council-business.[2] With necessary precautions the king was to enter the chamber lest the proceedings of the council should be divulged.

[1] Bk. I, Ch. 15.
[2] *Ibid.*

Kauṭalya did not believe the members for they were liable to let out secrets through the unconscious channels of signs and gestures (*iṅgita* and *ākāra*). Hence according to the *Arthaśāstra* they should also be kept under some restraint until the resolution of the council was given effect to (*ayuktapuruṣarakṣaṇaṁ ākārya-kālāt*).

The composition of the council

Next our discussion centres round the composition of the council, the number of members and their qualifications.[1] There are different schools of opinion on this question. Viśālākṣa discarded the *mantra* with a single member and advocated a number of men grown grey in wisdom, though young in age. In the opinion of Piśuna, only those who were experts in the special business to be undertaken were to be consulted if *mantra* had to fructify at all. He had made a distinction between ability to offer counsel (*mantrajñānam*) and ability to keep it secret (*mantrarakṣaṇam*). Kauṭalya did not subscribe to this view, for such a position is *anavasthā*. In other words, the number of works, their variety and nature are such that a consultation with experts in each and every business needs a number of heads, and to hold counsel with a good number is an impossibility and an impracticability. Hence three or four are generally to be consulted. The consultation with a single member would lead to no resolution. The minister would be all in all. Nor is consultation with two desirable. For if they happen to take two opposite views, the king has to favour one view against

[1] *Ar. śās.*, Bk. I, Ch. 15.

the other. He who is not in the good grace of the king will try to bring about the ruin of that undertaking. Hence three or four are recommended as the safest number. That would enable a king to decide a definite action (*arthaniścaya*).

Choice of councillors

Much attention was bestowed on the appointment of councillors. The subjects dealt with by the council being varied and large in number, special care was taken in the choice of members to this all important institution. Just as the deserving few are fit to take part in the *śrāddha* of a *śrotriya,* so also the eminent few are considered fit to be members of a king's learned council.[1] What qualifications were expected of these is mentioned in another chapter of the same book. They are to possess the following twenty-five qualities: being a native of the soil, coming of a noble family, self-controlled, versed in all arts and crafts, learned in the *Arthaśāstra,* wise, of retentive memory, clever, sweet in speech, generous, being a good debater, full of enthusiasm and energy, enduring, of tested honesty, of amicable nature, of unimpeachable loyalty, possessing good conduct, good physique, good health and courage, humble, of resolute nature, possessing an attractive personality, and being one who is ever for reconciliation. It may be pointed out here that the *purohita* was a member of the council,[2] and only a duly qualified man was appointed *purohita.*

[1] *Ar. śās.,* Bk. I, Ch. 15.

[2] See *Proceedings of the Third Oriental Conference,* p. 615. It is refreshing to note that Dr. M. Winternitz has agreed with this viewpoint, see *note* on p. 34, *Sir Asutosh Memo. Vol., Patna.*

The king and the council

The next question is whether the king who was of course the President of the Council was expected to act in administrative affairs with the previous consent of the council or he could act on his own initiative. As an answer to this Kauṭalya definitely lays down the significant statement[1] that the administration of the kingdom is learnt from personal knowledge (*pratyakṣa*), and from devoted friends (*parokṣa*), members of the cabinet to speak in modern political parlance. Kauṭalya is repeating this statement which he has already given in the chapter entitled *mantripurohitotpatti.*[2] In fact he seems to lay emphasis on this point with the implication that the king expected the assistance of *mantrins* and the *purohita* for all rājakarmas, *i.e.*, carrying on the government of the state.[3] Again it is said that a government, which is carried on according to the injunctions of the *śāstras,* where the *purohita* plays a significant role, and where definite action is taken on the resolution of the council, attains unqualified success, without any resort to field engagements.[4]

The interpretation of the term dharmavijaya in the Edicts

This ideal government of the *Kauṭalīya* became actually realised under Aśoka. His *dharmavijaya*[5]

[1] pratyakṣaparokṣānumeyā hi rājavṛttiḥ|

[2] Bk. I, Ch. 9.

[3] See commentary of Gaṇapati Śāstri: pratyakṣaparokṣetyādivākyena rājakarmaṇaḥ sarvasya sahāya-sāpekṣatvam mantripurohitotpattiprakaraṇoktam smārayati| Vol. I, p. 73.

[4] Bk. I, Ch. 9.

[5] R.E. XIII.

has been anticipated by Kauṭalya to a large extent. Besides this mere inference from an elaborate statement of the means enabling the *dharmavijaya,* Kauṭalya gives us elsewhere[1] three kinds of victories which depend on the nature and quality of the rulers for the time being.[2] These are *dharmavijaya* where the conquering king is satisfied with the mere acknowledgment of his suzerainty by the conquered, *lobhavijaya* where the aim of the conquering monarch is to covet the territory and treasure of the enemy and then continue him in his kingdom, and *asuravijaya* where the enemy is deprived of his kingdom, treasure, sons and wives, and is himself captured as a prisoner of war, or slain. In the light of these statements in the *Arthaśāstra,* it would be incorrect to give a new interpretation to the term *dharmavijaya* occurring in the Aśokan inscriptions. F. J. Monahan who followed the old interpretation of *dhammavijaya* has remarked as follows: "As to the precise nature and effects of this 'conquest' we are left in the dark; it is unfortunate that Greek records are silent on the subject. From the edict we gather that 'conquest' was made through envoys (*dūta*). They were sent to the various countries to preach, not Buddhism, but 'dhamma', and in Aśoka's view, as we know, 'dhamma' was compatible with adherence to various creeds. We may infer that the envoys were politely received."[3]

The true position becomes intelligible in the light of the *Arthaśāstra.* What Aśoka aimed at was to make known to the conquered states, as well as to neighbouring states through ambassadors or special messengers

[1] Bk. XII, Ch. 1.
[2] Cf. *Mhb. Śānti,* Ch. 59, 38.
[3] *Early History of Bengal,* p. 219.

(*dūtas*) that the king had given up *lobhavijaya* and *asuravijaya* in which he had indulged in the early part of his rule, and had taken his stand at the pedestal of *dharmavijaya.* In other words, the emperor informed his subjects and the kings of other states that he would be satisfied with mere obeisance from them and he expected them at the same time to follow the *śāstraic* injunctions without recourse to any rebellion or war.[1] Any other meaning will have no legs to stand on. No wonder the Buddhist tradition has utilised this material for its own purpose when it mentions the conversion of Chandāśoka to Dharmāśoka, furnishing the occasion for untenable theories. This then forms an unimpeachable evidence to demolish the theory that Aśoka was a Buddhist. For, this term *dharmavijaya* has been a convenient peg with scholars to hang the Buddhist theory on.

King consulted the council even on emergencies

That the king could not by himself pledge to anything relating to the state, even in extraordinary cases urging immediate attention, and that the decision of the council was binding on him is testified to by a remarkable statement of the *Kauṭalīya.* Whenever urgent and unexpected occasions arose for prompt action, the king summoned his council and placed the matter before them for final decision. He was to act on the considered advice of the best men in the council.[2]

Unanimity, no majority opinion

Here the term *bhūyiṣṭhāḥ* as has been elsewhere said,[3] does not connote majority opinion but refers to

[1] śāstrānugamaśastritaṁ.

[2] *Ar. Śās.,* Bk. I, ch. 15: yadbhūyiṣṭhāḥ kāryasiddhikaram vā brūyuḥ tat kuryāt|

[3] *Hindu Adm. Inst.,* p. 139, *note.*

the mature opinion of the highly learned members, if we interpret the term in the light of the expression *buddhivṛddhāḥ* in the same chapter. This does not mean that the voice of the other members was not heard. On the other hand there is evidence to show that a frank discussion was allowed in the council and every one including the absentee members had his say. For the absentees had to send their views for discussion in the council.[1] But final decision rested with the council as a whole. In other words the ministers were consulted individually and then jointly.[2] It was the onerous task of the king as the president to convert the opposition to his side and thus act on the unanimous decision.

The Aśokan Pariṣad

That such emergent matters were also debated upon even in the provincial *pariṣads* of Aśoka is evident from more than one inscription.[3]

The texts of these Edicts throw a considerable light on the procedure of the council meetings. The term *nijhati* in the Edicts is interpreted in different ways: 'meditation,' 'reconsideration,' 'amendment,' 'adjournment,' and 'appeal'. Hultzsch renders it as 'amendment'. This seems to fit in with the first part of the statement which says[4] that sometimes the king

[1] anāsannaissaha patrasampreṣaṇena mantrayet|

[2] Cp. *Kāmandaka,* XI, 68.

[3] R. E. VI, *Corpus,* p. 34; Dhauli and Jaugaḍa VI, *Corpus,* pp. 88 and 106.

[4] yaṁ pi ch [ākichi mukhate ānapayāmi] [hakaṁ dāpakaṁ vā sāvakaṁ vā ye vā punā mahāmate hi
atiyāke ālopite ho(t)i tā(yeth)ā(ye) vivāde nijhati vā saṁtaṁ palis(ā)ye anaṁtaliyenā paṭi. . . .viye me savatā savaṁ kālaṁ|
Corpus, p. 34.

sent oral orders to the *mahāmātras,* and these were discussed and generally agreed upon in the council. It might be that disputes arose on the point resulting in amendments. But such amendments were to be committed to the king wherever he was. This means that full weight was not attached to the oral orders, though the latter was in practice. This practice became quite discredited by the time of the *Śukranītisāra* where the king issuing an oral order is regarded as a thief in law.[1]

anusaṁyānam

The tenure of office for the ministers is not exactly given in the *Arthaśāstra.* Still it prescribes transfer of officers.[2] The tenure of office seems to have been restricted to five years in certain cities[3] and three years in certain other places.[4] The latter term of office was applicable to the ministers at Takṣaśīla and Ujjayini. The special Edicts—so are called the Kaliṅga Inscriptions by the Epigraphists—reaffirm this principle of retirement and transfer. The technical term for this process of retirement and transfer is *anusaṁyānaṁ.*[5] In the light of the *Arthaśāstra* it would be a far cry to take the term as meaning administrative tour. As it often happened that the provincial ministry arrogated to itself too many powers, which led to risings of the citizens, as for instance in Takṣaśīla. It is reasonable to assume that no permanent council was aimed at, and new ministers were appointed

1 II.293 (Oppert ed.).

2 Bk. II, sec. 9.

3 Dhauli R. E. I and R. E. III.

4 Kaliṅga Edicts II.

5 *J.B.O.R.S.*, V.36ff. Smith, *Asoka,* p. 164. According to Hultzsch, Mookerjee and other scholars, the term has reference only to periodical administrative tours and not transfer of officers.

ordinarily every three or five years, to quote V. A. Smith 'designed to prevent the abuses apt to arise when officials remain too long in a particular locality.'[1]

Functions of the council

What were, then, the functions assigned to the council? From the fact that the king sought its advice on the administration of the land including home and foreign policy, and acted on it, the main functions of the council were executive in character. Enjoying the confidence of the king, as it did, the council was largely responsible in shaping the policy of the government. Among others the following five points engaged its attention. They were (1) means of undertaking works including expedition into the enemy's territory (karmaṇām ārambhopāyaḥ); (2) gathering of resources in men and material in relation to the internal and external policy of the kingdom (puruṣadravya-saṁpat); (3) use of discrimination in undertakings with reference to place and time (deśakālavibhāgaḥ); (4) means of averting possible dangers and calamities arising from his own state and from that of the enemy (vinipātapratīkāraḥ); and (5) results arising from such works undertaken (kāryasiddhi).[2]

Other functions

After a free and full discussion of the means, resources, and results in regard to a particular work or works, the council came to one of the following four decisions.[3] They resolved, first, to undertake new works in their own country (akṛtārambhā), second-

[1] See also Woolner, *Aśoka Text and Glossary,* Pt. II, p. 62 and Samaddar, *Glories of Magadha,* pp. 88-91.

[2] *Ar. Śās.,* Bk. I, ch. 15. Cf. *Kāmandaka,* XII.36-40.

[3] *Ibid.*

ly, to complete works which had been already begun in their own state (ārabdhānuṣṭāna), thirdly, to improve works already executed (anuṣṭitaviśeṣa) with an eye to their importance and necessity, and lastly, to effect changes and improvements affecting the services of the state comprising both the civil and military departments (niyogasampat). The above functions allotted to this institution show its importance and paramount necessity of the mature deliberation on which the whole administrative edifice was allowed to rest.

The council not a mere advisory body

It is not altogether correct to take a narrow view of the functions attributed to the council. It has been contended that the deliberation was of an advisory nature and the *minister* was all powerful, but not the *council* of ministers.[1] These statements are untenable for various reasons. First, if the council was merely an advisory body, and if the final voice rested with the king, what is then the force of the statement that even in matters of urgency the council should be summoned and the decision of its best men be adopted?[2] Secondly, there is another prescription of the *Kauṭalīya* which says that "all kinds of administrative measures are to be preceded by deliberations in a well-formed council".[3] Thirdly, there is the interesting statement, namely, kingship is possible through assistance. One wheel is useless by itself. Hence the king must appoint councillors and act up to their advice.[4] Fourthly,

[1] See *Glories of Magadha*, pp. 92-97.
[2] *Ar. Śās.*, Bk. I, ch. 15.
[3] *Ibid.* See also Bk. VIII, ch. 1.
[4] Bk. I, ch. 7.

there is the statement which we have already quoted that government is dependent not only on the personality of the king but also on the help of his friends, the councillors. Fifthly, even in the matter of appointing superintendents and heads of departments, it was done with the approval of the ministry including the *Purohita.*[1] It is thus evident that the council enjoyed executive powers, and that the king did not generally go against its wishes. Thus neither the minister alone nor the king alone could act, but the king with the body of ministers did act.

Sec. ii. THE PAURA-JĀNAPADA

That the state policy of the Mauryan empire was much influenced by the conduct and mode of the assemblies of the *Paura* and the *Jānapada* is evident from the *Arthaśāstra.* The *Arthaśāstra* distinguishes *Jānapada* and *Durga*[2] while the *Rāmāyaṇa* (roughly 500 B.C. to 200 B.C.) refers to the *Jānapada* and *Nagara.*[3] The terms *Nigama, Durga* and *Nagara* denote one and the same territorial unit, and mean either the provincial Capital or the Headquarters of the empire. It transpires that these assemblies were a feature of both the provincial and the imperial Headquarters. Hence the commentator of the *Kāmasūtra* interprets *nāgarikāḥ*[4] as *Pāṭaliputrikāḥ.* The term *Janapada* in the *Arthaśāstra*[5] refers to the

[1] Bk. I, ch. 10.
[2] Bk. I, ch. 1.
[3] *ayodhyā,* ch. 79, 12.
[4] Bk. II, ch. 5.
[5] Bk. II, ch. 1.

area covered by villages and towns of the whole kingdom, except perhaps the capital, as a distinction is made between the *Janapada* and the *Durga.*

The Jānapada located in the capital

That the *Jānapada* assembly hall was located at the capital is testified to us by the *Mṛcchakaṭikā.* The news of the deposition of the reigning king and the election of his brother to the throne were brought by a messenger to the *Jānapāda-Samavāya* or the assembly hall of the *Jānapada* institution.[1] Thus the term *Jānapāda-Samavāya* is significant as it shows in unmistakable terms an assembly of the whole of the *Janapada* having its headquarters at the Capital city and not a miscellaneous assemblage as some scholars would have it. True the materials are lacking in regard to a number of particulars as to the working of that body, viz., the method of election, system of voting, writ to the members, spokesman of the assembly, etc., which are all features of modern democracies. But it is misreading history to import modern ideas into ancient systems of democratic government. Nevertheless the *Kauṭalīya* throws helpful light even in these respects.

Procedure

The terms *buddhivṛddhāḥ, bhūyiṣṭāḥ, śrotriyaḥ* indicate that the best and wise men were always chosen to these representative bodies. These were returned unanimously. There was no system of voting, though some scholars would even extend the

[1] Act X.

principle of voting. It may be granted, however, that there was a kind of voting in the meetings of the assembly, the voting even here ultimately reducing itself to unanimous resolutions. The term *patrasaṁpreṣaṇa*,[1] used in connection with the absentee members of the *pariṣad* may well permit us to infer that some kind of writ was in use. Again whenever there was occasion for the mention of a spokesman (*mukhya, śreṣṭin*) it was mentioned.[2] Under these circumstances to characterise these assemblies as mere crowds of the inhabitants of the city and from the village parts is positively meaningless.

The Paura-Jānapada in Pāṭaliputra

It is obvious that there were two assemblies in the capital with the designation the *Paura* and the *Jānapada*. Pāṭaliputra had a *Paura* association, and the members of the *Paura* can be identified with the city magistrates of Strabo.[3] It is said that these city magistrates exercised municipal administration in addition to their other functions by resolving themselves into six committees of five members each. The *Pañcika Saṁghas* of Patañjali may be the equivalent for these committees of the Greek writers. The *Paura* attended among others to the industrial and commercial concerns of the capital, watched the interests of foreigners resident in the city, and were in charge of the census. They also looked after the health and sanitation, besides police and magisterial functions. In addition they were in charge of the buildings like the assembly halls, temples, resthouses and public parks.[4]

[1] Bk. I, ch. 15.
[2] See *Mhb.*, XV, ch. 8-10, (Trans. by Dutt).
[3] Bk. XV, 50, 4-10, Meg.
[4] *Ar. Śā.*, Bk. II, ch. 36.

These were not all. The Negama coins[1] and the coins bearing the name of towns, for example, *Ujeniya,*[2] which were taken to be coins issued by the merchant guilds are possibly coins which the *Paura* got minted at the capital on behalf of the city. For the *Śreni* or the merchant guild was a sub-committee of the *Naigama* which is a synonym for the *Paura.*[3] The *Arthaśāstra* shows that the *Jānapada* too had the coins struck at the royal mint.[4] It is said that a king of small treasure would be a nuisance to the *Paura-Jānapada.*[5] From the fact that these assemblies are frequently referred to in connection with taxation, it is reasonable to assume that these assemblies exercised some control over taxation. Any additional tax was to be sanctioned by them. Kauṭalya says that the king had to beg of the *Paura* and the *Jānapada* towards this end.[6]

Jānapada in Aśoka's Inscriptions

A similar circumstance perhaps actuated Aśoka to employ Rājukas in such a manner as would win the affection and goodwill of the *Jānapada* assembly. In the Pillar Proclamations IV,[7] the term *Jānapada* occurs in three places where it is said that the Rājukas were to discharge their duties so as to secure the goodwill and affection of the members of the *Jānapada* and grant

[1] Cunningham, *Coins of Ancient India,* pp. 63-65, Pl. III.

[2] *A.S.R.,* Vol. XIV, p. 148.

[3] See Caṇḍdeśvara *V. R.,* pp. 177, 180, Naigamāh Paurāḥ naigamah-paurasamūha, quoted by Jayaswal, *Hindu Polity,* Pt. II, p. 77n. Cf. Nasik Cave Inscriptions *Ep. Ind.,* VIII, 82.

[4] suvarṇikaḥ paurajānapadānām rūpyasuvarṇamāveśanībhiḥ kārayet|—Bk. II, ch. 14.

[5] *Ar. Śās.,* Bk. II, ch. 1.

[6] etena pradeśena rājā paurajānapadān bhikṣeta|—Bk. V, ch. 2. Cp. Bk. XIII, ch. 5

[7] *Corpus,* pp. 147-8, pp. 122-123.

them *anugrahas.*[1] The discontented among them were to be brought round. The officers were to conduct themselves in such a manner as the *Jānapada* would not get offended. Aśoka attached so much importance to the *Jānapada* that he discussed with them the ways and means of propagating *dharma* in the land.[2] It appears from the fact that the phrase *Paura-Jānapada* occurs together whenever there is occasion for its mention, that these two bodies severally and conjointly carried out the political functions devolved on them. That they had to attend to such functions daily is evident from the kings' time-table where the second portion of the day is devoted to attending to the business of the *Paura-Jānapada.*[3]

As in the Capital so also in the provincial Headquarters, the *Paura* and the *Jānapada* assemblies had important functions to perform. The tenure of the local ministry depended on its harmonious relations with these organisations. If the ministers abused their powers, the citizens who had apparently the moral sanction of these assemblies, rose in rebellion and continued the struggle until their grievances were redressed. In Takṣaśila this was the case both during the reigns of

[1] kaṁmāni pavatayevū janasa jānapadasā hitasukhaṁ upadahevū anugahinevu chā sukhīyana-dukhīyanaṁ jānisaṁti dhṁma-yutena cha viyovadisanti janaṁ jānapadam kiṁti hidatam cha pālataṁ cha. . . hevaṁ mamā lajūkā kaṭā jānapadasa hitasukhāye yena ete abhītā asvatha saṁtaṁ avimanā kaṁmāni pavatayevūti||

Corpus, pp. 122-23.

[2] R. E. VIII (Girnār):
bāmhaṇasamaṇānaṁ dasaṇe cha dāne cha thairānaṁ dasaṇe cha hiraṁṇapaṭividhāno cha jānapadasa cha janasa daspanaṁ dhaṁmānusasṭī cha dhamaparipucchā cha . . . .

—*Corpus,* p. 14.

[3] dvitiye paurajānapadānām kāryāṇi paśyet|

—*Ar. Śās.* Bk. I, ch. 19.

Cp. *Mhb., Śānti,* 40, 19.

Bindusāra and Aśoka. *Kumāras* or princes were sent to rectify the wrongs perpetrated by the ministry. This so highly pleased the citizens who demonstrated that their loyalty to the emperor was unflinching.

The story of Tiṣyarakṣita

These assemblies again were entrusted with responsible executive work. A story[1] goes that once Tiṣyarakṣitā, the queen of Aśoka, made overtures of love to Kunāla, the son of Aśoka by another wife. Kunāla's righteous nature rebelled at the very idea. This drove Tiṣyarakṣitā to severe wrath and she resolved to punish him at the next available opportunity. Aśoka fell ill and Tiṣyarakṣitā attended on him carefully that the king promised to do her anything she wanted. Her request was that she should be at the helm of the empire for a week. It was agreed upon. The queen sent an order sealed, as if from the king, to the *Paura-Jānapada* at Takṣaśila to get Kunāla, the provincial governor of that city, blinded. The members of the assembly met and discussed the unpleasant duty which had fallen on their shoulders. They informed the prince of the royal orders, to which he readily consented. The assembly got him blinded. The rest of the story is not relevant to our purpose. The story may or may not be true. What we are concerned with here is the administrative detail thrown out by the story. The *Paura-Jānapada* enjoyed executive powers amounting to punishing even the provincial heads of the empire. It would be idle to deny the existence of such institu-

[1] See author's article in the *Ind. His. Quarterly*, Vol. VI (1930), pp. 181-4, with N. N. Law's reply thereon.

tions or to underrate the nature of the onerous work which fell to their lot.

Sec. iii. DEPARTMENTS OF TAXATION AND ACCOUNTS

The Mauryan state like any other Hindu state had for its aim the realisation of the *trivarga*—the trinity group of Dharma, Artha and Kāma. Of these the author of the *Arthaśāstra* attaches greater importance to the second, namely, Artha or wealth, for on this depended the realisation of Dharma and Kāma.

artha eva pradhānaḥ arthamūlau dharmakāmau|

This does not mean that Artha or wealth is superior even to Dharma. But it does mean that wealth is the means, nay the indispensable means, towards the realisation of the two ends, namely, Dharma and Kāma. This statement is conformable to another statement which says

kośāpūrvāḥ sarvārambhāḥ[1]

that every activity of the state was to be necessarily preceded by a well-formed treasure. The idea is further traced and it is remarked that with an insufficient treasury the king would be forced to resort to resources which would invoke popular discontent, revolt and revolution.[2]

In the absence of a sound treasury the consequences could be well imagined. There would be no proper

[1] Bk. II, ch. 8.

[2] alpakōśo hi rājā paurajānpadāneva grasate|

—Bk. II.1.

kṣiṇāḥ prakṛtayo lobham lubdhā yānti vīrāgatām|
vīraktā yāntyamitram vā bhartāram ghnanti vīrāgatām|

—Bk. VII.5.

exercise of *daṇḍa,* for neither the army nor the officials would be loyal.[1] This discussion of the pros and cons of a well-furnished, partially furnished, and non-furnished treasury, bears the test that Kauṭalya was more than a theorist. In short Kauṭalya seems to drive at the fact that a fully furnished treasury alone can ensure the successful working of the administration, home and foreign.

Sources of revenue

What were, then, the direct sources which tended to swell the king's exchequer? The primary source constituted the different kinds of land-tax, such as *sīta* or the produce of crown lands,[2] and *bhāga* or share of revenue apparently from private owned lands.[3] This was invariably the traditional one-sixth of the produce. *Bhāga* is itself termed in the chapter entitled *kōṣṭhāgārādhyakṣa, saḍbhāga.*[4] Megasthenes informs us that one-fourth went to the king's share, and mentions another tax which was one-fourth of the produce of the soil, which also the husbandman paid into the treasury. This seems to be entirely wrong. Professor Hopkins is right when he remarks "the fourth part evidently declared by Megasthenes to be the proportion exacted, contradicts the perpetual statement of native authorities, that the proportion on grain is one-sixth, and one-fourth only in emergencies."[5] Normally and generally the king's share is one-sixth as testified to by the *Arthaśāstra.* Aśoka who collected a sixth share of the grain harvest

1 kōśābhāve dhruvaṁ daṇḍavināśaḥ|
2 Bk. II, ch. 15.
3 Bk. I, ch. 13.
4 Bk. II, ch. 1; cp. Manu, VIII, 304-5.
5 *J.A.O.S.,* XIII p. 88.

made an exception in favour of the village of Lumbini by reducing it to a eighth share. The text of the inscriptions has the term *aṭhabhāga*. While Bühler took *aṭha* to mean *artha*,[1] others took it to mean *aṣṭa*.[2] According to Bühler's interpretation the term *aṭha-bhāgīya* means 'partaking of riches'. We cannot follow this interpretation. 'Partaking of riches' is misleading. We are in the dark as to the 'riches' which Lumbini village contained and which the king made use of. Besides if Aśoka meant *artha* by the term *aṭha* he could not have added the suffix *bhāga*. This suffix *bhāga* itself implies a numerical connotation. Therefore *aṭha* cannot be *artha* but only *aṣṭa*. *Aṣṭabhāga* means 'entitled to an eighth share', as Fleet would have it, or 'paying a eighth share', as Thomas[3] and Hultzsch[4] would have it. The latter meaning is more appropriate in the light of the use of the term *bhāga* in the *Kauṭalīya*.[5]

Other items of rural revenue

Other items of income which came under the category of rural revenue are mentioned. *Piṇḍa-kara* was a fixed commuted tax paid by the village community from time to time. *Senābhaktam* was a kind of punitive tax imposed on the country parts whenever the army was marching through them It is natural to suppose that this was in kind, such as, oils and rice. *Bali* is another kind of impost on the land coming down from early Vedic times[6] and seems to

[1] *Ep. Ind.* V, p. 5. See also *Z.D.M.G.*, 68, pp. 721-22.
[2] See, for example, Fleet *J.R.A.S.*, 1908, pp. 479-80.
[3] *J.R.A.S.*, 1914, pp. 391-2.
[4] *Corpus*, p. 165.
[5] Bk. II, ch. 24.
[6] R. V. X, 173.

have been an annual contribution to the central exchequer.[1] It is again different from *ṣaḍbhāga* which is a separate tax though Kullūkabhaṭṭa takes both of them as one and the same tax.[2] It is not a religious tax as suggested by Shāmā Śāstri.[3] This is again mentioned in the Lumbini inscription of Aśoka where it is said that Aśoka caused that village free from the impost of *bali*[4] in honour of his visit to the place, and as already mentioned, further reduced the traditional *ṣaḍbhāga* into *aṣṭabhāga*.

lummini-gāme ubalike kaṭe aṭha bhāgiyccha|

—*Corpus*, p. 164.

The term 'ca' meaning 'and' connecting *bali* with *aṣṭabhāga* in the inscriptions is an evidence to show that separate taxes were meant. From this it is evident that Aśoka accepted and followed the system of revenue collection and fiscal policy enunciated by his grandfather Candragupta.

Next comes *kara* which is apparently the share of produce from fruit and flower-gardens.[5] Shāmā Śāstri's interpretation as 'contribution by subdued princes' does not fit in at all. For, it must be remembered that it finds a place in the group of taxes arising from the *rāṣṭra,* literally, country parts.

Income from trade and commerce

Another source of revenue, next only in importance to the taxes connected with the land, is trade and com-

1 Manu, 7.80.

2 See the commentary on verse 30 of the chapter viii., Manu.

3 Cp. *Raghu,* I.18.

4 *ubali* (skt. *ud-bali*) has the analogous form *ucchulka* in the *Ar. Śās.,* Bk. II, ch. 21. See Thomas, *J.R.A.S.,* 1909 pp. 466-67.

5 Gaṇpati Śāstri Ed., Vol. I, p. 230.

merce. The *Kauṭalīyan* state recognised the value of this unfailing source of revenue and hence endeavoured its best to encourage trade and commerce.[1] What we understand to-day by the nationalisation of industries was, to a great extent, realised in the Mauryan epoch. The state undertook manufactures and industries. State manufacturies were established. These were in charge of the Superintendent of Commerce.[2] But private individual efforts and co-operative activities of guilds were not interfered with. Discrimination was used in the imposition of taxes on commerce. Foreign merchants were allowed a good deal of freedom. Illicit transactions (*vyavahāra*), misappropriation (*upabhoga*)[3] and defalcation (*apahāra*) were severely dealt with. To this list of punishable offences were added the offence of tampering with weights and measures[4] and offering forbidden and bad articles for sale in the market.[5]

The income under this head of trade and commerce included tolls which varied according as the articles were necessaries or luxuries—;[6] *dvāradeya* (literally, the gate dues), road-cess probably collected by the *antapāla*[7] and profits earned from weaving and spinning. This last was pursued by women of different castes and age for both, time and piece, wages.[8] Under this head came also incomes from ocean, and river, traffic. Fishermen generally paid one-sixth of the value of their

[1] pracārasamardhiḥ—II.8; paṇyabāhulyam—(*Ibid.*).
[2] Bk. II, ch. 16.
[3] Bk. II, ch. 8.
[4] Bk. II, ch. 19.
[5] Bk. II, ch. 21.
[6] *Ibid.*
[7] Bk. II, ch. 21 and 22.
[8] Bk. II, ch. 23.

haul. Customs duties were levied on ships touching the port towns. Income also came from coastal traffic.[1] Ferry dues (*taradeya*), tax on markets (*paṭṭanam*),[2] fee from licences of different kinds of passports, tax from the guilds of the artisan classes (*kāruśilpigaṇaḥ*), monopoly of income from salt and other commodities, tended to swell the revenues of the State from commerce. Special mention may be made here of the encouragement given by the State for exports of indigenous goods.[3]

Other items of income

The other category of income to the state comprising of those items arising from the State-owned properties like forests,[4] wastelands including the public pasturage,[5] land and ocean mines,[6] treasure finds, the mintage,[7] unclaimed properties, forced labour (*viṣṭi*), and fines of different descriptions for transgression and trespass of law. Added to these were the incomes collected by the excise department (*surādhyakṣa*),[8] the department of gambling (*dyūta*)[9] which was centralised lest

[1] Bk. II, ch. 28.

[2] Bk. II, ch. 34.

[3] See *Kauṭilya,* p. 200.

[4] Bk. II, ch. 17.

[5] Bk. II, ch. 29. Rock Edict XI refers to the superintendent of pastures. The term *vaḉhamhi* in R. E. VI is *vraja* of the *Artha-śāstra* (II.6), meaning a herd of cattle and other animals. This *vraja* is said to have been inspected by Aśoka. If we consider the great attention paid to the preservation and upkeep of cattle in the *Kauṭalīya* as indispensable for agriculture, Aśoka's interest in livestock only shows how the king interested himself in the material welfare of his people as in their moral welfare.

[6] Bk. II, ch. 12.

[7] Bk. II, ch. 12.

[8] Bk. II, ch. 25.

[9] Bk. III, ch. 20.

the evil should spread widely, from the institution of prostitutes (*veśya*),[1] the department of slaughter-house,[2] and other miscellaneous taxes collected from religious and charitable endowments, heads of cattle, building sites (*vāstuka*), spoils of war, tributes, voluntary contributions and other several minor dues like *utsaṅga, pārśva,* for which there was no absolute and fixed rate.[3] In cases of emergency extraordinary taxes and enhanced exactions (*praṇaya*) were collected.[4] The resources of the rich were primarily but carefully tapped.[5] Normally the State kept in stock half of the grain collections, to meet unforeseen circumstances[6] like the setting in of famine.

Principles of taxation

Remark has been elsewhere made that the theories of early writers like Maine who called the Hindu states 'tax-collecting institutions' have little justification at any rate in regard to the Mauryan times.[7] Or in other words let us examine the principles under which taxes were imposed and expended. Kauṭalya is a strong advocate of a gradual system of taxation. Says he: "A king should endeavour to gather the revenue from his subjects in the same way as the fruits of a garden are gathered as often as they become ripe. Just as the gardener would abandon the unripe fruits lest their source should be disturbed, so that the State

[1] Bk. II, ch. 27.
[2] Bk. II, ch. 26.
[3] See *Hindu Ad. In.*, pp. 176, 177, 179, 180.
[4] Bk. IV, ch. 2.
[5] karśanam vamanam vā kuryāt|—Bk. II, ch. 1.
[6] tato ardham rakṣet āpadartham jānapadānām|| Cp. *Ind. Ant.*, 1896, p. 261.
[7] *Hindu Ad. Ind.* p. 190.

should abandon the unripe sources of the kingdom lest they should cause anger to the people.[1] Grant of im munities from taxes and escheat was another feature of the Kauṭalīyan system. This was always shown in the case of the deserving—the needy cultivators and the *śrotriyas,* the latter being wedded to the promotion of the public good of the country as the custodian of the education of the people in addition to other public services according to the belief of those days. Misbehaviour on the part of the tax-collecting officials was anticipated by a statesman of the type of Kauṭalya. Hence proper safeguards were taken to keep a check on these revenue officials who would collect either twice the levied tax or more than what was due, by unduly harassing the subjects at large. To prevent such corruption and extortion special Intelligence officers were appointed, and it was their duty to see that the regulations of the State were properly carried out. Any infringement was reported and severely dealt with.[2] Taxes were so collected that the people did not feel them to be a strain on their purse. In the light of these healthy principles there is least justification to call the Kauṭalīyan recommendations as in any way immoral or even unmoral.

Public expenditure

The vastness of the empire and the many-sided activities in which the Mauryan state displayed itself chiefly from the point of view of the *yogakṣema* of the citizens involved a costly machinery and consequently heavy expenditure. Public expenditure depended pri-

[1] Bk. V, ch. 2.
[2] Bk. IV, ch. 9.

marily on the various functions which the State imposed on itself. The functions of the Mauryan State were political, economic, social, religious, and sociological. One of its chief political functions was to afford proper defence from internal dangers through an elaborate police system, and external dangers through the organization of the army and navy. In this direction the State built fortresses on the frontiers of the empire and garrisoned them under the control of the officers known as *antapālas*. There are the *antamahāmātras* mentioned in the Edicts of Aśoka.[1] In the interior the rural divisions of the *sthānīya, droṇamukha, kharvaṭika* and *saṅgrahaṇa* were primarily headquarters though the officials in charge of those places there were entrusted with various other duties.[2] In addition to these arrangements in the frontiers and the rural parts, the central administration maintained a large army and navy if we are to believe the Greek accounts. A fragment speaks of the Maurya army as consisting of six-hundred thousand footmen, thirty thousand cavalry-soldiers and thirty-six thousand elephant-men and twenty-four thousand chariot-men. The same source testifies to the fact that the naval force was equally elaborate. These are corroborated by the *Kauṭalīya*. Under the category of political functions mention must be made of the civil side of the administration and its establishment though it must be borne in mind that the Mauryan State did not draw any line of demarcation between the military and civil establishments.

[1] See Delhi-Topra Pillar, *Corpus*, pp. 119-120.

[2] *Ar. Śās.*, Bk. III, ch. 1.

The civil list

The civil list which includes the establishment of royal household, the religious establishments, pay and pension of other officials including the menial services, is a long one involving again heavy items of expenditure.

The following is the civil list as found in the *Kauṭalīya*[1]:

Allowances for the *ṛtvik, guru,* minister, *purohita, senāpati,* crown-prince, king's mother, and queen consisted of 48,000 *paṇas* each.

The chamberlain, controller of the household, *praśāstṛ,* revenue officer, and *sannidhātṛ* each got 24,000 *paṇas.*

The other sons of the king, nurse, *nāyaka,* superintendents of the city, judge, superintendent of manufactories, members of the ministry, superintendent of country parts, and boundary guards were paid 12,000 *paṇas* each.

The leaders of the military corporations, of elephantmen, cavalry and chariots, each got 8,000 *paṇas.*

The captains of infantry, cavalry, chariots, and forest-guards were paid 4,000 *paṇas.*

The chariot-driver, physician, horse-trainer, carpenter, trainer of other animals, each was allowed 2,000 *paṇas*.

The astrologer, *purāṇa* reader, bards, assistants of the *Purohita,* and all superintendents of other departments were paid 1,000 *paṇas* each.

[1] Bk. V, ch. 3.

The pay of the soldiers, accountants, and clerks was 500 *paṇas* each. While the musicians got 250 *paṇas,* artisans 120, the menials were paid each 60 *paṇas.*

Other items of expenditure

In addition to this regular establishment the following were other items of expenditure incurred now and then by the state. Officers on special duty were paid 1,000 *paṉas,* Intelligence officials 500 *paṉas,* while travelling allowances were calculated according to distance. Honoraria for the learned ranged from 500 to 1,000 *paṇas.* Whether the above allowances were annual or monthly has been raised by N. N. Law in a note to the *Indian Historical Quarterly.*[1] On the strength of two significant statements in the *Arthaśāstra, viz.,* that the pay was so fixed that the officials were above wants[2] and that 60 *paṉas* could be substituted only for 1 *ādhaka* or 32 seers of the staple food gram[3] it is argued that the wages must have been monthly and not yearly. As there is no statement in the text to warrant that it is an yearly allowance, it is reasonable to assume the allowances to have been monthly.

Productive expenditure

The economic purposes for which the State expended lavishly were many and varied. Some of these were industrial and manufacturing establishments, such as factories, manufactories, exploitation of the forests, mines, and treasure troves, construction of big irrigation works, and aid to co-operative irrigation

[1] Vol. V, No. 4.
[2] Bk. V, ch. 3.
[3] Bk. V, ch. 3; Bk. II, ch. 19.

schemes, construction of dams and embankments, help to the new settlements of villages, grants and loans to agricultural classes, regulation of trade and commerce, and regulation of banking and currency etc. In fine the State aimed at the nationalisation of industries including that of agriculture. Need it be said that the investments under these heads were heavy and even abnormal?

Poor relief

The social functions came in for a large item of the expenditure. Public poor relief was deemed as one of the functions of the State. The State undertook to protect the aged, the starving, and the disabled poor It also helped otherwise poor people who deserved consideration at its hands like the *śrotriyas* and the ascetics. It was again the patron of the Brahman and the Śramaṇa.[1] It guarded the interests of the orphan and the widow. Relief of distress was also regarded as one of the kingly duties. The state anticipated dangers, providential and otherwise, like famines and epidemics, and made provision for such emergent purposes by keeping in reserve half of the total revenues collected possibly both in kind and cash. Whenever the unexpected happened, relief came by advances from the storehouse.

Works of public utility

Other works of public utility consisted in constructing lakes and other reservoirs of water and laying out roads well furnished with medicinal herbs, plants, and trees.[2] The Sudarśana Lake under Candragupta and

[1] See *Meg. Fg.*, *Rock Edicts* IV and XI.
[2] See *Aśoka's Inscriptions, Corpus*, pp. 3-4.

the Grand Trunk Road leading to Pāṭaliputra are evidences.

Some more items of expenditure

Closely connected with these are the sociological functions which entailed also an appreciable expenditure. Under this category mention may be made of educational grants and educational pensions. In the *Arthaśāstra* while the *śrotriyas* were teachers of the sacred branches of learning, the *ācāryas, vidyāvantas, vaktāraḥ,* and *prayoktāraḥ* were the other teachers imparting instruction in scientific and technical arts including practical training. Students including those from the artistocratic classes flocked to the cottages of these teachers which were the seats of learning. There was no fixed salary paid to them. But generally the state endowed them with gifts of lands tax-free called *brahmadeya,* and sometimes with *agrahāras* with the sole right of enjoyment. Occasional gifts of money were not uncommon. Teachers who were in charge of secular branches of learning got pensions ranging from 500 to 1000 *paṇas* each according to his worth.[1]

The state extended its hospitality in different other ways the object being the *lokayātrā* of the world. Provision was made to the families wherein the earning member had given up his life in war for the sake of the country. To avert distress and suffering, hospitals for man and beast were founded throughout the empire. The State administered to the general health of the community and its moral progress.

[1] āryayuktārohakamāṇavakaśailakhanakāssarvopasthāyina ācāryā vīdyāvantaśca pūjāvetanāni yathārhaṁ labheran pañcaśatāvaraṁ sahasraparam|—*Ar. Śās.,* Bk. V, ch. 3.

The Religious Establishment

This leads us on to examine the vast expenditure on the religious establishment of the State. Reference has already been made to the salary of the *purohita, ṛtvik, guru,* the assistants of the *purohita,* and the astrologer according to the civil list. In those days people had strong belief that the performance of sacrifices, rites, and ceremonials could enable them to avert calamities or to achieve desired results. Besides, no fine distinction was made between secular and religious duties. Both were regarded as complementary to each other. The *śrotriya* was the recipient of all honours at the hands of the king. So also the *siddhas* and *tāpasas.* Sannyāsins as a class were looked upon with regard and esteem. Toleration was the keynote of the administration, whatever be the king's personal religion. Religious sects including those of the heterodox found favour with the State. Thus the activity of the State was many-sided and hence incurred great expenditure.

Department of Accounts

The total income of the Mauryan State was large and the expenditure was equally enormous. This income and expenditure then necessitated an elaborate machinery of administration for receipt and audit. At the apex of this department were the Sannidhātā or the Finance Minister and Samāhartā or the Collector-General. The Samāhartā was the supreme controlling agency of the fortresses, mines, agricultural works, forests, roads and cattle. One of his duties was to look to the proper classification of the villages for the purpose of revenue collection.[1] The Sannidhātā on the other hand, was a sort of Receiving Officer whose duty it was to see that the revenues were properly received and the same kept in safe custody.[2] He wielded equally other onerous duties. He kept custody of precious stones, metals and coins as well as grains in charge of Koṣṭhāgārādhyakṣa, forest produce sent in by the Kupyādhyakṣa and other articles received in kind. We need not be detained by his other functions, among which figures his control over the buildings in respect of the armoury, the prison house, and courts of justice. A review of the duties pertaining to his office as outlined in the *Kauṭalīya* shows that he was in charge of both the state-treasury and the store-house.

The Treasury

To the treasury of the Mauryas came pearls from the Pāṇḍya and Keraḷa States, from Persia and the Himālaya regions, gems of varied value from the Vindhya and the Malaya mountains, diamonds from Kaliṅga, Kośala and Benares and coral from the Isle of the Yavanas.[3] To the capital came also varieties of sandal, perfumes of all sorts, different kinds of skins from the Himālayan forests and of woollen blankets and other fabrics including silks and fibres. These demonstrate the richness of the treasury under the Mauryas. The store-house was equally rich in grains of different kinds, varieties of oil, sugar, pungents, salts and other necessaries of life. Both the treasury and the storehouse maintained records of income and expenditure running

[1] For details see *Hindu Ad. In.*, p. 201-ff.

[2] Bk. II, ch. 5.

[3] Bk. II, ch. 11.

over a hundred years.[1] The office of the Sannidhātā was again engaged in preparing budgets and presenting the same. The accounts were systematically maintained under three heads: opening balance (*vartamāna*), balance on hand (*paryuṣita*) and windfalls (*anyajāta*).[2]

How accounts were kept

The account-books were to be submitted each year at the commencement of the month of Śrāvaṇa in sealed covers for auditing and approval.[3] Wrong entries and defalcations were severely dealt with.[4] To prevent bribery and corruption among the revenue officials Kauṭalya introduced the system of periodical transfers of the State officials from one place to another.[5] Aśoka too followed the same line and had his officers transferred in some cases every three years and in other cases every five years.[6] It may be noted in passing that certain offices like those in charge of the palace, fortress and country parts were exceptions to this general rule.[7] The official year was reckoned as 354 days and nights. The budget session was towards the close of the month Āṣāḍha or roughly the middle of July.[8]

1 Bk. II, ch. 5.

2 Bk. II, ch. 6. The terms may also mean 'current,' 'arrears' and 'miscellaneous'.

3 Bk. II, ch. 7.

4 *Ibid.*, also ch. 8. *Note* Kauṭalya refers to forty forms of embezzlement by Government servants. See *Hindu Ad. Ins.*, pp. 208-10.

5 *Vikṣepa,* Bk. V, ch. 3.

6 Inscriptions at Dhauli and Jaugaḍa.

7 Bk. V, ch 3

8 triśataṁ caturpañcāśaccāhōrātrāṇāṁ karma saṁvatsaraḥ| tamāṣāḍhīparyavasānamūnaṁ pūrṇaṁ vā dadyāt|—Bk. II, ch. 7.

The *akṣapatala* of Kauṭalya is not only the Accounts Office but also a general record room.[1] The assumption is that while the current accounts were maintained in the Department of Accounts, past records were kept in custody in the Record office which was under the supervising control of the Accounts department. Here were preserved, in addition to the above records, title deeds of the immovable properties, documents concerning royal grants, copies of ultimatum issued to neighbouring kings, and of treaties with other states, records generally relating to the civil list and the military administration of the land.[2]

Gaṇanāyam

The same was also the case in the administration of Aśoka as is evident from a significant expression in the Edicts (R. E. III)—the *Gaṇanāyam* which simply means the Department of Accounts referred to in the *Arthaśāstra*.[3] We shall quote here the whole of the Edict as it bears relation to the topic in question.

devānaṁpiyo piyadasi rājā evaṁ āha|
dhādasavāsābhisitena mayā idam ājñpitaṁ|

śarvata vijite mama yutā cha rājūke cha prādesike cha panchasu panchasu vāsesu anusaṁ-yānāṁ niyātu etāyeva athāya īmāya dhaṁmānuṣasṭiya yathā ajñāya pi kaṁmāya|

sādhu mātari cha pitari cha susrūsā mitrasaṁstutajñātīnaṁ bāmhaṇa-samaṇānaṁ sādhu dānaṃ prāṇānaṁ sādhu anāraṁbho apavyayatā apabhāḍatā sādhu

[1] Monahan, *Early History of Bengal*, p. 45.
[2] Bk. II, ch. 7. For different kinds of official documents see Bk. II, ch. 10.
[4] Bk. II, ch. 7.

parisā pi yute ājñāpayisati gaṇanāyaṁ hetuto cha vyaṁjanato cha|—*Corpus,* p. 4.

"King Devānāṁpriya Priyadarśin speaks thus. (When I had been) anointed twelve years, the following was ordered by me. Everywhere in my dominions the *yuktas,* the *rājuka* and the *prādeśika,* shall set out on a complete tour (throughout their charges) every five years for this purpose (viz.) for the following instruction in morality as well as for other business. 'Meritorious is obedience to mother and father. Liberality to friends, acquaintances, and relatives, to Brahmanas and Śramaṇas is meritorious. Abstention from killing animals is meritorious. Moderation in expenditure (and) moderation in possessions are meritorious.'

The council (of *Mahāmātras*) also shall order the *yuktas* to register (these rules) both with (the addition of) reasons and according to the letter."—*Ibid.,* p. 5.

V. A. Smith's transaltion is more to the point and it is as follows:—

Thus saith His Sacred and Gracious Majesty the King:

"When I had been consecrated twelve years this command was issued by me:—

"Everywhere in my dominions the subordinate officials, the Governor and the District Officer must every five years proceed in succession (*anu*) on transfer, as well for their other business, as for this special purpose, the inculcation of the Law of Duty (or Piety) to wit: —

"An excellent thing is the hearkening to father and mother: an excellent thing is liberality to friends, acquaintances, relatives, Brahmans, and ascetics; excellent is abstention from the slaughter of living creatures: excellent is small expense with accumulation."

"The council also will inculcate (the same) on the officials in the Accounts Department, with regard both to the principle and the text (of the order)."

From this some facts emerge. (1) The *mantripariṣad* was the executive authority which issued orders of the king to the various departments of the State. (2) The accountants were transferred every five years. (3) Aśoka attached great value to small expense with its inevitable accumulation though small enough. It is interesting to note that these correspond to the prescriptions in the *Kauṭalīya* which have been already examined.

The Department of Finance under the Mauryan Government thus possessed many attributes of modern administration supervised by two officials of the state, the Samāhartā and Sannidhātā. It was run on efficient lines as attested partly by the fact of an elaborate machinery, and partly by the healthy principles on which the administration was based. The Kauṭalīyan State endeavoured in the direction of augmenting the sources of income with the consequent increase in the receipt with a proportionate diminution in the expenditure.[1] This does not mean that the state was chary of public expenditure but it does mean that the State recognised the value of a replenished treasury by cutting money on useless and unproductive works but without prejudice to works of public utility.

[1] Bk. II, ch. 6.

Sec. IV. ADMINISTRATION OF JUSTICE

Heads of Law

Mention has already been made of the peculiar concept of Indian Jurisprudence that the law of the land was the *de facto* if not *de jure* sovereign of the land, and that the monarch of the kingdom was bound by it and should act according to it.[1] In other words, the ancient Indian king was no law-maker. His function was to administer the law already established. This is one of the powerful weapons by which the people were able to check and curb the arbitrary powers of the king. We shall now examine what constituted this law or in clear language, what were the different heads of law. This is not the place to discuss the various heads of law as adumbrated in the *Dharmasūtras* or *Dharmaśāstras*. Confining ourselves to the contemporary work of the Mauryan epoch, we find that four heads of law are mentioned in the *Arthaśāstra*: *dharma* (to give out what has actually happened), *vyavahāra* (to rest on evidence), *caritra* (customs and precedents), and *rājaśāsana* (royal proclamations).[2] It may be noted *en passant* that these royal proclamations amounted to promulgation of laws fallen into disuse and not introduction of new laws altogether.

Equity

Equity (*nyāya* also *dharma-nyāya*) again is given due prominence and in conformity with the law-giver Yājñavalkya, Kauṭalya mentions it as a source of law

[1] See above p. 91.

[2] Bk. III, ch. 1.

to be applied, in case the positive law of the *smṛti* cannot properly provide equality of justice. In other words equity came in very handsomely so far as the interpretation of the law was concerned. Perhaps the term *dharmayutena* in the Aśokan inscriptions is another form of *dharmanyāya.*[1] The term 'equity' is not used in the same sense, in which it is used in Roman Law but in the broad sense of supplementing in some cases, or interpreting in other cases, the law of the land. Again it is remarked that in India law was *dharma.* This is no doubt true. But what is more important is that *dharma* alone did not constitute law. There were other heads of law also.

Courts of Law

The *Arthaśāstra* mentions two kinds of law-courts; the *dharmasthīya* or courts where civil law was administered and the *kaṇṭakaśodhana* or the criminal court of law. Kauṭalya devotes two books[2] to the province of jurisdiction of these two important courts of law. A study of the nature of the cases which came under the purview of the *kaṇṭakśodhana* court, and an examination of the functions allocated to that department lead us to the conclusion that in addition to its administrative functions, that court acted also as a police court. For, the detection and prevention of crimes as well as the award of corporal and capital punishments rested with it.

Though it would be interesting to study in detail the cases which came before the *dharmasthīya* court for disposal, still lack of space forbids us an attempt at

[1] Pillar E. IV. *Corpus*, p. 123.

[2] Bks. III and IV.

it. As it is, a passing mention of these cases will itself be of much interest. These may be categorically stated.[1]

1. Contracts of a general nature (vyvahārasthāpana).[2]

2. Agreements of service, etc., (samayasyānapākarma).[3]

3. Duties and rights of the employer (svāmyadhikāraḥ).

4. Duties and privileges of the employed (bhṛtakādhikāraḥ).

5. Questions concerning the slaves (dāsakalpaḥ).

6. All relating to loans (ṛṇādānam).

7. Deposits of different kinds (aupanidhikam).

8. Sales and pre-emption (vikrītakrītānuśayam).

9 Presents and gifts (dattasyānapākarma).

10. Highway robbery (sāhasa).

11. Assault (daṇḍapāruṣyam).

12· Cases relating to defamation (vākpāruṣyam).

13. Questions concerning gambling (dyūtasamāhvayam).

14. Irregular sale of property (asvāmivikrayaḥ).

15. The right of possession (svasvāmi sambandha)·

16. Formation of boundaries of lands and settling of disputes arising from them (sīmāvivāda, maryādasthāpanam).

17. Cases regarding the immovables (vāstukam).

[1] For further details see *Hindu Ad. Inst.*, p. 228-ff. See also N. N. Law, *Studies in Hindu Polity*, pp. 119-120.

[2] Bk. III, ch. 1.

[3] *Ibid.*

18. Destruction of crops, pastures, roads, etc. (vivītakṣetrapatha hiṁsā).

19. Laws of marriage (vivāhadharma, strī dharma-kalpaḥ).

20. Questions relating to co-operative enterprise (sambhūyasamuthānam).

21. Cases of inheritance and succession (dāyavibhāgaḥ, dāyakarma).

22. Rules of procedure (vivādapadanibandaḥ).

Jurisdiction of the Criminal Law-Court

The criminal law-court on the other hand dealt with the following cases[1]:

1. Protection of artizans and merchants (kārṁikavaidehakarakṣaṇam).

2. Protection and regulation of the claims of labour.[2]

3. Protection of the prostitutes (gūḍhājīvinām rakṣā).

4. Tracing criminals through spies (māṇavaprakāśanam).

5. Arresting the suspicious or real culprits (saṅkārūpakarmābhigraha).

6. Post-mortem examination (āśumṛtakaparīkṣa).

7. Maintaining discipline in the different departments of the State (sarvādhikaraṇarakṣaṇam).

8. Punishment for mutilation (ekāṅgavadhaniṣkrayaḥ).

9. Capital punishment with or without torture (śuddhaścitraśca daṇḍakalpaḥ).

[1] the whole of Bk. IV.

[2] Bk. IV, ch. 2.

10. Ravishment of immature girls (kanyāprakarma).

11. Examination by word of mouth and action thereon (vākyakarmānuyoga).

12. Other criminal offences (aticāradaṇḍaḥ).

A survey of the cases that came within the purview of the criminal law-court shows the combination of police functions with magisterial duties. Much of the police control was by means of informants who sometimes acted as *agents provocateurs.* One of the functions assigned to these informants was the shadowing of the suspected, and in this respect it resembles that of the modern secret police organisation. The procedure prescribed for investigating cases of theft and homicide[1] is a test to prove the perfect organisation of the judicial department. In regard to suicide committed by men or women, equal punishment was awarded. The idea was to check such a heinous offence as far as possible. Neither burial nor cremation was allowed. The bodies of persons who committed suicide were exposed on thoroughfares by having them drawn on public roads by *caṇḍālas* and were cast away uncared for.[2] Thus the seemingly arbitrary punishment was to put down such crimes as they would otherwise become numerous.

[1] Bk. IV, ch. 4 and 5.

[2] ghātayetsvayamātmānam strī vā pāpena mohitā||
rajjunā rājamārge tām caṇḍālenāpakarṣayet|
na śmaśānavidhisteṣām na sambandhikriyāstathā||
bandhusteṣām tu yaḥ kuryātpretakāryakriyāvidhim|
tadgatim sa caretpaścāt svajanādvā pramucyate||
—*Ar. Śās.*, Bk. IV, ch. 7.

Capital punishment

Punishments were of different kinds: fines, imprisonment, mutilation and death penalty.[1] It is often remarked that the *Kauṭalīya* does not mention the method of trial by jury but recommends torture to the suspected persons to elicit confession of guilt.[2] The statement is of course misleading, and is the result of a wrong interpretation of the *Arthaśāstra* texts. The chapter entitled *vākyakarmānuyoga*[3] means 'examination on evidence and action to be taken thereon.'

The technical sense in which the word *karma* is used, is 'examination' or 'cross-examination' and does not mean 'torture'.[4]

The interpretation of the title of the chapter goes a long way in settling an important issue. A careful study of the chapter in the light of the above interpretation goes to prove that only avowed culprits were

[1] Bk. IV, ch. 2. See R.E. V, *Corpus*, p. 19; IV Pillar Edict, *Corpus*, p. 123.

[2] *Early History of Bengal*, p. 109.

[3] Bk. IV, ch. 8. Shāma Śāstri translates: 'Trial and torture to elicit confession'; Monahan 'the questioning of an accused person by word and by act'.

[4] The technical term for 'torture' is *parikleśa* the *palikleśa* of Aśokan inscriptions. Hultzsch who takes *'karman'* in the *Kauṭalīya* in the sense of 'torture' is obliged to interpret *parikleśa*—'harsh treatment': The inscription runs thus: baṁdhanaṁ va paliklesaṁ (*Corpus*, p. 93) meaning imprisonment or torture.

Parikleśa cannot be merely 'harsh treatment' for two reasons: First imprisonment itself is harsh treatment; secondly *parikleśa* in the sense of 'torture' to which Senart and Lüders agreed, is found used in the *Arthaśāstra* (IV-9). According to the latter authority the superintendent of the jail was liable to be punished if he would imprison persons without assigning reasons, torture them and kill them. See also R.E. V where imprisonment, death and torture seem separately referred to in the terms bandhana, vadha, and palibodha, bandhana—badhasa paṭvīdhanay(e) apalibodhaye mo(ksaye) ayi anuba. (*Corpus*, p. 56.) See also Mookerjee's *Aśoka*, p. 143, note 2.

subjected to torture and not the 'suspected'.[1] Kauṭalya no doubt does not mention the ordeals of fire, water, etc., recommended in the law-codes. These ordeals were in vogue for long after Kauṭalya. Hence the author of the *Arthaśāstra* could not be charged with ignorance of that age-long institution. What is therefore reasonable to infer is that Kauṭalya regarded these ordeals as questionable expedients, the application of which was restricted to cases involving more than a thousand *paṇas*[2] and introduces the more healthy method of judicial enquiry, thus sowing the seeds of the modern jury system. That punishment was meted out only after the guilt had been proved is evident from the following, among other statements of the *Kauṭalīya*. It is said that the guilt of a suspected person should be proved by the production of such evidence as the instruments used in committing the crime, accomplices and abettors, the stolen articles and persons concerned in their sale or purchase. In the absence of such evidence the accused should be acquitted."[3]

Here there is no mention of torture to elicit confession of a crime. On the other hand there is evidence to show that the judge was empowered to act on the circumstantial evidence which any judicial enquiry must take into account. This is corroborated by another equally important statement—

[1] See also *Proceedings of Third Or. Conf.*, pp. 628-29; *Hindu Adm. Inst.* p. 236-ff.

[2] Yāj. II.101.

[3] śaṅkāniṣpannamupakaraṇamantrisahāyarūpavaiyāvṛtyakarānniṣpādayet|
karmaṇaśca pradeśadravyādānāmśavibhāgaiḥ pratisamānayet|
eteṣām kāraṇānām anabhisandhāne vipralapantamacoraṁ vīdyāt|
—Bk. IV, ch. 8.

āptadoṣam karma kārayet

meaning that action was to be taken only in case where guilt had been proved, and not in doubtful cases. Thus torture is recommended as a kind of punishment for proved cases.

The nature of capital punishments in practice in the 4th century B.C. in India and the principle on which such punishments were inflicted are clearly furnished in the chapter on *śuddhścitraścadaṇḍakalpaḥ* of the *Kauṭalīya.*[1] Death-penalty was not the rule. Two classes of criminals are distinguished—those who are cruel in their offences, and those who are not cruel. Death-penalty without torture to the former is recommended. Even in this prescription the *Arthaśāstra* distinctly mentions that this ruling had the authority of the *śāstras* behind.[2]

Again in inflicting banishment to the Brahman culprits, Kauṭalya shows himself a follower of the *Dharmaśāstras.* Thus it is seen that in this, as in other respects, Kauṭalya has not broken any fresh ground but has consistently adopted the basic principles of the *Dharmaśāstras.*

That there was judicial trial for criminal suspects and that judgment was passed on the strength of the evidence is obvious from the Fourth Pillar Edict of Aśoka. Though one of the punishments involved death-penalty, still a grace (*yote*) of three days was granted to those on whom the sentence of death had been passed.[3]

[1] Bk. IV, ch. 11.

[2] ete śāstreṣvanugatāḥ kleśadaṇḍō mahātmanām|
akliṣṭānām tu pāpānām dharmyaḥ śuddhavadhassmṛtaḥ||

[3] ava ite pi cha me āvuti
baṁdhana-badhānaṁ munisānaṁ
tīl(i)ta-daṁḍānaṁ pata-vadhānaṁ
tiṁni divasā(n)i me yote diṁne|—*Corpus,* p. 123.

There is an exaggerated statement in the *Aśokavadāna* where Aśoka is said to have totally abolished capital punishment on account of his repentance for having caused death to a monk who was his own unfortunate brother.[1] How this statement has no basis in fact is proved by the inscriptions themselves where the sentence of death is recognized as the punishment for extreme forms of criminal offence. But Aśoka was prepared to mitigate the severity of punishment provided somebody interested in the culprit would get the sentence revoked by satisfying the judicial officers concerned as to their innocence. This reminds us of Kauṭalya's advocacy of the release of prisoners on payment of proper compensation price.[2]

Referring to the case of those on whose account no body was forthcoming to effect their rescue, there was no escaping the judgment. Hence they are advised to act in such a way as to win enjoyment in heaven.[3]

Other Courts

In addition to the High Court of Judicature, which we have examined above, there were a number of local courts in the provinces and districts. They were generally located in the chief towns of the different administrative districts: janapadasandhi, saṅgrahaṇa, droṇamukha, and sthānīya. Three judges and three commissioners conducted the cases in each of these courts.[4]

[1] See *Divyāvadāna, aśokavadāna* section.

[2] puṇyaśīlāssamayānubadhā vā doṣaniṣkrayam dadyuḥ—Bk. II.36.

[3] *Corpus,* p. 123.

[4] dharmasthāstrayastryomātyā janapadasandhisaṅgrahadroṇamukhasthānīyeṣu vyāvahārikānarthān kuryuḥ|

—*Ar. Śās.,* Bk. III, ch. 1.

In addition to these, the *Arthaśāstra* recognises the authority of the village courts which were self-sufficing and independent of imperial control. Here the *grāmavṛddhas* or the village elders, decided the cases arising in the village. They had magisterial functions which were binding on the villagers.[1] The State felt called upon to accept as valid every local usage, customs of the caste, community, clan, and family, every bye-law of the corporate bodies, the guilds and such other organised non-political communities.[2]

Thus there was a gradation of the Courts of Justice ranging from the local courts of the village community to the supreme courts of judicature. The local usages and customs were respected by the central government and an appeal lay from the lower court to the higher court. Inasmuch as the king received complaints from his subjects and dispensed justice according to the nature and urgency of the case he with his councillors represented the highest court of appeal and also acted as the court with original jurisdiction over certain cases.

Legal Procedure

It has been already mentioned that the *Arthaśāstra* mentions four bases of law in the order of their increasing importance: *dharma, vyavahāra, saṁsthā,* and *rājaśāsana.* Every case was decided on its merits. Generally honest and truthful witnesses were let in to depose. *Śrotriyas,* the king, members of the interested party, degraded criminals, etc., were ineligible

[1] Bk. III, ch. 9.

[2] sve sve tu varge deśe kāle ca svakaraṇakṛtāḥ
sampūrṇacārāśśuddhadeśādṛṣṭarūpa-
lakṣaṇa pramāṇaguṇāḥ sarvavyavahārāḥ
siddhyeyuḥ|—Bk. III, ch. 1. cp. *Anc. Ind. Polity,* p. 54.

to depose as witnesses.[1] Only those who came of an honourable family and whose character had been put to test were eligible. These took the oath in the usual procedure before they were cited as witnesses.[2] The court allowed them travelling and halting allowances, which appear to have been met by the defeated party.[3]

Cross-examination was a feature of the legal procedure. So far as the criminal cases were concerned the suspected was not to be apprehended after the lapse of three days from the day on which the crime was committed. The suspected was arrested and kept in police custody (*caraka*) until the next day when he was tried. That the Judge should not decide a case on mere circumstantial evidence is the opinion of Kauṭalya, as he cites the case of Māṇḍavya where injustice was done, relying, as the judge did, on the strength of such circumstantial evidences.

The following court offences (*paroktadoṣa*) among others are mentioned by the *Kauṭalīya*, as punishable by the Court whether committed by the defendant's party or the plaintiff's party.[4] These are:

(1) Evading a straight answer to the question.

(2) Inconsistent statements.

(3) Seeking advice from undesirable sources.

(4) Not continuously answering the question at issue.

(5) Adducing irrelevant points.

[1] *Ar. Śās.*, Bk. III, ch. 2.

[2] *Ibid.*

[3] puruṣabhṛtiraṣṭāṅgaḥ|
pathi bhaktamarthaviśeṣataḥ|
tadubhayam niyamyo dadyāt|—*Ar. Śās.*, Bk. III, ch. 1.

[4] *Ar. Śās.*, Bk. III, ch. 1.

(6) Contradicting the statements given by his own witnesses.

(7) Talking in secret to the witnesses without obtaining permission from the court.

(8) Meeting the arguments of defence on the same day.

(9) Failure to defend or to prove one's case within the time fixed for the purpose.

(10) Unwarranted statements.

The fines for these offences are said to be *pañcabandha* and *daśabandha,* the fifth and tenth parts of the sums sued for.[1] The *Arthaśāstra* rules that creditors of high social status, guilty of *parokta,* shall pay a fine, equal to one-tenth of the amount sued for, and creditors of lower status one-fifth of the amount.[2]

The judge and other court officials

The judge or the *dharmādhikārin* was the chief official of the High Court of Justice.[3] In this connection the *dharmasthas, amātyas* and *pradeṣṭāraḥ* are mentioned. The *dharmasthas,* from the very nature of the term, were men versed in the law of the land and of unimpeachable character. They were judges who adjudicated cases and dispensed justice on the nature of the evidence tendered by the witnesses on examination. These were probably assisted by a panel of counsel who went by the name of *amātyas.* The *pradeṣṭāraḥ* were commissioners who occupied somewhat lower status, and answer perhaps to our modern District Judges and District Magistrates. One feature of the administra-

1. Bk. III, ch. 11. Cp. Vijñāneśvara's commentary on verse 171, (II) of Yājñavalkya: Also Śrimūlam commentary, Vol. II, p. 68.
2. See for details *Hindu Ad. Inst.,* p. 258.
3. *Ar. Śās.,* Bk. IV, ch. 9.

tion was to entrust dispensation of justice not to a single judge or commissioner but a panel of judges or commissioners. The usual number was three. When the Court was proceeding with the case, a class of officials known as *lekhakas,* literally writers, took down the evidence tendered by both the parties of the plaintiff and the defendant and presented it for the judge to decide the case on its merits. If the judge on the other hand misconducted himself and did not do proper justice, he was also punished like any other citizen. It is evident from the chapter entitled *sarvādhikāraṇarakṣaṇam* that the judge guilty of offence was tried in the Samāhartā's court, the Samāhartā being assisted by the Pradeṣṭāra officials.[1] Perhaps this reminds us of the Administrative law-court of France (De Droit Administratif) instituted for the trial of officials. Thus as in modern France there were two sets of courts (*a*) ordinary courts for the trial of private individuals; and (*b*) administrative courts for the trial of officials.[2] The offences punishable on the part of a judge are (*a*) offending the contending parties for no reason whatsoever, (*b*) causing insult to the parties by raising irrelevant points (*c*) tutoring witnesses, (*d*) showing partiality to either party (*e*) or otherwise infringing the rights of the parties concerned. The punishment was in the first instance fines, and then, dismissal, if the judge was found guilty of the same for a second time.[3]

The officers of the jail were known as *bandhanāgārādhyakṣa* and *caraka.* The former was the Sup-

[1] *Ibid.*

[2] Gilchrist, *Principles of Political Science,* p. 319, (Third ed.).

[3] punaraparādhe dviguṇam sthānātvyaparopaṇam ca.

erintendent of the Jail and the latter was one of his assistants. If these officers were found charged with the ill-treatment of the prisoners or with violating the rule of law they were also punished. Some of the offences punishable were the infliction of punishments more severe than what was due, ill-treatment of the prisoners in the matter of rations and bedding, transfer of prisoners from one jail to another without assigning sufficient reason, and illicit intercourse with female prisoners. From the duties expected of the *dharmamahāmātras* of Aśoka's Edicts, it would appear that these officials correspond to the *dharmasthas* or judges of the civil and criminal courts mentioned by the *Kauṭalīya*. The suffix *mahāmātra* like the term *adhyakṣa* in the *Arthaśāstra* is a technical term for an official. According to Aśoka, these officials were to be engaged with the employers and employees, and were employed for taking steps against unjust imprisonment, and the release on insufficient grounds of those already imprisoned. They were also to see that the people did not molest one another. Some of these were the functions of the *dharmasthīya* court of the *Kauṭalīya*. At the least the *dharmamahāmātras* of the Edicts can be compared to the Superintendents of the Jails found mentioned in the *Arthaśāstra*. According to Aśoka[1] these dispensers of justice must be impartial as between one citizen and another. All men were equal in the eyes of law, and proper award of punishment not only entitled the judges but also the king whom they represented, to merit heaven.[2]

[1] First separate R.E.: Dhauli, *Corpus*, pp. 93-94. See also *Ind. Ant.* 1890.

[2] viyohala-samatā daṇḍa-samatā—IV P.E., *Corpus*, p. 123.

Elsewhere Aśoka expects these judicial officers to behave towards the people as a father towards his son. He realises that this is in a majority of cases an ideal rather than the actual. For, says he, 'some single person only learns this (and) even he (only) a portion (but) not the whole'.[1] On the negative side Aśoka expects his judicial officers to be bereft of unhealthy dispositions like envy, anger, cruelty, hurry, want of application, laziness and fatigue. In his opinion the possession of some of these dispositions would lead to maladministration of justice, and this would in the long run retard the progress of the State.[2]

It is noteworthy that the *Kauṭalīya* mentions some of these as tending to mar the administration of justice, and provides for the punishment of such judges as those who failed to discharge their duties properly.[3] It was the sincere wish of the emperor that none of his subjects suffered from unjust imprisonment or undeserved capital punishment. To see that his officers fulfilled their duties impartially and justly, certain commissioners were sent out from the headquarters to watch their conduct and report to the authorities at the capital.[4] This reminds us of the *Kauṭalīyan* prescription to set members of the Intelligence department over these officials among others. Again, as under every civilised government the Mauryan kings gave a general amnesty to prisoners on certain occasions. According to the *Kauṭalīya* the young, old, diseased and destitute prisoners had to be set free

1 First separate R.E., Dhauli.
2 *Corpus*, p. 95.
3 *Ibid.*
4 *Corpus*, p. 95.
5 *Corpus*, p. 93.

on the king's birthday and on the full moon days. Prisoners were also released on the acquisition of a new territory, on the anointment of the crown prince, and on the birth of a son to the king.[1]

This is confirmed by the Aśokan inscriptions especially by the Fifth Rock Edict. Some portion of the Girnār Edict is unfortunately not traceable while the Mānsehrā gives the following text:—

> bhaṭamayeṣu bramaṇibhyeṣu anatheṣu vudhreshu
> hida-su(khaye) dharma-yuta-apalibodhaye viya(p)uṭa te
> bandhana-badha(sa) paṭivi(dhanay)e apalibodhaye
> mokshay(e) (cha iyaṁ) anubadha p(r)aja t(i) va kaṭrabhikara
> ti va mahalake ti va viyapraṭa te
> *Corpus,* p. 75; see also p. 32, Kālsi version.

Perhaps a new interpretation of these lines is required in the light of the *Arthaśastra* texts. It is evident that Aśoka was familiar with the ruling of the *Arthaśastra* in this particular instance as in others. For Aśoka speaks of as much as twenty-five jail deliveries effected by him in the course of 26 years since his anointment to the throne.[2] Yet another healthy regulation relating to the jail was the frequent visits to the prisoners made by the authorities concerned once a day, sometimes once in five days, to enquire into their conditions in regard to their specific work and health, and some-

[1] bandhanāgāre ca bālavṛddhavyā dhitānāthānām
ca jātanakṣaṭrapaurṇamāsīṣu visargaḥ . . . .
apūrvadeśādhigame yuvarājābhiṣecane|
putrajanmani vā mokṣo bandhanasya vidhīyate||
Bk. II, ch. 36.

yāva saduvīsati vasa-abhisitena me etāye
aṁtalikāye paṁnaṿāsati baṁdhana-mokhāni kaṭāni.

[2] Pillar E. V. *Corpus,* p. 126.

times grant them money perhaps for their personal upkeep. This is evident from the following verse:—

divase pañcarātre vā bandhanasthān viśodhayet|
karmaṇa kāyadaṇḍeṇa hiraṇyānugrahena vā||
—II, 36.

The translation of this śloka by Shāma Śāstri is faulty. It runs as follows: 'Once in a day or once in five nights, jails may be emptied of prisoners in consideration of the work they have done, or of whipping inflicted upon them, or of an adequate ransom paid by them in gold."[1]

[1] P. 179. *Trans.* (Second ed).

CHAPTER V

THE CENTRAL ADMINISTRATION—(*Contd.*)

THE MILITARY SYSTEM

Sec. i. INTRODUCTORY

With the commencement of the Mauryan epoch the military system of the ancient Hindus becomes more perfect and more practical. The theories of diplomacy which have been in vogue from the earliest times of the Vedic period are formulated into a diplomatic code for princes to copy and follow. The well-known diplomatic means were four:—*sāma* (conciliation), *dāna* (gifts), *bheda* (creating division among his ranks or subjects), and *daṇḍa* (open war). The first three means were pursued one after another, and the institution of war was only the last resort though the Hindu political philosophy recognised it as the chief political weapon to bring to subjection recalcitrant chiefs and troublesome neighbours. The *Kauṭalīyan* code of diplomacy is a great improvement upon the original standard. During the epoch of the *Ṛgveda Saṁhitā* there is evidence to show that deceit was practised upon the enemies to turn them back.[1] Though Kauṭalya seems to accept the basic traditional principles, still the methods recommended for employing the means of diplomacy are not unmoral. Kauṭalya no doubt mentions different kinds of warfare including

[1] IV, 15-4; III, 18-1.

treacherous wars or *kūṭayuddha.*[1] This does not mean that Kauṭalya is recommending such a course of action for all time. As a writer on the different aspects of the subject, Kauṭalya could not avoid mentioning them and explaining what he meant by them. This aspect has been misunderstood and there has been a tendency on the part of some scholars to equate the principles formulated by Kauṭalya with the immoral teachings of Kaṇika, the Brahman Minister of Dhṛtarāṣṭra in the *Mahābhārata.*[2]

It has been shown elsewhere that Kauṭalya's political philosophy more agrees with that of the sage Nārada in the same epic.[3] The fundamental ideas common to both are that conquest is not an end in itself. The victory is counter-balanced by responsibilities, and acquisitions by the necessity of having to provide for safeguarding them. The general principle of the *Kauṭalīya,* then, is the practice of the first two means of diplomacy, *sāma* and *dāna* towards the local chieftains, and the last two means *bheda* and *daṇḍa* towards foreigners. This prescription is in accordance with that of Manu the law-giver.[4] In formulating this policy Kauṭalya, being a sound politician, discriminates between local people and foreigners, and shows his leniency towards the former. Kauṭalya is practical when he concludes this portion of the discourse by saying that internal risings must first be dealt with. He is of opinion that, without internal peace and security, foreign expeditions should not be launched upon. The following is the reflection of Kauṭalya on

[1] Bk. III, ch. 6.
[2] *Ādi Parvan,* ch. iii.
[3] *Sabhā Parvan,* ch. v.
[4] *Manu* VII, 106-ff.

diplomacy. "An arrow shot by an archer may or may not kill a person, but the skilful diplomacy of a wise man kills even those unborn."[1]

Sec. ii. FOREIGN POLICY

Kauṭalya divides the foreign rulers under four classes—*ari* (the enemy), *mitra* (ally), *madhyama* (intermediary), and *udāsīna* (neutral).[2] The inter-state relations are determined by the respective situations which each state possesses in the circle of states. While the second, the fourth and the sixth states are inimical, the third and the fifth states are allies.[3] Kauṭalya distinguishes three kinds of international relations: *vigraha* (war), *sandhi* (peace), and *āsana* (neutrality).[4] According to Vātavyādhi there are only two divisions, war and peace. But this division is questioned rightly by the *Kauṭalīya*. According to this there is a six-fold policy of action.[5] The remaining three attitudes are *saṁśraya* (policy of alliance), *yāna* (preparation of march), and *dvaidhībhāva*.

These three are minor divisions which are, properly speaking, absorbed in the three major divisions of war, peace and neutrality. The last aspect of international law discussed in the *Kauṭalīya* is a prominent feature of the *Kauṭalīyan* policy in relation to the other states or nations. The relation of the *Kauṭalīyan*

[1] *Ar. Śās.*, Bk. X, ch. 6.

[2] *Ibid.*, Bk. II, ch. 2.

[3] *Ibid.*

[4] *Ibid.*, Bk. VII, ch. 1.

[5] *Ibid.*

states was that each state acknowledged the sovereignty of the central power. The *Arthaśāstra* recommends territorial expansion by the policy of conquest.[1]

Diplomatic Agents

These new acquisitions were treated as protectorates or vassals, in modern political parlance. The border-peoples to which repeated reference is made in the Edicts of Aśoka[2] come under the category of these protectorates. The principle underlying the foreign policy was the maintenance of the balance of power.[3] This was effected by the diplomatic agents of the Empire. Kauṭalya makes mention of different classes of such agents.[4] Some of them correspond to our ambassadors. The *cāras* are those employed in secret service. There is the *ubhayavedana* who was perhaps the permanent ambassador in a foreign court. It is difficult to interpret the term as it comes under the common title of Gūḍhapuruṣas. These latter were the secret informants in war in addition to their office in the rank and file of the Mauryan bureaucracy.[5] They gathered news about the strength or otherwise of the enemy-state, and reported the same to the head-quarters. In accomplishing their ends they assumed different guises—, of a trader, an ascetic, a physician, an agriculturist, lest they should be unable to get at the required information, and lest they should be detected, and the real state of affairs be kept from them. These perhaps are meant by Megasthenes' 'supervisors'.

[1] Bk. X, ch. 5 and 6.
[2] R.E. II and XIII.
[3] *Ar. Śās.*, Bk. VI, ch. 2.
[4] Bk. I, ch. 11, 12 and 14.
[5] *Ibid.*

The inscriptions of Aśoka furnish us with a specialised kind of reporters designated *prativedaka* who were engaged in a similar work of furnishing to the capital, information collected about the enemy's country.[1] As these officers were entrusted with responsible duties Kauṭalya recommends the appointment of only tried men to these posts. The state was to render all possible help to them when they were in service. It is said that the king gave audience to them only at nights. This was perhaps to avoid the common people and interested men, lest the secrecy should be divulged. Whenever they put down some information in writing, they did it in a special form of writing *gūḍhalekhya* translated as 'cipher writing.' The idea was that even if it were miscarried the ordinary citizen could not make out its contents. Though the state had implicit confidence in its employees, still it did not hastily resort to action on a single report. Unless the report was confirmed by two sources, other than the one received, no action was taken.[2]

Dūtas or Ambassadors

The other class of diplomatic agents who were entrusted with still more responsible work to discharge were the *dūtas*. The term can be translated as ambassadors or envoys. The *dūta* is an open spy. While the *cāra* collected secret information, the *dūta* delivered the message in person without fear or favour sometimes at the risk of his own person. The qualifications for this office were by no means simple. A *dūta* must be

1 R.E. VI, *Corpus,* p. 58.

2 trayānām ekavākye saṁpratyayaḥ|
Ar. Śās., p. 21; cp. *Rāma*: Ayod., ch. 100; p. 36.

one who belonged to a well-known high-class family versed in the science of land, of a towering personality, humorous, eloquent, bold, faithful, and capable of meeting trying situations. Tactfulness and a resolute mind were his other characteristics.[1] The envoy went to the foreign court only with previous instruction. There were letters of credence, *śāsana,* containing the message of his king. There is a significant statement in the *Kauṭalīya* which says that letters of credence are important to the kings. On these depend cessation and outbreak of hostilities.[2] The *dūta* was the king's representative and hence his person was sacred.[3] However unpleasant the mission he was engaged in and the message he delivered, he was not to be slain. When once the message had been delivered the *dūta* could leave the station with or without the sanction of the king of the country.[4] In addition to these ambassadors, there were consular officers as is evident from the records of Megasthenes. Referring to the second Municipal Board mentioned by the Greek writer, V. A. Smith remarks that this Board performed duties which in modern Europe are entrusted to the consuls representing foreign powers.[5] The term *dūta* also occurs in the inscription of Aśoka. The mission entrusted to them seems to be the spreading of peace and goodwill between the respective states and the empire.

[1] *Ar. Śās.,* Bk. I, ch. 16.

[2] śāsanapradhāna hi rājānaḥ; tanmūlatvāt sandhivigrahayoḥ—*Ar. Śās.,* Bk. II, ch. 10.

[3] dūtamukhāvai rājānaḥ.—*Ibid.*

[4] *Ibid.*

[5] *Ind. Ant.,* 1905, p. 200.

Foreign Embassies

The Mauryan Empire grew in extent under Candragupta and got further expanded under Bindusāra and Aśoka. Candragupta succeeded to the throne immediately after Alexander's invasion and the latter incident involved him in international relations. After having consolidated his empire Candragupta turned his attention to the countries which were under the Macedonian rule. Seleucus Nikator who was in charge of the Greek kingdoms in the Indian frontier relinquished his rights to that portion of the country belonging to the Indian Empire, the satrapies of the Paropanisadai, Aria, Arachosia, and Gedrosia, and he was presented in return with 500 elephants. Seleucus felt the strength of the arms of Candragupta and arranged for peace through negotiations. This peace was effected with success by Megasthenes, the Greek ambassador of Seleucus in 303 B.C.[1]

The friendly relations between India and the Hellenistic kingdoms begun by Candragupta continued during the reigns of his successors. Dionysius came to Bindusāra as the envoy of Ptolemy Philadelphus of Egypt, and Daimachus as the envoy of Antiochus I Soter of Syria. It is not yet settled whether Dionysius delivered his letters of credence to Bindusāra or his son Aśoka, for the rule of Ptolemy Philadelphus extended from 285 to 246 B.C.[2] It is evident that both these envoys followed the example of Megasthenes and left records of their observations with regard to the country. Very few of the notes of Daimachus are preserved

[1] Smith, *Early History of India,* pp. 125-26.

[2] *Ibid.,* pp. 155-156; *C.H.I.*, p. 433.

while those of Dionysius are lost. About the latter Pliny mentions in his *Natural History,* VI, 17 and 58.[1]

It seems that Aśoka had unbroken friendly relations not only with the states within the country but also without. The Hellenistic kingdoms to which Aśoka sent his envoys were Syria under Antiochus Theos, Egypt under Ptolemy Philadelphus, Cyrene under Magas, Macedonia under Antigonus Gonatus, and Epirus under Alexander.[2] We do not hear of any foreign embassy in India during the reign of Aśoka, nor return embassies from India to foreign courts during the reigns of Candragupta and Bindusāra. It is however reasonable to assume that mutual and unbroken intercourse went on continuously under the first three Mauryan monarchs, if not later.

Alliances and Treaties

Mention has already been made that the ambassadors played a prominent part in effecting political combinations and peace negotiations. Let us now examine the nature and kinds of alliances contracted between the different states. The alliances were both offensive and defensive in character. The motive and time for such alliances are examined *in extenso* in the *Kauṭalīya.* These alliances were sometimes voluntary (*pratibhūḥ*) and sometimes effected by purchase (*pratigraha*). The former contained elements of permanence (*sthira*) and the latter elements of impermanence (*cala*).[3]

Alliances are again definite (*paripaṇita*) and indefinite (*aparipaṇita*).[4] The former are to be effected

[1] *Ibid.*
[2] R.E. XIII, *Corpus,* pp. 46-48; *C.H.I.,* I, p. 502.
[3] *Ar. Śās.,* Bk. VII, ch. 17.
[4] *Ibid.,,* ch. 6.

according to the place (*deśa*), time (*kāla*), and purpose in view (*artha*). Five kinds of agreements are mentioned. These are to win an ally (*mitra-sandhi*), to acquire wealth (*hiranya-sandhi*),[1] to acquire territory (*bhūmi-sandhi*),[2] to achieve some specific purpose (*karma-sandhi*),[3] and lastly the agreement contracted with no determined aim (*anavasita-sandhi*).[4] Kauṭalya next explains under what conditions these alliances are to be effected. First, when the king feels his inability to march against the enemy, he must ally himself with equals, inferiors, or superiors.[5] Secondly, alliance is generally made with one who is more powerful than the enemy.[6] Thirdly, if a powerful ally is not available the king should try to win the goodwill of his neighbours.[7] Fourthly, a king between two strong powers must ally himself with the stronger of the two, or with both, or with a neutral.[8]

Lastly, coalition is recommended for the king devoid of strength.[9] Coming to practical politics, according to Justin, Candragupta defeated the Nandas with the help of a lion and an elephant identified with the King of Simhāpura in Rājputana, and the Gajapati King of Kaliṅga.[10]

[1] *Ibid.*, ch. 9.
[2] *Ibid.*, ch. 10.
[3] *Ibid.*, ch. 12.
[4] *Ibid.*, ch. 11.
[5] samahīnajyāyobhissāmavāyikaiḥ sambhūya yāyāt|—*Ar. Śās.* Bk. VII, ch. 4.
[6] yatbalaḥ sāmantaḥ tadviśiṣṭabalamāśrayeta|—*Ibid.*, ch. 2.
[7] tādviśiṣṭabalābhāve tamevāśritaḥ|—*Ibid.*
[8] balīyasorvā madhyagatastrāṇasamarthamāśrayet| yasya vā antardhisyāt; ubhau vā kapālasamśrayastiṣṭet|—*Ibid.*
[9] saktihīnasamśrayeta|*Ibid.*, ch. 1.
[10] McCrindle, *Invasion of Alexander the Great*, pp. 327-28. See S. V. Visvanātha, *International Law in Ancient India*, p. 95 and S. V. Venkateśvara in *Ind. Ant.*, 1916, p. 30.

Three kinds of treaties are mentioned *sama* or equal, *viṣama* or unequal, and *hīna*, inferior.[1] Other forms of peace were not unknown. The following three *ātmāmiṣa, puruṣāntara* and *adṛṣṭapuruṣa* entailed supply of army and the giving of a woman of high rank as a hostage. Peace on payment of money was of four kinds: *parikraya, upagraha, suvarṇasandhi* and *kapāla*. Other treaties were concluded on payment of raw materials and by ceding territory.[2]

Sec. iii. ETHICS OF WAR

Though wars were fought on a large scale in Ancient India, still they were resorted to only as the last means. When once war was declared, the warrior was expected to fight to the finish. All glory was to the soldier who died in the field of battle. Appeal was so made by the Purohita to the soldiers as to stimulate their heroic spirit. It is said that the valourous soldiers who give up their lives in righteous warfare reach the worlds of heaven much more quickly than the Brahmans who wish to attain heaven through performance of sacrifices and austerities.[3] The idea is that once in the field, the soldier must not desert it or even retreat.

kūṭayuddha

A detailed reference to the *kūṭayuddha* or warfare by deceit by the author of the *Arthaśāstra* has made some scholars draw the conclusion that the *Arthaśāstra*

[1] Bk. VII, ch. 3.
[2] *Ibid.*
[3] Bk. X, ch. 3.

attaches importance to that kind of warfare where considerations of morality are subordinated to those of expediency and practical gain.[1] But later on it is stated that even in the *Arthaśāstra,* the *kūṭayuddha* occupies only a secondary or less honourable place.[2] The *Arthaśāstra* being a text-book on polity considers all the aspects of that polity. In speaking on the different kinds of warfare it is natural for the author to refer to every one of them and supply such details as were then available to him. This does not mean that the *kūṭayuddha* is recommended at all times. This kind of warfare is justified only in certain cases, and under peculiar conditions. Kauṭalya advocates only fair fighting and this is seen from the way in which he discusses the different methods of capturing a fortress. He condemns incendiarism by saying that the use of fire is an offence against God inasmuch as it would cause destruction to men, grains, cattle, gold, raw materials, etc.[3]

attention to the sick and the wounded

Special attention was devoted to the sick and the wounded. Physicians accompanied the army with surgical instruments (*śastra*), mechanical appliances (*yantra*), healing balm (*sneha*), dressing cloth (*vastra*), and nurses (*striyaḥ*). They took their stand in the rear and inspired the soldiers.[4]

[1] S. V. Viśvanātha, *Inter. Law,* p. 121.

[2] *Ibid.,* p. 124.

[3] aviśvāsyo hyagniḥ daivapīḍanam ca| apratisaṁghāta prāṇidhānyapaśuhiraṇyakupyadravyakṣayakaraḥ|—Bk. XIII, ch. 4.

[4] Bk. X, ch. 3. Cp. *Śānti,* 95, 12.

Non-combatants unmolested

Another feature of the ancient warfare was that the non-combatants were left unmolested. Megasthenes says: "Nor would an enemy coming upon a husbandman at work on his land do him any harm, for men of this class being regarded as public benefactors are protected from all injury. The land thus remaining unravaged and producing heavy crops supplies the inhabitants with all that is requisite to make the life very enjoyable."[1] Again with regard to the treatment of the conquered, Kauṭalya is of opinion that the conquered people should not be disturbed from the observance of their own laws and customs (*dharma*).[2] This is perhaps in keeping with what Aśoka says concerning the unsubdued borderers. 'The King desires that they should not be afraid of me, that they should trust me and should receive from me happiness and not sorrow. The king will bear patiently with us so far as it is possible to bear with us........the king is to us even as a father: he loves us even as he loves himself: we are to the king even as his children."[3] It is ordained that the family members of the slain soldier should not be deprived of their property or lands. On the other hand they must be reinstated.[4] There is thus a record of humane laws of war expounded by Kauṭalya in accordance with tradition and corroborated by the Greek contemporary writer.

[1] Fg. 1, p. 39 (Cal.) 1926.

[2] Bk. VII ch. 6; Bk. XIII, ch. 5.

[3] Smith, *Aśoka*, p. 177.

[4] na ca hatasya bhūmidravyaputradārānabhimanyeta|
kulyānapyasya sveṣu pātreṣu sthāpayet||—Bk. VII, ch. 16.
Cp. *Śānti*, v. 57.

Sec. iv. THE ORGANISATION OF THE ARMY

The army primarily constituted of the Kṣatriyas, well-trained and well-disciplined. In discussing the merits and demerits of forces consisting of the Brahmans, Kṣatriyas, Vaiśyas, and Śūdras respectively, Kauṭalya would attach no value to an army composed of Brahmans. He would prefer only a pure Kṣatriya host, though under certain circumstances a mixed host could be recruited which would be only bales of cotton signifying thereby the uselessness of that army. Much discrimination was urged in the matter of recruitment. There were of course the hereditary troops (*maula*) and these certainly constituted the standing army to which there is the evidence of Diodorus.[1] According to this authority this army was paid a handsome salary and was regularly supplied with arms, ammunitions, etc., by the state. This corresponds to the *Kauṭalīyan* arsenal department under the lead of the Āyudhāgārādhyakṣa. Under the latter's management weapons of war and other accessories to a military expedition were manufactured and kept in store for the supply of soldiers whenever there was an occasion for it. What these were and what the nature of the equipment was are given in detail.[2] The reference to the Board of supply and commissariat in the Greek records can be fitly compared with this department of the *Arthaśāstra*.

Besides the standing army, the fighting force consisted of hired men (*bhṛtakas*), contingents supplied by corporate associations (*śreṇibala*), contingents supplied by the ally (*mitrabala*), and members

[1] II, 41.

[2] *Ar. Śās.*, Bk. II, ch. 18.

of forest-tribes (*āṭavibala*). From the nature of the recruitment and from the significant statement in the *Kauṭalīya, hrasvaḥ pravāsaḥ* it can be safely assumed that this part of the army was engaged only for the time being, and when once their service was not required it was disbanded. There is no evidence on record to show that either conscription was in use or the army was a militia. If the records of Pliny[1] and Plutarch[2] could be believed the army of Candragupta consisted of as many as 9,000 elephants, 30,000 horses, and 60,000 footmen besides chariots. This means that the traditional four-fold division of the army continued in existence and was in the employ of the state. This division of the army also finds a mention in the *Kauṭalīya* with the respective uses to which each limb of that organism was put.

We have the evidence of Arrian to show that there was more than one method of equipment in vogue. The common mode is here furnished. "The foot-soldiers carry a bow made of equal length with the man who bears it. This they rest upon the ground, and pressing against it with their left foot thus discharge the arrow, having drawn the string far backwards: for the shaft they use is little short of being three yards long, and there is nothing which can resist an Indian archer's shot,—neither shield, nor breastplate, nor any stronger defence if such there be. In their left hand they carry bucklers made of undressed ox-hide which are not so broad as those who carry them, but are about as long. Some are equipped with javelins instead of bows, but all wear a sword, which

[1] VI, 19.
[2] Alex., ch. 62.

is broad in the blade, but not longer than three cubits; and this, when they engage in close fight (which they do with reluctance), they wield with both hands, to fetch down a lustier blow."[1]

With regard to the equipment of the cavalry Arrian remarks: "The horsemen are equipped with two lances like the lances called *saunia,* and with a shorter buckler than that carried by the footsoldiers. But they do not put saddles on their horses, nor do they curb them with bits like the bits in use among the Greeks or the Kelts, but they fit on round the extremity of the horse's mouth a circular piece of stitched raw ox-hide studded with pricks of iron or brass pointing inwards, but not very sharp: if a man is rich he uses pricks made of ivory. Within the horse's mouth is put an iron prong like a skewer, to which the reins are attached. When the rider, then, pulls the reins the prong controls the horse, and the pricks which are attached to this prong goad the mouth, so that it cannot but obey the reins."[2]

The equipment of the chariot of Poros can be taken as the standard in vogue in the Mauryan epoch. Each chariot was "drawn by four horses and carried six men, of whom two were shield-bearers, two archers posted on each side of the chariot and the other two charioteers as well as men-at-arms, for, when the fighting was at close quarters they dropped the reins and hurled dart after dart against the enemy."[3] Three archers besides the mahout or driver rode an elephant.[4]

[1] Mccrindle, *Arrian* XVI, pp. 225-26, (Cal.).

[2] *Ibid.*, p. 226.

[3] *Curtius,* VIII, 14..

[4] See *Strabo,* XV, 52; *Aelian,* XIII, 10.

Of all the figting forces the elephant force was deemed the best and full reliance was placed on its strength. On this depended victory or defeat.[1] It is said that the superiority of this force attracted the attention of the Seleucid monarchs who took to the oriental mode of warfare and especially employed elephants.[2]

Sec. v. THE WAR OFFICE

The control and the organisation of the army and navy were under an efficient staff of six boards consisting of thirty commissioners in all. Five members constituted each board. The boards were those of the infantry, cavalry, chariots, elephants, the admiralty, and the commissariat.[3] Kauṭalya makes no mention of such management by boards. According to this authority the six departments were under the control of different superintendents, such as the padyādhyakṣa, the aśvādhyakṣa, the rathādhyakṣa, the hastyādhyakṣa, the nāvādhyakṣa, and the āyudhāgārādhyakṣā, the last possibly the commissariat department of the Greek chronicles. Coincidences exist between the board of infantry and the department of padyādhyakṣa, the board of cavalry and the department of aśvādhyakṣa, the board of chariots and the department of rathādhyakṣa, the board of elephants and the department of hastyādhyakṣa, and the admiralty and the department of nāvādhyakṣa. Suffice it to say here that every department looked after the proper training of animals and

[1] *Ar. Śās.* Bk. VII, ch. 2.

[2] E. R. Bevan, *The House of Seleucus,* Vol. II, p. 289 (1902, London).

[3] Fg., 35 and 36.

men, their feeding, their health, their equipment, and their discipline. It is unnecessary to enumerate here every one of these. Though there is no pointed reference to the naval force and a department of admiralty in the *Kauṭalīya,* still we can assume that Kauṭalya has in mind a similar institution by his regulations to prevent smuggling, and other regulations as regards instruments of warfare, native vessels leaving for foreign countries, and foreign vessels entering the native ports. This assumption is well supported by the Greek evidence.

The commander-in-chief

Among the chief army officers the commander-in-chief played a significant role. He who was skilled in every kind of tactical and strategical mode of warfare and in handling weapons of war, and who could decide easily action or inaction in the circumstances of the situation, was qualified to be a commander. The following were among his other duties. He was to select the field of battle and camping grounds. He was to reinforce the strength of his army and take advantage of the time and the place for march, for engagement and for retreat. He was to maintain discipline of the host. He should employ such means as to create a dissension in the ranks of the enemy.[1] He was a permanent officer of the imperial government drawing a liberal salary of 48,000 *paṇas.*

Other Army Officers

Other officers of the army were commandants of cavalry, infantry, chariots, and elephants.[2] There was

[1] Bk. II ch. 33.
[2] Bk. II, ch. 30-32.

yet another officer designated as *nāyaka*.[1] The salary fixed for him was 12,000 *paṇas*. Hence he held a status lower than that of a commander-in-chief. The *nāyaka* is the chief of ten *senāpatis* or commandants. Next in rank to the latter is the *padika* who is the chief of ten smaller military officials. The *nāyaka* attended to the array of different army constituents, to collect the scattered soldiers, to arrange for the halt, march, and retreat. He also arranged these army constituents by various signs, such as, the trumpet-sounds, flags, and standards.[2] Besides the various military officials there were other officers and servants who were non-combatants and were attached to the department of transport and co-ordinate supply. There were, first of all, cooks for the supply of food to the fighting men under the head-cook *mahānasa*. There were the *purohita* and war musicians with drums and gongs to encourage the troops to fight with enthusiasm. Medical men followed the army for the treatment of the sick and the wounded, besides nurses.[3] Sappers, miners, and engineers (*vardhaki* and *viṣṭi*) under the command of an official designated *praśāsta* went in advance of the army in the course of the march repairing roads and constructing wells wherever necessary. They had also to attend to raising fortifications or demolishing them. They were again in charge of the construction of camps.

[1] Bk. V, ch .3.

[2] *Arthaśāstra,* Gaṇapati ed., Vol. III, pp. 141-2.

[3] purastādadhvanassamyak praśāstā grahṇāni ca|
yāyādvardhakiviṣṭibhyāmudakāni ca kārayet||—Bk. X, ch. 1.

Sec. v. CONCLUSION

Thus the organisation of the army was efficient and excellent. It was so ably managed that the first Mauryan emperor succeeded in bringing a great part of India under his control besides effecting the expulsion of the Macedonian chieftains. The latter were so much impressed with the superior force of not only Candragupta but also his successors that they sought permanent alliance with the Mauryan emperors. The superior arms again enabled Bindusāra to effect other conquests in the Dekhan and South India. They further enabled Aśoka to effectively resist the Kaliṅgas who also possessed an equally formidable force. We shall close this section with the observation of V. A. Smith: "The military organisation of Candragupta shows no trace of Hellenic influence. It is based upon ancient Indian model and his vast host was merely a development of the considerable army maintained by the kingdom of Magadha."[1]

[1] *Early History*, p. 153.

CHAPTER VI

PROVINCIAL AND LOCAL GOVERNMENTS

Sec. i. *A GENERAL SURVEY*

It has been already shown (Ch. II) that the empire of Candragupta extended from Afghanistan to Mysore and that of Aśoka was far greater in extent including all the Dekhan and South India upto the frontiers of the Tamil kingdoms. The vastness of the empire under Aśoka can be easily gauged from the distribution of the Pillars, Edicts and the Topes[1] which are usually associated with his name. A significant fact is that Aśoka has invariably caused the Minor Rock Edicts to be located on the borders of the empire. A study of the sites wherein all Aśoka's dumb monuments were located is in itself an interesting one. The chief places where the Major Rock Edicts are found are the following[2]:—

[1] In regard to the topes of Aśoka we have no reliable authority except a few legends in the Buddhist books. [Watters, *Yuan Chwang*, II, pp. 21 and 159; also *J.R.A.S.*, 1901, pp. 397-410.] The statement by Chinese pilgrims, Yuan Chwang and Fa-Hien, that as may as 84,000 topes were set up for Aśoka by Yakṣas or even human agents cannot be credited with any trustworthiness. (Pp. 88-91.) But in his tour beginning with the country of Kapis, through Gāndhāra, Taksaśīla, the Ganges and the Jumna, Kānyakubja. Kośāmbi, Lumbini, Vaiśāli, Tāmralipti, Kośala, Cola, Drāviḍa, Mahārāṣṭra to the middle Sindh, Yuan Chwang refers to as many as fifty topes seen by him. Hence it is reasonable to attribute a few topes to Aśoka's credit. Or even it may be that later on some of these topes were associated with this great name to establish the authenticity of Aśoka's faith in Buddhism. Yuan Chwang also refers to about eight pillars of Aśoka of various dimensions standing near Kapilavastu, Lumbini (p. 14), Kusinara (p. 28), Vaiśāli (p. 65), Pāṭaliputra (p. 93), and Rājagṛha (p. 162).

[2] A reference may be made with profit to a map appended to his note on the new finds of the Edicts of Aśoka in the *Ind. Ant.* (Feb.), 1932 by C. E. A. W. Oldham.

(1) Shāhbāzgārhī, in the Peshawar district of the North-West Frontier Province.

(2) Mānsehrā in the Hazāra district of the North-West Frontier Province.

(3) Kālsī, in the Dehra-Dūn district of the United Provinces and near the hill-station Masuri (also Mussooree).

(4) Sopārā of the Thāna district, Bombay.

(5) Girnār, near Junāgāṛh in Kathiawar.

(6) Dhauli, seven miles of Bhuvaneśvar, Orissa.

(7) Jaugaḍa in the Ganjam District, Madras.

The Minor Rock Edicts are found at the following places:—

(1) Maski, Raichur District.

(2) Śiddhāpura, Jaṭiṅga Rāmeśvara and Brahmagiri in the Chitaldroog District of Mysore.

(3) Sahasrām in South Bīhār.

(4) Rūpnāth in the Central Provinces.

(5) Bairāṭ in the Jaipur State of Rājputāna.

(6) Barābar Hill.

The Pillar Edicts are at the following places:—

(1) Toprā in the district of Ambāla.[1]

(2) Mīrāt[3] (Delhi-mirath) in the United Provinces.[2]

(3) Kauśāmbī (Kośam) about thirty miles from Allahabad.[3]

[1] But this Toprā Pillar is now located near the "Delhi Gate" removed thereto by Emperor Firoz Shah in the fourteenth century.

[2] This Mirāth Pillar has also been removed by Firoz Shāh and now stands on the ridge to the north of Delhi.

[3] A column is now found at Allahabad.

(4) Laurīyā-Ararāj, Laurīyā-Nandangaṛh and Rāmpurvā, all in the Champāran District of Bihar.

(5) Sārnāth near Benares.

(6) Sāṁchi in Bhopāl State, Central India.

(7) Rummindeī (identified as the site of the Lumbini garden, the birth-place of the Buddha) in the Nepal Tarāi.

(8) Niglīva (Nigālī-Sāgar), about 13 miles north-west from Rummindeī in the Nepalese Tarāi.

This geographical distribution of the Edicts and Pillars bears infallible testimony to the limits of the empire in the hey-day of its existence.

Administrative Divisions

This wide and extensive empire of the Mauryas was then a union of states, loosely called provinces, under the supreme dominion of the Emperors like Candragupta, Bindusāra, Aśoka and his successors. With such extensive territory it is impossible for the central executive machinery, however efficient, to function properly. Hence in those days, as is now being done, the empire was split up into different administrative units, these in their turn into smaller divisions, so as to facilitate the smooth course of the general administration. These administrative divisions may be termed for the sake of convenience, provinces, districts and villages. It cannot be said with any definiteness that the government of the provinces was an innovation of the Mauryas. It is perhaps reasonable to take the view that provincial government began with the Śaiśunāgas, and the Nandas under whom the empire was growing.

Mauryan Provinces

Coming to the Mauryas we know there were several viceroyalties under Candragupta. Unfortunately we are not in possession of the full materials to make a definite statement as to the number of provinces, the names of viceroys and such other details. There is evidence to show that Girnār was the headquarters of one of the provinces of Candragupta, and its governor (rāṣṭrīya) was one Puṣyagupta Vaiśya, apparently a local chief.[1] It is evident from the Buddhist books that prince Bindusāra was the viceroy of the southern provinces.[2] It is reasonable to assume that the provincial administration continued to be growing under Bindusāra as gathered from the Buddhist legends. Under him Taxila and Ujjain were among the provincial capitals. At these places Bindusāra appointed his sons Sumana (otherwise known as Susīma) and Aśoka as governors.[3] This is further corroborated by the *Divyāvadāna* which mentions a revolt of the citizens of Taxila during the reign of Bindusāra, when Aśoka was sent to take up the governorship and pacify the people.[4]

Under Aśoka

We have both literary and epigraphical evidence, as we shall see subsequently, to show that the government of the provinces was an accomplished fact under Aśoka. That the wealthy city of Taxila[5] continued to be

[1] Ep. Ind., VIII, pp. 46-47.

[2] *Mahāvaṁśa,* Ch. V.

[3] *Ibid.,* Ch. V, pp. 45-46, (S.B. Ceylon) Vol. I.

[4] Pp. 371-72.

[5] That Taxila was one of the richest cities when Aśoka ascended the throne, Cunningham mentions on the authority of Burnouf's "Introduction a' l'histoire de Buddhisme Indien" (p. 373). The passage is taken from his *Ancient Geography of India.* "At the time of Aśoka's

the capital of the *uttarapatha* or the northern province is evident from the *Divyāvadāna*. We hear of a similar rising of the citizens under Aśoka when he sent his son Kunāla as governor.[1] Viewed from the present geographical situation, Taxila was the ancient Headquarters of the North-Western Province which probably included the Punjab. Sind, the country beyond the Indus, and Kāṣmir. Besides this, there were certainly three more provinces whose respective capitals were Ujjaini (modern Ujjain in the Gwālior state), Tosāli and Suvarṇagiri. The latter was probably the headquarters of the southern provinces beyond the Nerbudda river.[2] The jurisdiction of the governor of Tosāli extended to the eastern provinces including the Kaliṅga country. Ujjain was the capital of the western provinces which included Mālva, Gujarat, and Kathiawar.[3] According to an inscription of Rudradāman, Girnār continued to be the capital of one of the provinces of Aśoka, under whom the governor was the Yavana chief Tuṣaspha.[4] Other cities which were seats of gover-

accession the wealth of Taxila is said to have amounted to 36 kotis or 360 millions of some unnamed coin, which, even if it was the silver *tangka* or six pence, would have amounted to nine *crores* of rupees, or £9,000,000. It is probable, however, that the coin intended by the Indian writer was a gold one, in which case the wealth of this city would have amounted to about 90 or 100 millions of pounds." This statement goes to prove the reputed wealth of Taxila within fifty years after Alexander's expedition.

[1] Pp. 407-408.

[2] Suvarṇagiri Dr. W. Geiger identified with a mountain of that name near Girivraja in Magadha (*Mahāvaṁśa,* Intro., p. xxvii). It is now identified with Kanakagiri in the Nizam's dominions, south of Māski, famous for an Edict of Aśoka. (See *Hyderabad Arch. Series No.* 1, p. 1. Hultzsch, *Aśoka,* Intro., p. xxxviii: Bühler, Ep. Ind. III, p. 134-ff.

[3] See *Early History of India,* p. 172.

[4] *Ep Ind.,* VIII, pp. 46-47.

nors were Samāpa (Jaugaḍa) and Kauśāmbi, the modern Kośam in the west of the Magadha province.[1]

Kumāras or Āryaputras

The governors of these provinces were either the local chieftains like the Yavana Tuṣaspha or royal princes who accepted the suzerainty of the emperor. Ordinarily members of the blood royal were deputed as viceroys to distant provinces. Bindusāra and Aśoka were in their turn the recipients of this honour at the hands of the Imperial government. There are two Rock Edicts[2] according to which the *kumāras* or *ārya-putras* were generally appointed as heads of the provinces. From the Rock-inscriptions of Aśoka we find that the governors at Ujjain and at Tosāli were *kumāras*[3] while the governor at Suvarṇagiri was an *āryaputra.*[4] Hultzsch is of opinion that the two *kumāras* were probably the sons of the king himself and the *āryaputra,* some other member of the royal family.[5]

Districts and villages

For purposes of administration the provinces were divided into districts and these again into villages. The term meaning a district is *āhāla* (Sanskrit *āhāra*), occurring in the Rupnāth

[1] See Kauśāmbi Pillar Edict of Allahabad-Kośam (Hultzsch, pp. 159-160). Also Cunningham's *Inscriptions of Aśoka,* p. 39.

[2] Jaugada First Separate R.E., *Corpus,* p. 112; Mysore Edicts, ib. pp. 175-178.

[3] Dhauli Separate R.E. I & II. *Corpus,* pp. 93 and 97.

[4] Brahmagiri and Siddapura R.E., *Corpus,* pp. 175 and 178.

[5] *Corpus,* Intro., p. xi.

Edict[1] and *āhāla* in the Sārnāth Edict.[2] There is again the mention of the district of Īsila[3] which was probably under the supervising control of the viceroy at Suvarṇagiri. For, the king's orders were not directly communicated to the district officer at Īsila, but went through the officials at the headquarters of the Suvarṇagiri province.[4] The next administrative division was the *grāma* or a village, or a group of a number of villages which formed the political unit. That these were also under some sort of control of the district officials is borne out by an important record, viz., the Soghaura copper-plate inscription whose interpretation remained unsettled for a long time.[5] This inscription which is accepted to be of the period of Aśoka is an order to the villages of Mānavāsitikṛtaśrīmanta and Ūṣagrāma by the mahāmāttras of Śrāvasti. Śrāvasti was apparently a district. Though we are not at present concerned with the object of the grant, still it may be noted in passing that it was an order to the respective villages to put up two temporary storehouses on the road with full provisions. Thus we are enabled to see in an outline how the local government was carried on during the epoch of the Mauryas.

[1] *Corpus,* p. 166.

[2] *Ibid.,* p. 162.

[3] *Ibid.,* pp. 175 and 178.

[4] See for more details, the Mysore Edicts at Brahmagiri and Siddhapura, *Corpus,* pp. 175-179.

[5] For a discussion on the subject see the proceedings of *A.S.B.,* 1894, p. 87ff: *J.R.A.S.,* 1907, pp. 523ff: *Annals of the Bh. R. Institute,* Vol. XI, pt. 1, pp. 32-48.

Sec. ii. LOCAL ADMINISTRATION IN THE KAUṬALĪYA

The four divisions of the Janapada

Before we proceed to examine the details in regard to the government of the provinces let us pass in review the scheme of provincial administration as outlined in the extant *Arthaśāstra*. The whole Janapada is divided into four convenient parts, the *sthānīya, droṇamukha, kharvaṭika* and *saṅgrahaṇa.*[1] These divisions were different stations where government officials were posted primarily for the purposes of police and secondarily for revenue purposes. The *sthānīya* is the largest division in the midst of 800 villages. The *droṇamukha, kharvaṭika* and *saṅgrahaṇa* were the headquarters for 400, 200, and 10 villages respectively. The area of the Kauṭalīyan village extended from one to two *krośas,* a *krośa* measuring 2250 yards.

The Antapālas

The officers at these respective divisions were graded officials all subordinate to the *Samāhartā* or the Collector-general. We are not able to fix the exact functions assigned to these rural officials. That these headquarters were not fortified garrisons for purposes of defence is evident from the fact that in the next line of the same book,[2] we find a set of officials called *antapālas* who were placed in charge of the frontier-territories. In each of these were military stations at least one recalling to our memory the Palatine earldoms under William the Conqueror. That the officials at these rural head-quarters had some-

[1] Bk. II, ch. 1; cp. Bk. III, ch. 1.

[2] Bk. II, ch. 1.

thing to do with the revenue collection is evident from the fact that these were answerable to the Collector-general. Added to this is the fact that this division occurs in the chapter entitled the *Janapada niveśa*[1] where the question of the settlement of the villages is discussed. If it is then conceded that these officials had the supervising control over the collection of revenue and were partly answerable to it, then it is reasonable to take the view that the central government entrusted the same agency to guarantee safety and security to the rural areas. This means that these officials undertook to defend the people from thieves and robbers, for the *antapālas* guarded the entrance into the kingdom. This position, it is possible to take, for in those days there was no fine distinction between the police functions and revenue functions.

Other officials

In addition to these the Central government appointed other agencies to ensure internal peace. The trap-keepers (*vāhurika*), archers (*śabara*), hunters (*pulindas*), outcastes (*caṇḍālās*), and wild tribes (*araṇyacara*) were set about to reconnoitre the country parts including the forest regions, and whenever they anticipated disturbance or danger of any sort, they sent information to the capital. The means of carrying this news was by the blowing of conch shells or the beating of drums. Sometimes it was by flying the pigeons with writs (*mudrā*), or causing fire and smoke at respectable distances.[2]

1 Bk. II, ch. 1.
2 Bk. II, ch. 34.

Classification of villages

The administrative classification of the villages is not without interest to the antiquarian. Kauṭalya speaks also of three-fold classification of the villages.[1] These were, first, villages exempted from taxation (*parihāraka*), secondly, villages supplying soldiers *āyudhīya*), and thirdly, villages liable to taxation in cash or kind.[2] In the same chapter[3] a further sub-division of the villages according to the quality of the soil is given. These are again classified under three heads—the superior, the middling and the inferior. Apparently such considerations weighed with the settlement officers in regard to the assessment of the revenue. Barring this the central administration did not interfere in the rural politics which were in the hands of the village communities. These villages, economically self-sufficient, enjoyed complete rural autonomy.

Duties of the Gopa

In every village there was an official who went by the name of *Gopa*.[4] He was the official of the Central government appointed over a small area ranging from five to ten villages. He held the jurisdiction of this area for which he was responsible. He was primarily a revenue official. Among the functions assigned to him the following may be noted:

[1] For a correct interpretation of the term *grāma* see K. A. Nīlakanta Śāstri's article in the *J.O.R.* (1930), part 3, being a reply to the ingenious interpretation of Prān Nāth in his *A Study in the Economic Condition of Ancient India.*

[2] See the excellent comment of Gaṇapati Śāstri on this passage Vol. I, pp. 344-45.

[3] Bk. II, ch. 35.

[4] *Ar. Śās.*, Bk. II, ch. 35.

(1) He maintained proper records of the accounts relating to the village or villages under his jurisdiction.

(2) He set up boundary limits of villages, fields, forests and roads.

(3) He numbered the plots of ground under respective heads: cultivable and non-cultivable, dry lands and wet lands, number of gardens including fruit, flower and vegetables.

(4) He also kept a note of the grounds covered by temples and altars, cremation grounds, rest-houses where food and water were supplied, pasture grounds and roads.

(5) He maintained another register wherein were noted down gifts, sales, charities and the cultivable lands remitted of revenue.

(6) He kept yet another register showing the number of houses in his charge, both tax-paying and tax-free. In this he further noted the number of inhabitants, their castes and professions, their income and expenditure besides the heads of cattle in each household, as well as other domestic animals.

These rural officials were not left to themselves. The Central government appointed as many as three commissioners in every headquarters of the rural areas. They went about the country and kept watch over the revenue officials lest they should prove tyrannical or harass the people unduly with unjust taxes. These commissioners were then an effective check on the conduct of these government servants who were thus given no opportunity to misuse their powers.[1] If any comparison could be made, the *sthānīyas* and the *droṇa-*

[1] *Ibid.* Also see Bk. III, ch. 1.

mukha officers were the viceroys and provincial governors, while those at the *kharvaṭika* and the *saṅghrahaṇa* were district officers. The *gopas* were the members of the subordinate civil service who were in charge of the accounts.

Sec. iii. THE GOVERNMENT OF THE PROVINCES

The relation between the central government and the provinces

It would be particularly interesting to examine how far the scheme of provincial administration in the *Kauṭalīya* coincides with such aspects of that administration as can be gathered from the inscriptions of Aśoka. It is indeed difficult to define the exact relations between the central government and the local government. It is evident that at the head of each province there was a viceroy or a governor. He was invariably a member of the royal dynasty and preferably a royal prince. But in the provinces where it was felt that a local chief might prove a better administrative head, the local man was appointed.[1] This governor was assisted in his work of administration by a body of officials known by different designations, the *mahāmātras,* the *rājukas* and the *pradeṣṭṛs.* These were executive officials appointed again by the Central government. Their chief functions appear to have been the collection of revenue, and defence by means of an elaborate police organisation. These provincial heads were also the channel of communication between the Central government and the rural officials. The

[1] See above, pp. 201-2.

orders of the imperial Headquarters were communicated to the provinces by Edicts and royal prescripts of which we have some specimens in those of Aśoka to the officers at Tośāli and Kauśāmbi.[1] These officers at the Headquarters of the provinces in their turn communicated the orders of His Majesty to the rural officers. For instance, the prince and the *mahāmātras* of Suvarṇagiri communicated to the *mahāmātras* at Īśila what the Devānāmpriya had commanded.[2] If the administrative details contained in the *Divyāvadāna,* undoubtedly a later work, could be relied upon, then there were, in addition to those officers above mentioned, political organisations in the provincial capitals which went by the name of the Paura, the Jānapada and others.[3]

The mahāmātras

Let us now examine the status assigned to and the functions expected of the *mahāmātras,* the *rājukas,* and the *pradeṣṭṛs* one after the other. The term *mahāmātra* occurs in several places in the *Arthaśāstra* and has been translated by Shāmā Śāstri as 'minister'.[4]

There is also another term *mahāmātrīya*[5] meaning 'the official-chamber of the ministry'. Excepting the fact that these *mahāmātras* were ministers or high officials of the state, no other functions definitely marked as such can be gathered from the *Arthaśāstra.* A comparative study of the *Arthaśāstra* and inscriptions of Aśoka[6] where the designation *mahāmātra* occurs,

[1] *Corpus,* pp. 92, 191, 155, etc.
[2] Brahmagiri R. Ins., p. 175.
[3] *Divyāva,* p. 411.
[4] Bk. I, ch. 12.
[5] Bk. II, ch. 5.
[6] Rock Edict V, XII, Minor Rock Edict I, Kalinga Edicts, Pillar Edict VII, Kauśāmbi and Sārnāth Edicts. Cp. Vātsyāyana, *Kāma-*

beȧrs the possibility of equating the term *mahāmātra* in the Edicts with that of the *adhyakṣa* in the *Artha-śāstra*. This possibility of change was only in designation but not in function. This correspondence of *adhyakṣa-mahāmātra* does not negative the special interpretation of *mahāmātra* meaning a minister. It would seem that whenever the term is used without any prefix it may be generally taken to denote ministers. More of this later on.

Similarity of offices in the Arthaśāstra and the Edicts

As Kauṭalya mentions a number of *adhyakṣas* in charge of the respective departments of the state Aśoka speaks of a number of superintendents in charge of different departments. We shall mention here such officers from the *Arthaśāstra* as correspond to those under the *mahāmātra* officials of the Edicts. *Nāgaraka* who is the superintendent of the town[1] corresponds to *mahāmātra-nāgaraka*. The *paura-vyāvahārika*[2] corresponds to the *nagala-viyohālaka*.[3] These latter are found as administrators of justice for their cities, Tośāli and Samāpa.[4] Perhaps the *gaṇikādhyakṣa*[5] or the superintendent of courtesans can be compared with *Ithījhakha-mahāmāta*[6] or *strīadhyakṣamahāmātras*.[7] Probably these officials attended to the needs and comforts of the women members of the royal family. What their functions exactly were is not clear. A com-

sūtra, pp. 285, 287, and 300. See also H. C. Chakladar, *Social Life in Ancient India* (Greater India Society publication, No. 3), p. 106.

1 Bk. II, ch. 36.

2 Bk. I, ch. 13.

3 *Corpus*, p. 92.

4 *Ibid.*

5 Bk. II, ch. 27.

6 XII R.E. Girnār, *Corpus*, p. 20.

7 Mānsehrā, XII and Shāḥ., XII.

parison can again be made between the *dharmā-vasathinaḥ* of the *Arthaśāstra*[1] and the *dharma-mahāmātras* of Aśoka. In the former they were managers of religious and charitable institutions, who administered to the wants of the *śrotriyas* and ascetics, and who kept in check the *pāṣaṇḍis* and other heretical sects. They interested themselves in the promotion of morality and religion.[2]

Functions of dharmamahāmātras

More or less the same functions were expected of the *dharmamahāmātras* by Aśoka.[3] Their functions were as follows:—

"These are occupied with all sects in establishing morality, in promoting morality, and for the welfare and happiness of those who are devoted to morality (even) among the *yonas, kambojas,* and *gāndhāras,* and whatever other western borderers (of mine there are).

"They are occupied with servants and masters, with Brahmanas and Ibhyas, with the destitute, (and) with the aged, for the welfare and happiness of those who are devoted to morality, (and) in releasing (them) from the fetters (of worldly life).

"They are occupied in supporting prisoners (with money), in causing (their) fetters to be taken off, and in setting (them) free, if one has children, or is bewitched or aged, respectively.

"They are occupied everywhere, here and in all outlying towns, in the harems of our brothers, of (our)

[1] Bk. II, ch. 36.
[2] *Ibid.,* p. 10.
[3] R.E. V, XII and P.E. VII.

sisters, and (of) whatever other relatives (of ours there are).

"These *mahāmātras* of morality are occupied everywhere in my dominions with those who are devoted to morality, (in order to ascertain) whether one is eager for morality or properly devoted to charity."[1]

The antamahāmātras

The *antapālas* of the *Kauṭalīya* correspond to the *antamahāmātras* of the Edicts. The Empire had grown so huge and so vast that effective frontier administration was of paramount necessity. Clear instructions are laid down in the *Arthaśāstra* as to the duties

[1] Hultzsch, Trans., pp. 33-34. See above pp. 168, 173-5, for a slight modification in the interpretation of certain terms.

The statements in the inscriptions (V.R.E.):

atikātaṁ aṁtaraṁ na bhūta-pruvaṁ dhammamahāmātā nāma|
ta m(a)yā traidasavāsābhi(s)i(tena) dhammamahāmātā katā|
(Gīrnār, *corpus*, p. 9).

se atikaṁtam aṁtalaṁ nohuta-puluva dham(m)a-mahāmatā nāmā|
t(e)dasa-vasābh(i)sitenā mamayā dhaṁma-mahāmāt(ā) kaṭ (ā)|
(Kālsi, *corpus*, p. 32).

sa atikrataṁ atara no bhuta-pruva dhraṁma-ma(ha)ma(tra) nama|
so todaśavaṣabhisitena
maya dharma-mahamatra kiṭa
(Shāhbāzgārhi) *corpus*, p. 55.

This has been rendered by Hultzsch in his translation thus: "Now in times past (officers) called mahāmātras of morality did not exist before. But mahāmātras of morality were appointed by me (when I had been) anointed thirteen years." This interpretation has also been generally accepted. The words 'no' and 'na' may equate and mean 'indeed', 'now', etc. Hence the first line may be translated "In times past officers called dharma-mahāmātras indeed existed." What Aśoka apparently wants to make out is that this office which once existed did not exist during the period of his first thirteen years. He perhaps felt the necessity for such office and appointed special officers. In the light of the *Arthaśāstra* where there is evidence of a similar office, with most of the functions as found in the Edicts assigned to it, the interpretation that it did not exist before seems to be incorrect.

and responsibilities of the boundary guards and frontier chiefs and their relations with the central government. They had both political and economic functions to perform. The economic duties were to collect the road-cess (*vartani*) on imported goods, mark them with the royal seal and take charge of these goods until they passed beyond the toll house.[1] Kauṭalya advises a good number of frontier-guards to be appointed lest they should be won over by the enemy. If they were a good number, they would be afraid of betrayal from one another and conduct themselves loyally to the empire.[2] The frontier peoples, whether conquered or unconquered, forest-folk or others, were kept in good humour and the paternal principle of government was even extended to them as is evident from the Kaliṅga Edicts.[3] The *antamahāmātras* like the *antapālas* were chiefly occupied with the administration of the frontier provinces.[4] The *Arthaśāstra* refers to three kinds of *dūtas*—(1) those possessing ministerial qualifications, (2) those possessing lesser qualifications, and (3) those possessing ordinary qualifications.[5] It would appear that generally from among the first class of messengers, ambassadors were selected and sent to other states to determine the relation of states to one another. This practice corresponds to that in Aśoka's time. From a study of the Rock Edict V it can be safely said that from among the *mahāmātra* officials, ambassadors (*dūtas*) were selected. They were sent not only

[1] Bk. II, ch. 21.

[2] Bk. II, ch. 4.

[3] *Corpus*, pp. 98 and 102.

[4] First Pillar Edict—Delhi Topra, *Corpus*, p. 119.

[5] Bk. I, ch. 16.

to the neighbouring states but also to foreign countries with which the empire had diplomatic relations.[1]

The mantripariṣad of the provinces

As already mentioned the *Arthaśāstra* refers to the terms *mahāmātra* in the sense of a minister,[2] and the *mahāmātrīya*[3] as the official chamber of the ministry. It is significant to note again the term *mantripariṣad,* meaning thereby the council of ministers. Suffice it to say here that this council enjoyed the right of consultation by the king before he would launch on some business affecting the state. What is interesting is that Aśoka uses the terms *mahāmātra* and *pariṣad* in a similar sense. There are two important Edicts, R. E. III and V, which bear this out. The first is an order of the council to the officials in the Accounts Department,[4] and the second refers distinctly to the inner working of the councils.[5] It is refreshing to note that Hultzsch agrees with this interpretation.[6] He writes: "Jayaswal[7] has drawn attention to the occurrence of the term *mantripariṣad* 'the council of ministers,' in the *Kauṭalīya.* This meaning fits admirably both here and in the Rock Edict VI." That the *āryaputra* or the provincial chief did not act on his own initiative, but consulted his council before he took action, is seen from the fact that even the orders of the provincial Headquarters were sent both in the name of the provincial chief and his *mahāmātras* as is

1 See R.E. XIII, *Corpus,* p. 67.
2 Bk. I, ch. 13.
3 Bk. II, ch. 5.
4 Edicts R.E. III and VI.
5 *Corpus,* p. 4.
6 In a footnote on page 5.
7 *Ibid.,* p. 11. See also *I.A.,* 42, pp. 282-284.

evident from the phrase 'ayaputasa mahāmātāṇaṁ cha'.[1] Though the members of the *mahāmātra-pariṣad* seem to have enjoyed a good deal of freedom, still they did not go unchecked. They could not abuse their rights and privileges. If differences of opinion arose among them, the matter was reported to the king at the imperial Headquarters who was the final arbiter.[2] Again if they should conduct themselves badly the citizens would raise the standard of revolt, which would be duly reported to the King.

Revolt against provincial ministry

A practical instance of this is seen from the history of Aśoka. The citizens of Taxila, the capital of *uttarapatha* or the northern provinces, resented the insolent behaviour of the ministry at their provincial capital. When the matter reached the Emperor Bindusāra, Aśoka was sent to restore law and order. The citizens accorded the prince a cordial welcome with *pūrṇakumbhas* and other invaluable presents. They addressed him thus: "We are not hostile either to the Kumāra or even the king Bindusāra. But we are hostile to the ministers who by their high-handedness provoke us to excitement."[3] There was a similar rising in the same place under Aśoka who sent his son Kunāla. He was also warmly received by the *pauras* who ventilated their grievances against the ministry.[4] It has been shown

[1] See *Corpus*, p. 176, Brahmagiri R. E.

[2] See R.E. VI, *Corpus*, p. 11.

[3] śrutva takṣaśīlanivāsinaḥ paurāḥ| ardhatṛtīyāni yojanāni mārge sobham kṛtva pūrṇaghaṭamādāya pratyutgatāḥ| pratyutgamya ca kathayanti| Na vayam kumārasya viruddhāḥ, nāpi rājño Bindusārasya| api tu duṣṭāmātyāḥ, asmākam paribhavam kurvanti| mahatā ca satkārena takṣaśīlam praveśitaḥ|—*Divyāvadāna,* pp. 371-72.

[4] *Ibid.,* pp. 407-8.

already that these ministers retired from office in some places every three years as at Takṣaśīla, and in other places every five years.[1] Mention has again been made of the relations which existed between the ministry and the local assemblies of the realm such as the *paura* and the *jānapada.*

Rājukas

Another body of higher officials went by the designation of *rājuka* or *lājuka.* It would be indeed interesting here to examine whether this office of the *rājuka* is mentioned in the *Kauṭalīya Arthaśāstra.* The term occurs in the work with a prefix *'cora'*, and the full designation is *'corarajjuka.'*[2] It would appear that the designation *rajjuka* is the more correct technical term and not *'rājuka.'* It is not clear from what root the word derives its present form. Perhaps it comes from the old root *rasj* or *rajj.* Whatever this may be the passage in the *Arthaśāstra* throws welcome light on the rural administration of the land. Rural policy depended obviously on the nature of the territorial area. In the intervening places between any two villages was the officer in charge of the pasture lands (*vivītādhyakṣa*) and he was responsible to make good the loss occurring in his territorial jurisdiction. If the locality was not considered of sufficient importance from a commercial point of view, and the traffic was slack, there was the *cora-rajjuka* who was responsible for the security of the place. There were again other places where transactions were next to nothing, and in those places the people of the locality made their own arrangements

[1] See above p. 132.

[2] *Ar. Śās.*, Bk. IV, ch. 13.

for the upkeep of peace. Perhaps the responsibility was fixed in the village community.[1] In Chapter VI of Book II, the terms *rajjūḥ* and *corarajjūḥ* occur and are respectively interpreted as 'income from the territory' (*viṣayapāladeyam*), and as 'income from the village for protection against the thieves."[2] The officials in charge of such incomes were those who were connected with the department of revenue. Whenever they were chosen for specified interests, they were designated with a title, the prefix of which denoted the functions allotted to them. It may be presumed that they were officials connected with 'survey, land settlement and irrigation'.[3] This was also the interpretation which Bühler gave in discussing the phrase *mahāvalabham rajjūkam*[4] when examining the Śātavāhana inscription containing a grant of Hārītiputta Satakaṇṇi of Bānavāsi of the second century A.D. That such officials existed is corroborated by the Greek authority, Megasthenes.[5]

To turn our attention to the Aśokan inscriptions the term occurs in the Rock Edict III and the Pillar Edict IV. According to the latter the *rājukas* are set over hundreds of persons. An examination of their powers and functions shows that they occupied a status next in rank only to the viceroys. Says V. A. Smith: 'The modern term governor may serve as a rough equivalent.'[6] According to the same authority the word *rājuke* or *rāju* (Mānsehrā R. E.) is etymologically con-

[1] *Ibid.*

[2] coragrāhakāya grāmadeyam, *T.S.S.*, Vol. I, p. 134.

[3] See F. W. Thomas, *C.H.I.*, Vol. I, pp. 487 and 508.

[4] See *Z.D.M.G.*, xlvii, p. 466, *cp. Ep. Ind.*, II, p. 466, *n.*

[5] Fg. 34, p. 86 (Cal., 1926); see also Law, *Aspects of Ind. Polity, Intro.*, by Mookerjee, p. 36; *Contra* Stein, *Meg. und Kauṭalya*, p. 22.

[6] *Aśoka*, p. 94.

nected with *rāja,* and hence Bühler's construction cannot be accepted. If it is connected with the term *rāja,* he should have been one of the *mahāmātra* officials, since *rāja* in Pāli means *mahāmātra.* The term may therefore mean 'all those who have power of life and death'.[1] The Rājukas were very likely the chief provincial revenue officers. It appears that Aśoka invested them with extensive powers and allowed them the use of their independent discretion 'without the necessity of obtaining sanction for particular acts by reference to the Crown.'[2] Categorically their powers and duties may be stated as follows[3]:—

(1) They were the sovereign authority with regard to the questions of war and peace (*abhihara*) so far as the provinces were concerned. This means that they informed the Central government of the movements of the enemy and breaking up of hostilities in the neighbouring kingdoms or border tracts.

(2) They were the final authority in matters relating to the upkeep of internal peace. This was to afford protection by the proper exercise of *daṇḍa* and *daṇḍanīti.* That their decision was binding is evident from the term *ātmapatiye* in the inscription. Local affairs were left to the hands of local men who had first-hand knowledge of the locality. It was felt improper to dictate a policy from the imperial capital by members who had neither the opportunity nor the occasion to get themselves acquainted with the needs and aspirations peculiar to the locality.

1 See Childer's Pāli Dictionary.

2 See Pillar E. IV, *Corpus,* p. 123; also Smith, *Aśoka,* p. 203.

3 See P.E. IV.

(3) They exercised also civil and criminal jurisdiction. Wrongs were righted and grievances were redressed by an impartial administration of justice. They thus took cognizance of both civil and criminal causes within their territorial jurisdiction.

(4) They were to conduct themselves in such a way as to win the esteem and confidence of the Jānapada organisations. Co-operation was therefore sought with the Jānapada or popular assembly for awarding punishment or granting *anugrahas* (favours and concessions). In their acts and deeds they were to be like nurses whose only care was to look after the proper growth and progress of children.

(5) They were to discharge their responsibilities with a sense of duty, peace of mind, and with no feeling of hostility. They were to promote what was good for the *prajā* and the *loka* (people) and on behalf of the Jānapada. By taking a dispassionate view of things and acting selflessly with an eye to the welfare of the people, they realised their objects easily. They were, in short, expected to do what the common will dictated as tending for the common good.

Thus according to the *Arthaśāstra* and the Edicts of Aśoka, the Rajjuka or Rājuka was the officer of the Jānapada entrusted with duties of a varied character as warranted by the circumstances of the situation.

The Prādeśikas

We have now examined two institutions, thrown off to exercise, as their peculiar work, administrative and judicial functions of the provincial government, that is, the offices of the *Mahāmātras* and the *Rājukas.* The next body of officials was that of the *Prādeśikas.* The *Arthaśāstra* mentions a class of officers called the *pradeṣṭṛs.*[1] They were appointed by the Samāhartā.[2] They seem to have[3] been primarily revenue commissioners.[4] They had also magisterial functions to perform. It is said that a Board of three commissioners was formed, and that it was deputed to enquire after the disturbers of the peace including state officials in the locality, and to bring them to book so that the trade and industry which were the mainstay of the empire had an unhampered continuity.[5] The term *kaṇṭaka* in this passage is interpreted as artisans in the T. M. commentary.[6] But it is hardly acceptable. It is highly improbable that three ministers or three commissioners would have been appointed to look after the artisans. It is very likely that these officers resembled the justices of peace of the mediæval England who made extensive tours in the country parts and awarded punishment to men of criminal tendencies and acts.[7] In meting out justice the commissioners were to be impartial and equitable[8] and if not, they were liable to the same penalty.[9] These commissioners like the judges were

[1] Bk. I, ch. 12.

[2] Bk. IV, ch. 9.

[3] The pay of a *pradeṣṭa* officer is computed to be 8,000 *paṇās* equal to that of the president of the *śreni* and leaders of elephants, horses, and chariots. (Bk. V, ch. 3.)

[4] gopasthānīkasthāneṣu pradeṣṭārāḥ kāryakāraṇam balipragraham ca kuryuḥ|| Bk. II, ch. 35.

[5] Bk. V, ch. 1,4 and 9.
pradeṣṭārāṣṭrayastrayo vā amātyāḥ kaṇṭakaśodhanam kuryuḥ|

[6] See Shāma Śāstri Trans. p. 245-n.

[7] pradeṣṭa coramārgaṇam, Bk. IV, ch. 6.

[8] Bk. IV, ch. 10.

[9] *Ibid.,* ch. 9.

watched over lest they should become corrupt by accepting bribes. Those who were proved guilty were punished.[1] This shows that they were expected to discharge their functions with full responsibility.

Identical with these officers are the *prādeśikas* of the Aśokan Inscriptions.[2] The term has had the benefit of a Full and critical examination by scholars. F. W. Thomas renders it as 'thc head of the executive revenue and judicial service'.[3] Mookerjee translates it as the divisional commissioner[4] and surmises an ascending order of rank from the mention of the *yuktas, rājukas* and *prādeśikas* in the Rock Edict III. Samaddar holds that their position was equal to that of a minister and that they could not have been mere 'district' officers.[5] If the term is derived from *pradeśa* which means a territorial division and hence a specified area, the *prādeśikas* might be provincial officers entrusted with jurisdiction over a specified area. If the term *anusaṁyānaṁ* means 'tour,' then these officials toured round the country once in every five years.[6] But if it means 'transfer,' they were also transferred every five years, when new commissioners took their place. The latter seems to be more probable.

[1] Bk. IV, ch. 4.

[2] R.E. III, *Corpus,* pp. 4 and 5.

[3] *J.R.A.S.,* 1914, pp. 383-6.

[4] *Aśoka,* p. 56.

[5] *Glories of Magadha,* pp. 87-88.

[6] R.E. III, Shāh., Mān., Gir., and Kāl.

Sec. iv. MAURYAN CIVIL SERVICE

The Puruṣas

Administrative work, civil or criminal, or even military, would be impossible without an organised civil service. In the Mauryan empire we find that two classes of civil servants are distinguished. They were the *puruṣas and the yuktas.* While the *yuktas* belonged to the cadre of subordinate civil service, the *puruṣas* were of the superior civil service. The *Arthaśāstra* mentions *Gūḍhapuruṣas,* and they are mainly Intelligence Officers.[1] An examination of the functions assigned to them in the *Kauṭalīya* demonstrates corroboration with the writings of the classical writers like Megasthenes, Arrian and Strabo. "They spy out what goes in country and town and report everything to the king".[2] Again Megasthenes says: 'the sixth class consists of the overseers to whom is assigned the duty of watching all that goes on and making reports secretly to the king. Some are entrusted with the inspection of the city and others with that of the army. The former employ as their coadjutors the courtesan of the city and the latter the courtesans of the camp. The ablest and most trustworthy men are appointed to fill these offices.'[3] The *Arthaśāstra* uses the term *puruṣa* in both a general and a technical sense. Besides it speaks of *ayukta-puruṣas,*[4] *abhityakta puruṣas*[5] (outcaste men according to Ṣhāma Śāstri), *yogapuruṣas,* and *pravīrapuruṣas* (members of military associations).[6] There is besides in it a chapter

1. Bk. I, ch. 11-12.
2. *Ind. Ant.,* VI, pp. 124 and 237.
3. Fg. 36.
4. Bk. I, ch. 15.
5. Bk. II, ch. 5.
6. Bk. VII, ch. 14.

titled *puruṣavyasanavargaḥ*.[1] But this does not refer to the troubles of civil officials, but treats in general of *vyasanas* to which a man is liable to. There is a distinct mention of *puruṣas* and *yuktas* in the sense of civil servants in chapter V of Book II.

That they were employed in all departments and that misappropriation on their part was severely punished is seen from the same chapter also.[2] Perhaps the statement in chapter 20 of Book III in regard to the *puruṣas* and their qualifications is a reference to the civil servants. Regard was to be shown to those *puruṣas* who were learned, wise, bold, of high birth and skilled in discharging duties.[3] It would appear that only qualified men were appointed to this service.

The evidence of inscriptions

From the Edicts of Aśoka,[4] the *puruṣas* who were civil servants of the superior rank were appointed in three grades—the lower, the middling and the higher. This reminds us of our own civil service system where a civil servant who is started in the lower scale is promoted to the upper division after a certain period of service. From Pillar Edict IV where these *puruṣas* are said to be acquainted with the wishes of the king it seems that these government servants were appointed by the authorities at the imperial Headquarters, and they were hence answerable to them. The Edicts are valuable in as much as they refer to the duties expect-

[1] Bk. VIII ,ch. 3.

[2] sarvādhikaraṇeṣu yuktopayukta tatpuruṣāṇām paṇādicatuṣpaṇāh paramāpahāreṣu pūrvamadhyamottamavadho daṇḍāḥ|—Bk. II, ch. 5.

[3] pūjyāḥ vidyābuddhipauruṣābhijñakarmātiśayataśca puruṣāḥ.

[4] Pillar I, IV and VII.

ed of these officials. These two duties are mentioned. First, they were the inspectorate of the government, and in that capacity watched whether the provincial officers were loyal to the king.[1] Secondly, they were sent over to the common people[2] to get at the prevailing public feeling with regard to the government of the land. This, it may be remembered, is a function assigned to the *gūḍhapuruṣas* by Kauṭalya.[3]

The Yuktas

The other class of civil servants who were of the subordinate rank went by the technical name of the *yuktas.* Apart from its use in the Aśokan inscriptions, as we shall see presently, it occurs in the *Arthaśāstra* in different connections. There is a very informing chapter entitled *upayuktaparīkṣa.*[4] Two different classes of officials are mentioned, the *yuktas* and the *upayuktas* in the *Kauṭalīya.*[5] In every department there were *yuktas* and *upayuktas.*[6] They had again their own assistants. They were subject to punishment as every other government official was. The punishments were of a varied character.[7] Such of those civil servants as were employed in the collection and distribution of revenue could not easily avoid the temptation of tasting a portion of the king's revenue. Sometimes it would be impossible to detect the amount so misappropriated, just as it is not possible to find out whether

1 Pillar E. IV: also Mookerjee, *Aśoka,* p. 57.

2 bahune janasi āyaṭā P.E. VII, *Corpus,* p. 132 (Delhi-Topra).

3 See Bk. I, ch. 12 and 13.

4 Bk. II, ch. 9.

5 These may be also identified with the Āyuktas and Viniyuktas of the Gupta Inscriptions. (Fleet, *C.I.I.,* III, p. 169, n. 4 and 5.)

6 Bk. II, ch. 5.

7 *Ibid.*

fishes drink water or not. In Kauṭalya's opinion it is even possible to spot the birds flying high in the air, but it is an intricate task to ascertain the conduct of the government servants with dishonest motives. Hence it is recommended that those who would not covet the king's wealth but would show an increase through legitimate means, and who would prove loyal, are to be appointed as government servants.[1]

The title of Chapter 8 of Book II, *samudayasya yuktāpahṛtasya pratyānayanam* shows that the *yuktas,* generally accountants and clerks, had something to do with the collection of the revenue. It is reasonable to assume that they maintained accounts in regard to the various revenue items. This is obvious from the fact that in case of embezzlement, among the persons to be examined, is mentioned first in the order of importance the *upayukta.*[2] The translation of Shāma Śāstri has omitted *upayukta.*[3] The *upayukta* held a subordinate position and when he was found guilty, in cases of embezzlement, the punishment amounted to that of a *yukta* as is evident from the *Arthaśāstra*:

mithyāvāde caiṣām yuktasamo daṇḍaḥ|

Thus while the *upayukta* was one among the eight officers connected with the accounts, the *yukta* in the official staff of the department, held a position superior to that of the other eight officials, who were the *upayukta, nidhāyaka* (cashier), *nibandhaka* (prescriber), *pratigrāhaka* (the receiver), *dāyaka* (the paying shroff), *dāpaka* (officer in charge of the payment of the

1 Bk. II, ch. 9.
2 Bk. II, ch. 8, T.S.S. Vol. I, 157.
3 P. 73 (II ed.).

department), *mantrivaiyāvṛttikara* (ministerial servants).[1]

The mode of appointment

It is evident that each department was manned by an army of civil officials of different grades and status. The *yuktas* and the *upayuktas* had their own assistants as is evident from Chapter 5 of Book II of the *Kauṭalīya*. These servants of the government were appointed temporarily in the first instance.[2] In this connection the term *bahumukhya* is important and is the same as the word *anekamukhya* in chapter 4 of the same book. This shows that there were a number of temporary officials. These were in course of time taken to the permanent service, on the merits of the case in respect of qualifications, character and conduct. It is said that those who would not eat up the wealth of the state, those who would swell the wealth by fair and legitimate means, and those who would court the welfare of the king and kingdom were to be appointed as permanent servants of the state[3] (*nityādhikārāḥ*). Thus the tenure of service largely depended on the honesty and efficiency of the government servants.

The evidence of the Edicts

Coming to the inscriptions of Aśoka, we find the term *yukta* mentioned in the Rock-Edict III.[4] F. W. Thomas was correct in rendering the term into a subordinate official.[5] The *yuktas* of Aśokan Edicts may be identified with the *yuktas* and the *upayuktas* of the

1 T.S.S., Vol. I, p. 157.
2 bahumukhyamanityam cādhikaraṇam sthāpayet, Bk. II, ch. 9.
3 Bk. II, ch. 9.
4 *Corpus,* pp. 4-5.
5 *J.R.A.S.,* 1914, 387, 91.

Kauṭalīya. The duties of the *yukta* according to the Aśokan inscriptions are[1]:

(1) to go on tours like the Rājukas and Prādeśikas every five years if *anusaṁyāna* means 'tour'. From the position assigned to these officials we have to take that they accompanied their official superiors on tour. If the term *anusaṁyāna* means 'transfer',[2] this cannot be accounted as a part of their duties, but merely points to the administrative detail of transfer of officials.[3]

(2) to be in charge of the department of accounts. The last line of the Rock-Edict III[4] has been translated in different ways by scholars. The term *gaṇanāyam* has been a puzzle to many in spite of the fact that the same term occurs in the *Arthaśāstra* and means the department of accounts. D. R. Bhandarkar translates this line as follows: 'The Council (of Ministers) shall order the Yuktas in regard to the reckoning (of this expense and accumulation) both according to the letter and according to the spirit.'[5] From this it would appear that the *yuktas* maintained accounts of receipt and expenditure and were subject to the scrutiny and control by the council of the *mahāmātras.*[6]

1 Mookerjee, *Aśoka,* p. 57.

2 *J.B.O.R.S.*, IV, p. 36-ff.

3 See Smith, *Aśoka,* p. 164.

4 *Corpus,* p. 4.

5 *Aśoka,* p. 278.

6 Reference may be made to the untenable criticism of Samaddar in regard to the position of the ministers and the Department of Accounts in the light of the interpretation offered by Jayaswal. He asks "were the ministers whom Mr. Jayaswal has endowed with all executive powers, and who according to him were even more powerful than the king himself, at the mercy of the department of accounts? If the ministers were so powerful how could they be at the mercy of

Sec. v. ADMINISTRATION OF TOWNS

In regard to the administration of the city, Megasthenes, the Grecian ambassador of Seleukos, has given us elaborate details. According to this testimony the city of Pāṭaliputra was governed by thirty Municipal Commissioners who formed themselves into six committees of five each. These committees looked after the moral and material interests of the city. Of the functions assigned to these, Megasthenes says[1]:

"The members of the first look after everything relating to the industrial arts.

"Those of the second attend to the entertainment of foreigners. To these they assign lodgings and they keep watch over the modes of life by means of those persons who were given to them for assistants. They escort them on the way when they leave the country or in the event of their dying, forward their property to their relatives. They take care of them when they are sick, and if they die, bury them.

"The third body consists of those who inquire when and how births and deaths occur with the view not only of levying a tax but also in order that births and deaths among both high and low may not escape the cognisance of Government.

that department?" (*Glories of Magadha,* p. 92). It is a simple case of misunderstanding the true relations between the two departments. It is not here a question of inferior *versus* superior officers. It is about the question of accounts. So long as the accountants were accountants they had to maintain proper records. This does not mean that the accountants were more powerful than the ministers. To-day for example the Accountant-General can disallow the allowance or pay of any superior officer of the state on some audit objection.

[1] Fg. 34.

"The fourth class superintends trade and commerce. Its members have charge of weights and measures and see that the products in their season are sold by public notice. No one is allowed to deal in more than one kind of commodity unless he pays a double tax.

"The fifth class supervises manufactured articles which they sell by public notice. What is new is sold separately from what is old and there is a fine for mixing the two together.

"The sixth and the last class consists of those who collect the tenths of the prices of articles of food. Fraud in the payment of this tax is punished with death."

These committees and their duties are also found mentioned by Strabo, another classical writer.[1] Besides the special functions allotted to each one of these six bodies all of them in their collective capacity interested themselves in matters of general interest, such as, the upkeep and repair of public buildings, the regulation of prices, the care of markets, harbours, and temples.[2] Every writer on the Mauryan polity has not failed to quote this long extract of Megasthenes. It has been followed here, the object being to quote parallel passages from the *Arthaśāstra*.

Protection to artisans

The first committee interested itself in the promotion of industrial arts. The *Arthaśāstra* in more than one place refers to the work of artists and artisans. They were expected to work for a day in a fortnight for the

[1] See Strabo, 51; McCrindle, *Ancient India as described in Classical Literature*.

[2] *Ibid.*, XXXIV.

king. This enabled them to commute their payment to the state into their manual labour.[1] There is a special chapter[2] containing regulations affording protection to artisans. It is said that artisans shall carry on their business according to the engagement in respect of time, place and nature of the work. Such of those who put off their work under the plea that there was no definite engagement as regards time, place, and the nature of work were not only deprived of $\frac{1}{4}$ of their wages, but also punished with a fine equal to two times the prices of their labour except when they were in trouble, or visited by a calamity. Besides they compensated the loss of damage to the employer. Those who engaged themselves in contravention of definite orders forfeited their wages in addition to their paying a fine equal to two times the amount of their price of labour.[3] It is further said that such of those who were responsible for lowering the quality of the work by an artisan and who interfered in their transactions were to be severely punished with fines.[4] When we see the excellent standard to which artistic skill was developed in the days of Aśoka, what with lofty edifices in brick, wood and stone, massive embankments, handling of monoliths, construction of chambers, a profusion of spirited bas-reliefs, attractive statues of men and animals, masterpieces of some fine carvings, it is reasonable to take the view that Aśoka continued the patronage and protection of artisans like his grandfather.

[1] Bk. II, ch. 2 and 36.

[2] Bk. IV, ch. 1.

[3] Bk. IV, ch. 1.

[4] *Ibid.*, ch. 2.

Protection to foreïgners

In regard to the regulations affecting the foreigners to which the Greek ambassador has referred, we find numerous passages where Kauṭalya asks the officers of the state to show favour to them. For example, while the Superintendent of ships concerned himself with the weather-beaten ships, the Superintendent of Commerce attended to those who dealt in foreign merchandise.[1] Kauṭalya recommends the invitation of foreign traders to settle in the country with a view to foster the trade of the land. These merchants enjoyed certain privileges and could move about freely. They could not be sued in the ordinary courts of law. There were special courts which decided their causes.[2]

The citizens were to make a report of the strangers residing with them or leaving the station.[3] The boundary-guards or *antapālas* were to collect what is known as the road cess (*vartani*) and they were held responsible for the loss incurred by merchants in the part of the country under their charge. Thus adequate attention was paid to the safety and security of merchants, travellers, foreigners and others.[4]

Considering the extensive international relations that existed between Aśoka and other foreign countries and the healthy intercourse that existed between the empire and the neighbouring states, where Aśoka also is said to have established hospitals for man and beast, and considering again the great material prosperity attained

[1] Bk. II, ch. 16 and 28.

[2] parabhūmijam paṇyamanugraheṇāvāhayet| nāvikasārthavāhebhyaś-ca parihāramāyatikṣamam dadyāt| anabhiyogaśca artheṣvāgantū-nāanyatra sabhyopakāribhyḥ|—*Ar Śās.*, Bk. II, ch. 1.

Cp. Meg. Fr. I, p. 42 (Cal. 1926).

[3] Bk. II, ch. 36.

[4] Bk. II, ch. 21.

in his age as the outcome of the growing trade and commerce, it may not be far from truth to say that Aśoka simply continued the social and political institutions of his predecesors.

The census

Megasthenes next speaks of the census operations. From the *Arthaśāstra* we gather that the census of the Mauryas was a permanent institution manned by permanent officials. It was not a periodical one. The statistical information served political and economic interests. It furnished the total population of a certain village or town at a particular period, the division being made according to the castes and their professions. For example, here was noted the exact number of cultivators, cowherds, merchants, artisans, labourers, slaves, as also the heads of cattle and other biped and quadruped animals. The census further furnished details as regards the amount of income and expenditure in addition to free labour available. All this formed a basis on which perhaps taxation was assessed. The houses were numbered and classified as tax-paying and non-tax-paying. The number of inhabitants in each house according to their age, sex and profession was also noted down.[1] The remarks of V. A. Smith are apposite. "Even the Anglo-Indian administration with its complex organisation and European notions of the value of statistical information did not attempt the collection of vital statistics until very recent times, and has always experienced great difficulty in securing reasonable accuracy in the figures.[2]

[1] Bk. II, ch. 35-36.

[2] *Early History,* p. 125.

Trade and commerce

The fourth administrative board was that of trade and commerce. The *Arthaśāstra* asks the city merchants to entertain strangers on their own responsibility and make a report of these merchants who deal in forbidden articles of merchandise, and who sell these in any place or time without due regard for the orders of the authorities of the city. Ordinarily merchants were to deal in their own merchandise and not in those which belonged to others. Perhaps to deal in them required a special license which Megasthenes probably calls a double tax.[1] It may be pointed out also that Kauṭalya imposes stringent regulations in regard to weights and measures.[2] Even the slightest difference was not tolerated. Sale by public notice was exactly what the author of the *Arthaśāstra* has recommended. The process of this sale is given as follows: "In a place proximate to the flag of the toll house, articles of merchandise for sale are to be gathered each in their respective places. The owners of the articles in question were to proclaim the real quantity contained together with its value. Three times it was given aloud. Who will buy such a quantity of merchandise for so much price? Afterwards he who was willing to buy it for that price could purchase it."[3] The tax on sales was one of the sources of revenue, and hence the control of sale was under the Board of Trade, each article offered for sale being marked with the official stamp.[4]

1 Bk. II, ch. 36. See also ch. 16, 19, and Bk. IV, ch. 2.

2 Bk. II, ch. 19.

3 Bk. II, ch. 21.

4 *abhijñānamudra, Ibid.*

Control of manufacture

The fifth Board concerned itself with the control of manufactured articles. Here also the same regulations were in practice. Perhaps this refers to the manufactures run by the Department of the state in its manufactories. Kauṭalya is very particular in regard to the purity and good quality of the articles sold. A distinction was maintained between old commodities in stock and fresh supplies.[1] If articles inferior in quality were sold as good ones, the sellers were liable to a heavy fine.[2] In accordance with the economic laws of supply and demand the sale of manufactured articles like that of liquor was centralised or decentralised. It was an offence to sell bad liquor and bony flesh.[3] It is prescribed that only articles of good quality were to be sold. And if bad ones were offered for sale, the price was to be fixed considerably below the market-price.

Tolls and other charges

The sixth board attended to the collection of revenue on sales of merchandise. According to the *Arthaśāstra* the Superintendent of Tolls was generally the officer who was engaged in such business.[4] The rate mentioned by Megasthenes as 1|10th must have been a conventional one like the 1|6th share of land revenue. In practice however the rates varied according to the quantity and quality of the articles, their easy availability, necessity, or otherwise. Flowers and fruits which were luxuries were taxed 1|6th while cotton cloths,

[1] Bk. II, ch. 15.
[2] Bk. IV, ch. 11.
[3] Bk. II, ch. 25 and 26.
[4] Bk. II, ch. 21 and 22.

arsenic, metals, sandal, raw materials, carpets, and woollen goods were charged from 1|10th to 1|15th. The rate varied again from 1|20th to 1|25th for articles of absolute necessity—cattle, cotton, medicine, fibres, skins, clay pots, oils, sugar, salt, etc.[1] Towards the end of the chapter entitled *śulkavyavahāraḥ* Kauṭalya rightly remarks that agreeably to the customs of countries or communities, the rate of tolls shall be levied on commodities, old and new.[2]

Pāṭaliputra the capital

That Pāṭaliputra was the Capital of the Mauryas is evident not only from the records of the classical writers but also from the fifth Rock-Edict and the Sāranāth Edict where a distinct mention is made of it. It stood on the northern side of the river Son, a little above the confluence of the latter with the Ganges. Defended thus by two big rivers it formed a strong citadel for its occupants perhaps answering to the *nadīdurga* of the *Arthaśāstra.* Over this ancient site now stands the modern Patna with a number of villages surrounding it. The city presented to Megasthenes an appearance of a long narrow parallelogram nearly nine miles in length and 1½ miles in breadth.[3] A great fortress it was, containing 64 gates, 570 towers, surrounded on all sides by a deep moat of waters. It cannot be denied that Aśoka improved it by an outer masonry wall and decorated it with durable stone buildings as testified by the recent excavations. Unfortunately the excavations have been partial since the nature of the land does not easily

[1] Bk. II, ch. 22.
[2] *Ibid.,* cp. IV, ch. 2 and 7.
[3] Fg. 26. Cp. Smith, *Aśoka,* pp. 84-85.

admit of it. The depth of the overlying silt often reaching as far as twenty feet and the existence of numerous modern buildings make the excavation exceptionally difficult.[1] In this connection mention may be made of '*The Discovery of the exact site of Aśoka's Classic Capital* and the *Report on the Excavations at Pāṭaliputra*'[2] being the works of that enthusiastic writer L. A. Waddell directly dealing with the excavations of the imperial Capital of the Mauryas. Dr. Spooner of the Department of Archæology conducted further excavations and discovered a hall of 100 pillars.[3]

The nāgaraka and his duties

An examination of the administrative machinery shows that the *nāgaraka* was the chief official of the city, possibly a nominee of the Imperial Government. The *nāgaraka* may in some respects answer to the Corporation Commissioner of the modern day. He was an official of the state and was responsible to the imperial Govern ment for the conduct of the civil administration. His duties were many and varied. They can be categorically mentioned.[4]

1. He was to preserve the peace of the city by keeping watch over the movements of strangers and new-comers into the city.

2. He was to maintain an elaborate census of the houses and the residents therein noting their total income and items of expenditure.

1 Smith, *Aśoka*, p. 85.

2 (1903) (ed. Cal.).

3 *Annual Report of Archaeological Survey of India, E. Circle*, 1912-13, pp. 55—61.

4 Bk. II, ch. 36.

3. He took precautions against the outbreak of fire. People were forced to keep water-pots and other things which were useful to quench fire.

4. He looked after the health and sanitation of the city. Stringent regulations were promulgated under penalty of punishment for committing nuisance on public roads, and for throwing dead bodies carelessly on thoroughfares, and for offences of a similar nature.

5. He was to keep watch and ward by means of special watchmen especially during nights. No one was allowed to leave the city or move about in a late hour at night except in cases of necessity, when a permit was usually granted. Such of those who violated this were punished.

6. He attended also to the sluices, embankments, and other buildings connected with the city so that no damage of any sort was done to them as it would cause inconvenience to the neighbours.

7. He was to hold a supervising control over the *antapālas* at the military frontiers and the official in charge of the toll house. Perhaps they had to remit their collections through him.

8. He kept in safe custody articles either stolen and recovered or lost. These were however returned to the owners on their claim.

9. If among the guilty were children, old men, the diseased and others he could set them free by receiving proper compensation price. Other prisoners were liberated on the king's birthday, and on similar occasions.

10. He was also responsible for the public morals of the city. By means of police regulations he arrested and punished the suspicious and men of criminal tendencies. Those who misbehaved with slave girls and seduced the *kulastrī* or family woman were severely punished. He also looked after the religious and charitable institutions with the help of the managers of those institutions.

Mention has already been made of *nāgaravyavahārika* as occurring in the Aśokan inscriptions.[1] These officers are also styled as *mahāmātras* as is seen from the Dhauli and Jaugaḍa Separate Edict I. The officers mentioned are of the provincial towns like Tosāli and Samāpa and not of the capital city. That these exercised important judicial powers is evident from the fact that the officers are taken to task for having inflicted arbitrary punishment including imprisonment to some of the citizens. The *nāgaraka* could not be expected to shoulder such heavy responsibilities single-handed. He was assisted by a body of officials called the *sthānīkas* and *gopas*.

The sthānīka

For purposes of administration every city was divided into four divisions over each of which was placed a *sthānīka*. The *sthānīka* was then responsible for his ward. He was entrusted with large police powers. He was the intermediate official between the *gopa* and the *nāgaraka*.

The gopa

The *gopa* was the official next in rank to the *sthānīka*. He maintained registers showing the names of

[1] Separate Kalinga Edict I, *Corpus*, p. 92.

persons in his territorial jurisdiction together with the amount of property possessed by each. A *gopa* was expected to maintain the accounts relating from ten to forty households. It was also his duty to maintain a statistical record of the inmates of the households with their respective castes, *gotra* names, profession, income and expenditure. He was a small census officer. It is reasonable to assume that a number of *gopas* were under a *sthānīka,* for each *gopa* was entrusted with about forty households. The Managers of religious houses and charitable institutions sent reports to the *gopa* or the *sthānīka* as regards the movement of heretics (*pāṣaṇḍa*) and strangers. They further entertained ascetics and *śrotriyas* of pure character. Artisans, merchants, and other *gṛhasthas* were to report to them as to their movements, as well as those of their friends, who were strangers to the city. The sentinels and watchmen were also held responsible to some extent. They also sent their reports to the *gopa* or through him to the *sthānīka* who ultimately reported to the *nāgaraka.*[1]

Aśoka's interest in municipal affairs

From a study of the inscriptions of Aśoka it can be seen that parks, hospitals, rest-houses, educational institutions, and metalled roads with medicinal plants and herbs received the attention of the Mauryan city-administration. The inscriptions further tell us that on these roads banyan trees and mango trees were planted affording shade to cattle and men. At intervals of eight *kos* or one *yojana* wells were dug with flights of steps for easily getting to the water. It

[1] Bk. II, ch. 36.

appears that watersheds were also built here and there.[1] To these may again be added theatrical entertainments, public shows, and exhibition. In short the Mauryan state bestowed utmost care and attention to beautify the cities and make them centres of culture and light. In this direction Aśoka, more than any other monarch of the dynasty, did much and earned the eternal gratitude of his subjects.

[1] See Seventh Pillar Edicts; Delhi-Topra, *Corpus*, pp. 134-135.

CHAPTER VII.

MAURYAN STATE IN RELATION TO DHARMA

Sec. i. THE CONCEPT OF DHARMA

No question is more difficult to answer than the question—what is the true concept of *dharma* as understood and realised in the epoch of Hindu India? This question has been raised by a number of distinguished scholars, but it is still a problem requiring a definite answer.

As a tentative definition *dharma* may be taken to mean the totality of duties expected of every individual to his family, community, country, and God. The Vedas were believed to be revealed texts, and are still so believed, and hence whatever is ordained in them is absolute truth which ought to be pursued even at the sacrifice of one's life. The doctrines and rules found scattered in these works of high antiquity came to be generally known as the *vedic dharma*. It is also known as the *śrauta dharma*. These were in a highly technical language, the interpretation of which required special skill and expert knowledge. Hence the ancient sages and seers of this land felt called upon to impart this hidden knowledge to the masses by reducing them to an easily understandable style. This was the attempt of the different authors of the *Dharmasūtras* and the *Dharmaśāstras*. When these, what are now called Brahmanical codes, became popular, the *smārta dharma* became the accepted and accredited *dharma*

M—31

for both the ecclesiastic and the laity. While the *vedic dharma* was essentially religious, the *smārta dharma* constituted visible lay elements, though the religious element was still predominant.[1] From the statement that the *vedic dharma* was religious, it must not be taken that no lay element was in it. It was there but not predominatingly.

Smārta dharma

The *smārta dharma* or the *dharma* of the Law-codes was, then, an analysis of the symbolic *dharma* of the Vedic texts. The classification was secular and religious as well. But according to the old conception, nothing was purely secular, for the latter bore the tinge, a distinct tinge of religion to support it. The *dharma* of the Law-codes may be reduced broadly to two divisions: the *rājadharma* and the *prajādharma,* in other words, the duties of the state and the duties of the subjects. The *prajādharma* was the following of *svadharma* by every individual member of the society according to the rules prescribed. These came to be known as the *sanātana dharma,* the *dharma* for all times and for all places. The *rājadharma* came in to aid the progressive march of this *sanātana dharma* into accomplishment, by clearing the roads which lead to it, of the weeds and thorns, which might otherwise hamper the welfare and happiness of the world. Notwithstanding the trifle differences in doctrines these *dharmas* were common to orthodox as well as to heterodox sects prevalent then in the land, like the Buddhists, the Jains, the Ājivikas and others.

[1] See *Vāyu Purāṇa,* Ch. 57, st. 39-46.

The dharma of Buddhism

Perhaps what the late Professor Rhys Davids meant in speaking for the *dharma* of Buddhism is equally applicable to the Brahmanical notion, and may we add, even Jaina conception. "*Dharma* is not simply law but that which underlies and includes the law, a word often most difficult to translate and best rendered by truth or righteousness."[1] It is a difficult and intricate labour to attempt anything like a distinction as regards the conception of *dharma* according to the Brahmanical, Buddhist, and Jaina literature. In fact there is a significant statement in the *Aṅguttaranikāya*[2] according to which the *dharma* to the Buddha was the *dharma* formulated by the ancient seers and sages, like Devala and Asita. It is the correct estimate of Prof. Keith who remarks "Nor in choosing the term *dharma* for the system, was Buddhism without *Upaniṣad* precedent; the *Bṛhadāraṇyaka*[3] tells that Brahman created the *Dharma* than which nothing is higher, and the *Mahānārāyaṇa*[4] asserts that the whole universe is encircled by the *dharma* than which there is nothing harder to describe."[5] The concept of *dharma* can generally be viewed from two standpoints, namely, the standpoint of ethics and that of the doctrine. Examined under these particulars the coincidences are something striking, something phenomenal, that they defy a student of comparative religion to draw any line of demarcation.

1 *Buddhism,* p. 45.

2 II, p. 51.

3 I, pp. 4-14.

4 Bk. XXI, ch. 6.

5 *Religion and Philosophy of the Veda,* Vol. II, p. 550.

Views of Dr. Jacobi

The ripe scholar Hermann Jacobi who is competent to speak with authority on these matters has justification for holding the opinion which we quote below:

"From the comparison which we have just instituted between the rules for the Brahmanic ascetic and those for the Jaina monk it will be apparent that the latter is but a copy of the former. It may be assumed that the Nirgrantha copied the Buddhist Bhikku who himself was but a copy of the Sannyāsin. This suggestion is not a probable one, for, there being a model of higher antiquity and authority, the Jainas would probably have conformed rather to it than to the less respected and second-hand model of their rivals, the Buddhists."[1] We see that the germs of dissenting sects like those of the Buddhists and the Jainas were contained in the institute of the fourth *āśrama,* and that the latter was the model of the heretical sects; therefore Buddhism and Jainism must be regarded "as religions developed out of Brahmanism, not by a sudden reformation, but prepared by a religious movement going on for a long time."[2]

Jainism and Buddhism, only monastic sects

This means that the Vedic doctrines and ethics formed the convenient model for the Jainas and the Buddhists to copy. As a matter of fact, in the period of which we are now speaking, there were no religious systems, such as Jainism and Buddhism, though one cannot deny that there were monastic sects embracing the ideas and ideals inculcated by the foun-

[1] *Jaina Sūtras,* Pt. I, Intro., p. 29. *S.B.E.,* Vol. XXII.

[2] *Ibid.,* p. 32.

ders, Mahāvīra and Gautama. These monastic sects had not yet spread to the extent so as to assume the dimensions of what one may ordinarily understand by the term religion. Elsewhere this point has been examined[1] *in extenso,* and suffice it to say here that the history of Buddhism in the Mauryan epoch was still the story of the monastic sect looking for royal patronage and affording no *locus standi* to a lay man. If at this time Buddhism did not attain the status of a religion in the technical sense of the term,[2] it then naturally follows that Aśoka's conversion to that faith becomes a fiction. For, the examination of Aśoka's religion much depends on the evidential conclusion of the larger question whether there is justification for the assumption that Buddhism had been recognised as a religion, different from the established religion of the land. And yet we have strange, but as we shall soon point out, incredible stories about Candragupta becoming a Jaina, and Aśoka turning now to Jainism, and now to Buddhism.

Sec. ii. DHARMA AND THE STATE

Religion and politics

Before we actually enter into the subject of the religion of the Mauryas, personal religion as well as state religion, it would be better if we would try to understand and realise the exact position of the Mauryan state in relation to *dharma.* A state and its institutions are, if judged by modern notions of polity,

[1] See the author's article on *'The Early History of Buddhism in India,'* Bombay Hist. Society, Vol. II, pt. 1.

[2] Kern, *Manual of Ind. Buddhism,* p. 50.

secular. They aim at human welfare, moral and material. But the concept of *dharma* connotes a religious significance that permeates the whole. Did religion, then, function in politics? Did religion largely guide and control the state policy and administration? These are indeed questions which require a satisfactory answer. It must be taken as a matter of fact that religion, to the extent it meant *dharma,* law and morality, exercised a moderate and healthy influence on ancient Indian polity and politics. It had a smoothening effect on the machinery of administration. *Dharma,* doctrinal or ethical, was considered to be the eternal law as against the man-made law of our legislature.

Ancient conception of law

The ancient Indian conception of law was that it was something superhuman, and something transcendental. A great amount of sacredness was attached to it, not only by the people but also by the ruler with the result that law became the king of kings,[1] the *kṣatra* of the *kṣatra.* According to the Vedic tradition, which was handed down in unbroken succession, there is nothing higher than *dharma,* the observance of which will tend to universal moral welfare, and righteousness of a general kind. If we are to accept the definition of the term by the philosopher Kaṇāda that *dharma* is the source of material welfare in this world and spiritual welfare in the other,[2] then it is easy to realise the full import attached to it especially by the reigning sovereigns of the land. If the state emerged from a well-established society for the welfare of that society, and

[1] *Bṛhad. Up.,* I-IV, 11-14; *Chānd. Up.,* 11-23, 1-2.

[2] *Vaiśeṣika Sūtras* 1, 1-2.

if the state represented the common will of that society, by upholding principles which tended to the common good and the common welfare, (the *yogakṣema* of the Hindu literature),[1] then necessarily that institution which we call state, must take cognisance of the social order, peculiar to that society, and function in such a way that that social order is maintained intact, and that an orderly progress is the ultimate result.

With this end in view ancient Indian writers on polity rightly based their theories of state and its institutions on the lines of the *dharma* of the land. It proved an effective check on the arbitrary conduct of the monarch. For, the latter was expected to rule and reign according to the established law of the country. Transgression of that law would lead in the first instance to revolt from people, and ultimately to revolution and anarchy, disturbing the peace and security of the people.

The primary function of the state was, according to the *Arthaśāstra,* the upkeep of the social *sthiti* or in other words, the maintenance of the social order. Society, in those days was divided into castes and orders, the castes being an economic classification on the principle of the division of labour. Castes were, therefore, so many occupational groups with this peculiar difference that these occupations were to be deemed hereditary. Viewed from an economic point of view the motive for this classification cannot be questioned, for, it drove the last nail into the coffin of economic ills.

[1] See in this connection the interpretation of the phrase *ityai artham* occurring in the *Ṛg Veda* in the *Economiques et Politiques Dans L'Inde Ancienne,* by H. C. Joshi, pp. 17-18 (Paris, 1928).

The competitive principle, as we experience to-day, produces more of evil than good. This was avoided by the principle known as *svadharma,* so much insisted on by Indian writers, secular or religious. This is the very principle on which the author of the *Arthaśāstra* has worked out the theory of the State. The *svadharma* of the king is to endeavour and protect the people according to *dharma* or law.[1] And the fruit of such *svadharma* is the attainment of heaven. This is exactly what the authors of the *Dharmasūtras* and *Dharmaśāstras* have prescribed.[2] The *Arthaśāstra* clearly states that the social polity, entitled *varṇāśrama dharma,* and the prosecution by the king of his duty demanded that the castes and the orders did not err from the ordained path, but pursued the path of *dharma* by sticking on to their own duties. This shows that the state punished that member of the society who gave up his own *dharma* and interfered with the *dharma* of the other communities. In a word the state expected every citizen to discharge his obligations according to the *dharma* of his caste and order.

The doctrine of Trivarga

We thus gather that the *dharma* of the state was to see that the respective *dharmas* of the people were followed and to exercise the rod of punishment towards him or her who would misbehave. Hence the *Mahābhārata* views the *dharma* of the state or the *kṣatra dharma* superior to all other *dharmas.*[3] *Dharma*

[1] Bk. III, ch. 1.

[2] Āp. II, pp. 25-15; Baud. 1, 18, 1; Manu, VII.2; Yāj., I-335, etc. Also the article on '*Dharmaśāstra* and *Arthaśāstra* by Dr. Winternitz, in *Sir Asutosh Memorial Volume, Patna,* esp. pp. 31-32.

[3] *Śānti* 64, 6; 62, 30; 63, 29.

then, is the composite expression which, if properly analysed, will be the means for and the end of the progressive realisation of the *trivarga* or the *muppāl* of Tamil literature. This term is significant in more than one respect. It includes *dharma, artha,* and *kāma.* In other words every citizen of the state, whether male or female, was to pursue his or her *dharma,* which was the *svadharma* or the peculiar duties which he or she owed to the society at large. In performing these duties, let him or her use *artha* and *kāma,* so far as they help him or her to realise this object, namely, the fulfilment of his or her obligations. Over-indulgence would lead to the misuse of power with the result that there would be a conflict as regards the relations which exist among these three factors of life. The object underlying the principle of *trivarga* is the attainment of the last aim in life, namely, *mokṣa* or salvation, one form of which is heavenly bliss in after life. Life to the ancient Hindus of all faiths including the Buddhists and Jainas was a race to be run and the goal was absolute freedom from the fetters of the mundane world. The people required material comforts and welfare so as to realise this end. Towards this end the state came to function by looking after their material and moral welfare. These are exactly the motives which underlie the political philosophy of the *Kauṭalīya.* Kauṭalya envisages a social order of castes, and pinning his faith in the *trivarga* and the *caturvarga,* he prescribes means and methods by which the social order should be maintained. The means and methods laid down are *dharmaic* in the sense that they help the people to realise their chief aims in life. It is reasonable to assume that this idea must have profoundly influenced the administration of the first Mauryan emperor and his son, not to speak of Aśoka.

Sec. iii. *AŚOKA'S DHARMA*

The practical aspect

The *dharma* of *Aśoka's* inscriptions has a twofold aspect—the practical and the doctrinal.[1] Under the first category come:

1 Dutifulness (*śusrūṣā*) to parents.[2]

2. Reverence to elders[3] and teachers.[4]

3. Dutifulness towards superiors[5] *aghrabhūti*. The rendering of this term as 'men of high caste, or pay' is not convincing.

4. Regard for Brahmans and Śramaṇās[6] (*saṁpratipatti*). The term Śramaṇa means ascetic in the broad sense. It does not mean, as has been taken by almost all scholars, heretical sects of ascetics. Śramaṇa in Sanskrit literature of the period of our study is an equivalent and synonym for the *parivrājaka,* whatever might have been its meaning in later times. This *parivrājaka* is the Hindu Sannyāsin of the orthodox type. The term has been unfortunately taken to mean Buddhist and Jaina monks. But more of this later on.

5. Regard for family relationships.[7]

1 See Mookerjee, *Aśoka,* p. 194.

2 R.E. III, IV, XI, XIII and P.E. VII

3 R.E. IV.

4 R.E. XIII, P.E. VII.

5 R.E. XIII.

6 R.E. IV, P.E. VII.

7 M R.E. II, R.E. IV, and XIII.

6. Kind treatment of slaves (*dāsa*) and servants (*bhaṭaka*).[1]

7. Kindness to the poor and the suffering (*kapana-valāka*).[2]

8. Regard for friends, relatives, and others.[3]

9. Gifts (*dānam*) to Brahmans and ascetics.[4]

10. Gifts for friends (*mitra*), acquaintances (*saṁstuta*), and relations (*jñati*).[5]

11. Gifts of wealth to the aged.[6]

12. *prāṇānām anāraṁbha*[7] translated as 'abstention from slaughter of living beings,' *pāṇeṣu sayamo*[8] translated as 'restraint of violence towards living beings.' Again in M.R.E. (II) there occurs *prāṇeṣu drahyitavyaṁ.*[9]

13. Non-injury to living beings (*vihiṁsā bhūtānām*).[10]

14. *Sava-bhūtānāṁ achhatiṁ*[11] or non-violence towards all creatures.

Thus the practice of *dharma* involved virtuous qualities of *dayā* or sympathy,[12] *dāna* or gifts, *satya* or truthfulness[13] *śaucam* or purity of mind and body,[14]

1 R.E. IX, XI, XIII and P.E. VII.
2 P.E. VII.
3 R.E. XIII.
4 R.E. III, VIII, IX and XI.
5 R.E. III and XI.
6 R.E. VIII.
7 R.E. III, IV, XI and P.E. VII.
8 R.E. IX.
9 *Corpus*, p. 176.
10 R.E. IV, P.E. VII.
11 R.E. XIII.
12 P.E. II and VII.
13 P.E. II and VIII.
14 P.E. II and VIII.

mārdavam or kindliness,[1] *sādhutā* or goodness,[2] *apavyayatā* and *apabhandata* or economy in expenditure and in saving,[3] *saṁyama* or restraint of the senses,[4] *bhāvaśuddhi* or honesty of purpose,[5] *kṛtajñatā* or gratefulness,[6] *dṛḍhabahktitā* or abiding loyalty[7] and *dharmarati* or morality in act and deed.[8] To these are added also *dharma-kāmatā* or a desire to act righteously, *parikṣā* or confidence in ones' own self, *śusrūṣā* or dutifulness, *bhaya* or fear of wrong action, and *utsāha* or enthusiasm.[9] While the positive aspect of Aśoka's *dharma* consisted in doing good things,[10] the negative aspect constituted in *apariśravaṁ* or not doing evil deeds[11] generally caused by a host of dispositions like rage, cruelty, wrath, pride, and envy.[12]

The doctrinal aspect

In the category of the doctrinal aspect of Aśoka's *dharma* the doctrine of toleration occupies the first place. Every man was allowed religious liberty so far it did not undermine the social order. The next was that special care was taken to promote the noble virtues of all his subjects irrespective of their faith. The term *kalāṇāgama* of the inscriptions may be equated with the *kalyāṇaguṇa* of the Hindu literature.[13]

1 R.E. XIII P.E. VII.
2 P.E. VII.
3 R.E. III.
4 R.E. VII.
5 R.E. VII.
6 R.E. VII.
7 R.E. XIII.
8 R.E. XIII.
9 P.E. I.
10 *bahūni kayānāni*, P.E. II. *Corpus*, pp. 120-121.
11 R.E. X.
12 P.E. III, see Mookerjee, *Aśoka*, p. 71.
13 See *Bhagavad-Gīta*, Chap. VI, st. 40; R.E. XII (Girnār), *Corpus*, pp. 20-21.

Aśoka's special insistence on the moral and ethical relations[1] among men and women because of the fleeting nature of life, has been taken by some scholars to mean that Aśoka had no respect for the rituals and ceremonials pertaining to the religion of the land. There is no evidence to demonstrate that Aśoka condemned them. Insistence on a general principle is not the negation of the existing practices. For example, the *Bhagavad Gītā* which insists on the *svadharma* so much in all its eighteen chapters concludes by saying "Give up all *dharmas*. Identify yourself with me. I shall emancipate you from the bondage of all sins." On this account can we say that the *Gītā* teaches here against the practice of *dharmas* and prescribes giving them up? Certainly not. This is exactly the position with regard to the moral precepts of the Aśokan inscriptions.

The third was the principle of an all round exertion[2] as prescribed in the *Arthaśāstra*. In the opinion of the *Kauṭalīya, utthāna* is the chief requisite of a monarch. One should exert oneself and cultivate this habit even though one has to sacrifice other qualities (*sarvaṃ parityajya*). Likewise Aśoka simply glorifies active exertion, but does not recommend a serious giving up of other things.

Fourthly, the term *dharmadāna*[3] simply means gift to really deserving persons. *Dāna* is indeed one of the cardinal principles of the Hindu *sanātana dharma;* and various restrictions are ordained in the *Dharmaśāstras* regulating *dāna*. or gift. The law-books do not advise any indiscriminate gift. They draw a

[1] R.E. IX.
[2] R.E. X. See the *Mahābhārata, Śānti,* 57, 14-15.
[3] R.E. XI.

line of demarcation between righteous gifts and unrighteous gifts. Aśoka wished that the gifts went for a worthy cause. Charitable and religious institutions were abundant in those days, and no wonder that the state patronised all creeds by helping them. Hence the *stūpas, caityas,* and other monuments were raised by the kings of the land whatever be their religious conviction.

Fifthly, there are other and similar doctrines such as the doctrine of *dharmavijaya.*[1] The phrase *dharmavijaya* commonly translated into 'the conquest by morality' occurs in the thirteenth Rock Edict, immediately after describing the consequences of the Kaliṅga rebellion where there was heavy slaughter of men including innocents. Those who advocate Buddhism as the faith of Aśoka believe that the emperor susbtituted the 'conquest by morality' for the 'conquest by arms'.[2] This is interpreted so as to suggest that Aśoka gave up his arms and became a monk, and again the same principle found acceptance with his vassals and neighbours. The general belief, that the preaching and practice of simple virtues like *ahiṁsā* constituted the *dharmavijaya* of Aśoka, is difficult to be accepted for the following reasons:—

1. The Mauryan empire consisted of different peoples and tribes professing different faiths and creeds, and to them the cult of *dharmavijaya* in the sense of complete disarmament as is alleged could not have appealed.

2. The Edicts mention that envoys were sent to various kingdoms, which fact shows, if anything at

[1] See above p. 128.
[2] See *Corpus,* Intro., p. 53.

all, that there were extensive international relations between the empire and the frontier as well as the neighbouring kingdoms.

3. There is no testimony to believe that Ptolemy, Antiochus, Antigonus, Magas of Cyrene and Alexander of Epirus preferred 'conquest by morality' to conquest by arms. More unconvincing is that the peoples and states outside the pale of the empire like the Coḷa and the Pāṇḍya accepted this cult.

5. Aśoka feels satisfied that he has succeeded everywhere by extending the *dharmavijaya,* but adds that that satisfaction is of little consequence since his goal is the attainment of heaven. If *dharmavijaya* means 'conquest by morality', there is no occasion for Aśoka's remark that *dharmavijaya* is of little consequence and the heaven is of much consequence and that is to be won by peaceful means and will be more stable and more effective. To achieve this a separate department was instituted and it was manned by officers called *dharma-mahāmātras.* Anything relating to this department was prefixed by the term *dharma,* such as *dharma-lipi, dharma-gosha, dharma-maṅgala, dharma-saṁbandha,* etc. Though the details of this department are not found in the *Kauṭalīya,* yet there is mention in it of some kind of that institution. But Kauṭalya's recommendations are to a large extent creative and aid to spread a moral atmosphere and a moral force in the administration of the land. In fact, it is laid down that it is the duty of the best of kings to aim at the practice and observance of such moral virtues and qualities. Though this was expected of all the Kṣatriya monarchs, yet those who were occupied more with

wars and foreign policy, could have had no time to attend to the internal progress on peaceful lines.

6. According to the *Arthaśāstra* the expression *dharmavijaya* is a political term of much significance. There are three kinds of conquering monarchs—the righteous conqueror, the greedy conqueror and the demon-like conqueror. Of these the righteous conqueror is content with mere obeisance which is the acknowledgment of his overlordship[1] by other kings and chieftains.[1] Aśoka who indulged in *asuravijaya,* as for instance, in the Kaliṅga war, took to *dharmavijaya.*[2]

7. This position is confirmed by the Edict itself. "Even (the inhabitants of) the forests which are included in the dominions of Devānāṁpriya, even those he pacifies and converts (instructs?). And they are told of the power to (punish them) which Devānāṁpriya (possesses) in spite of (his) repentance, in order that they may be ashamed (of their crimes) and may not be killed."[3]

This means that the forest tribes who were independent or semi-independent, Aśoka was afraid, might or might not acknowledge his overlordship. Hence *dūtas* were sent to them with instructions that, if they did not do obeisance, they would be attacked and killed. This explains unmistakably that Aśoka did not relinquish conquest by arms, for does he not say that he still possessed power to attack them? This is exactly the Kauṭalīyan policy of *dharmavijaya.*[4]

[1] Gaṇapati Śāstri ed., Vol. III, p. 155. See also *Nayacandrika* comm., p. 213, *Pun. Sanskrit Series,* No. IV.

[2] See for a parallel Yudhiṣṭhira's feeling after the Kurukṣetra incarceration in the *Mahābhārata.*

[3] *Corpus,* p. 69, R.E. XIII, Shāhbāzgārhī.

[4] For similar ideas see the Pallava inscription published on p. 51, *Ind. Ant.,* Vol. V.

8. That same Edict of Aśoka instructs that his successors should not abuse their power and engage themselves into deadly wars actuated by the land-grabbing ideal. But, if certain states showed cause for provocation, Aśoka was for engaging in righteous war, where mercy would be shown and light punishment be awarded. Thus runs the Edict: (His successors) "should not think that a fresh conquest ought to be made (that) if a conquest does please them, they should take pleasure in mercy and light punishments, and (that) they should regard the *dharmavijaya* (conquest by morality) as the only (true) conquest".[1] It is therefore inferable that both the vassal and the independent states felt the might of Aśoka's arms fully and acquiesced in his overlordship. Hence the proclamation that the whole world has been won over by means of *dharmavijaya.*[2]

Aśoka who realised this point of view gave up further pursuit of territorial acquisitions and devoted his full attention to the promotion and prosecution of *dharma.*

Attainment of heaven, the end and aim of life

What were the guiding motives which impelled these monarchs of old to cling to this ideal? As has been already said, in those days the people believed, just as we do, in *svarga* or heaven, and the end and aim of life was supposed to be the attainment of that heaven. He who could not go to heaven would be condemned to the tortures of hell. Men feared hell and longed for heavenly enjoyment. It was a common belief shared both by the

[1] *Corpus,* p. 70.

[2] ye se(la)dhạ etakenā hoti savā vi(ja)ye piti-ase(se), *Corpus,* p. 46.

ordinary and aristocratic classes. So far as the Hindu king was concerned there were only two courses open to him to realise this end. One was to fight in the open field and heroically fall in battle. The other was to protect the people and administer justice according to *dharma* and thus earn heaven by well merited action in this world. The latter course appealed to Aśoka more effectively. "In this scheme of values he considered the other world as of supreme consequence and as the objective of life."[1] In the Rock Edict (X) there is the plain declaration as to why he was doing all that; it is all for the happiness in the next world.[2] In the Rock Edicts (VI), he re-affirms this by repeating once again that the one great obligation on the part of the ruler is to act in such a manner as would tend to the common good of the world.[3]

These sentiments and beliefs are more characteristic of the Brahmanical Hinduism. A student of Sanskrit literature knows that most of the ideas that find expression in the Edicts are in no way new but are found scattered in ancient Hindu literature, especially the didactic epics. The *dharma* entrusted to the Kṣatriya is something real and fruitful, testifying to one's own self, stable, and tending to the common good.[4] Perhaps *parikṣa* in the Edicts stands for *ātmasākṣikam* of the *Śānti parvan,* and *mahāphala* is the *phala bhūyiṣṭha* of the verse referred to above.

1 R.E. XIII; Mookerjee, *Aśoka,* p. 75.

2 Cp. R.E. IV and P.E. IV.

3 nā(sti)hi kāmatara(ṁ)sarva-loka-hitatpā, *Corpus,* p. 12.

4 pratyakṣaṃ phalabhūyiṣṭhamātmasākṣikamacchalam|
ṣarvalokahitaṃ dharmaṃ kṣatriyeṣu pratiṣṭhitam||
—*Śānti,* 63, 5.

The *utthānam* and *arthasaṁtīraṇā* which are said to be the roots of the administration in Edict (VI) are equivalent to the Sanskrit *utthānam* and *arthasaṁhitānam.* They are the main prescriptions of the *Kauṭalīya* and the epics. Bhīṣma in addressing Yudhiṣṭhira on the kingly duties says: "Oh Yudhiṣṭhira, you must ever cultivate exertion. Even gods do not help business (*artha*) of those kings devoid of activity."[1] The *Arthaśāstra* contains similar prescriptions.[2] In fact Kauṭalya speaks of these as the essential requisites for a government to conduct itself to the satisfaction of its subjects. Much stress is indeed laid on the requisite *utthānam* by the author of the *Arthaśāstra,* for, on it depends the prosecution of state business. These prescripts show that in the field of political administration as in others Aśoka was merely following the *Kauṭalīyan* tradition. We may now conclude this portion with Professor Kern's remarks: "Nothing of Buddhist spirit can be discovered in his state policy. From the very beginning of his reign he was a good prince."[3]

[1] utthānena sadā putra prayatethā Yudhiṣṭhira|
nahyutthānamṛte daivam rājñāmartham prasādhayet||
—*Śānti,* 55, 14.

[2] "*arthasyamūlam utthānam*", Bk. 1, ch. 19.

[3] *Ind. Ant.* Vol. V, p. 275. See also Ibid., Vol. III, pp. 77-81, where J. Muir gives an analysis of the essay of Prof. Kern on Aśoka's religion. Cp. *J.R.A.S.*, XII, pp. 238-50, where H. H. Wilson discusses the religion of Aśoka; *J.B.B.R.A.S.*, 1850 and 1853; Burnouf, *Lotus de la Bonne Loi,* Vol. I, Paris, (1925), Appendix X, pp. 628 ff.

Sec. iv. PERSONAL RELIGION OF CANDRAGUPTA MAURYA

The above discussion leads us on to the consideration of the personal religion of the chief Mauryan monarchs, and to the consideration whether the embracing of a faith by a king did prejudicially affect the state policy and practice during that period and after. Despite all progress of modern science it is an intricate task to attempt to define the term religion. It is a curious fact that everybody speaks of religion, but nobody is prepared to furnish us with the full meaning connoted by it. The fact is that no two thinkers of any nationality have agreed on a common definition of the term. Hence the term religion like our own popular term *dharma* is used in different senses. This is clear from a reference to the New Oxford Dictionary. It is a point of dispute whether ethics, metaphysics, doctrines, etc., form part of religion. It is a general notion that the kernel of religion consists in the belief in the existence of a personal Supreme God. If this is accepted can we speak of Buddhism as a religion? If it is no religion, then, what is it? Can we compare it to Theism which is reckoned to be a doctrine? If the question how far Buddhism is a religion still looms large in the province of hot controversy, much more was it so when the Buddha sowed the seeds a few centuries before the Christian era.

Buddhism, a child of Hinduism

"Buddhism began as a child of Hinduism."[1] So long as it continued to be so pursuing its own philosophic

[1] Gour, *Spirit of Buddhism*, p. 413.

speculation without encroaching upon the region of other sects, and other faiths, it secured the patronage of the state to whatever faith the king at its helm might have personally belonged. Hence it flourished for some centuries in the land of its birth. But it disappeared from the country because it became by slow but sure degrees a misguided child of Hinduism. In other words, when it assumed later on the garb of a serious rival and made an onslaught on its parentage by disowning its vital principles and tenets, the energy of its youth became extinguished. The old parent however was too strong to be supplanted. The result was Buddhism found shelter in countries outside India, though it left behind remnants of it, here and there, in its native home.

Jainism, a doctrine, not a religion

The same observation is true of another child of Hinduism, namely, Jainism. The influence and range of Jainism were much less than those of Buddhism. The followers of this sect did not seem to have spread beyond the confines of Bihar and Ujjain at the commencement of the Mauryan epoch, though there is testimony to show that towards the end of the reign of Candragupta there was a Jaina migration to South India. In spite of the seeming influence of this movement Jainism was still a sect not in conflict with the settled religion of the land. Jainism was a doctrine, but not a religion. Perhaps it is the correct estimate of the writer who, speaking of the time of Khāravela,[1] remarks "Jainism was yet more of a philosophy than a religion of dissenting Hindus".[2]

[1] 173-160 (B.C.).
[2] *J.B.O.R.S.*, Vol. III, p. 447.

Some assumptions

Among the various kings of the Mauryan dynasty we have some authentic records of Candragupta Maurya, Aśoka, and Daśaratha. A critical examination of the documents pertaining to these monarchs leads us to the conclusion somewhat different from what has been generally accepted.

Historical investigations have laid bare new materials to reconstruct the history of Ancient India though imagination still plays a significant role owing to the paucity of materials. In spite of a century and more of research we are not yet able to get at plain and reliable history, and one has need to seek the aid of imagination as well. Hence some possible and some probable theories and assumptions are set afloat in the wide sea of India's past. One such assumption is that Candragupta died a Jaina ascetic while Aśoka ended his career as a Buddhist monk. Among the old school of German historians, Lassen, who still holds the field as an acknowledged authority, gives it as his opinion that the Mauryan empire began with a Brahmanical reaction.[1] The Nandas had misused their authority and power so much that both the *śāstra* and *śastra* fell into desuetude, and king Dharma seemed transplanted from his exalted throne. Hence Cāṇakya, well-known as Kauṭalya, assisted Candragupta in effecting a revolution. The attempt proved fruitful. The Mauryan dynasty was established. There can be little doubt that Candragupta must have invoked further the assistance of Cāṇakya to guide him in the administration of the empire by awarding to him the office of Chancellorship. From

[1] *Int. Alt.*, II, pp. 209-11.

the extant *Arthaśāstra,* of which he was the author, it is transparent that the public religion of the state as well as the personal religion of the Emperor were the same, namely the Brahmanical religion.

Evidence of the Arthaśāstra

It has been pointed out elsewhere that the *Arthaśāstra* belonged to the school of early Hinduism when the Vedic modes of worship were still extant and when the Vedic sacrifices and rites were yet common.[1] Though it is impossible to build anything like a theory on the disputed phrase *śākyājīvikādīn* still there are scholars who wish to speak of the influence of Buddhism and even Jainism in the *Arthaśāstra.*[2] There was very little influence, if there was any influence at all. There is no denying the fact that religious speculation was rife in this age owing to the expansion of the philosophic sects of the dissenting Hindus. The prohibition of the *Kauṭalīya* in regard to householders from taking the fourth *āśrama* or *sannyāsa*[3] under penalty of punishment may go to prove the fact that the Maurya state extened so much patronage to the members of the ascetic sect by providing for free boarding and perhaps lodging, that every householder found the ascetic life more attractive and more advantageous than that of a family life (*saṁsāra*) with all its obligations and responsibilities. There are other circumstances in the book to warrant the belief that indiscriminate *sannyāsa* was the order of the day, and that, when once an ascetic did not find it profitable, he turned back to

1 See *Z.I.I.*, Vol. VII, pt. 2.
2 See *J.R.A.S.*, 1929.
3 Bk. I, ch. 19.

the mundane world. Him the state provided with some means of livelihood by employing him to set purposes, such as to act as a *cāra,* a *gūḍhapuruṣa.* The fact again that Kauṭalya wrote for his king (*narendra*), and the statement that the king gave audience to ascetics, physicians, ācāryas, and others from the chamber of the sacred fire (*agnyāgāra*) are further proofs that Candragupta was out and out Brahmanical in his religion. Heretics and members of dissenting sects were also shown due consideration by the state; and toleration was the principal doctrine, in matters religious and social.

According to Tāranātha, the Tibetan historian, Cāṇakya continued to be the chief minister of Bindusāra, son and successor of Candragupta.[1] If this tradition has any basis at all, it must be admitted that the same policy must have been continued and that Bindusāra's religion must have been the established religion of the land. This is further corroborated by the *Mahāvaṁśa.*

Identification of Prabhācandra

In his work on '*Jainism* or *the Early Faith of Aśoka,*' Thomas says: "the ṭestimony of Megasthenes would likewise seem to imply that Candragupta submitted to the devotional teachings of the Śramaṇas as opposed to the doctrines of the Brahmanas,"[2] and remarks that Candragupta and his successors Bindusāra, and Aśoka, at least in his early years of his reign, were Jainas, and that it was Aśoka who introduced Jainism in Kashmir as the *Rājataraṅgiṇi* would have

[1] See also *Pariśiṣṭaparvan,* ed. Jacobi, p. 62.
[2] P. 23.

it. The theory that Candragupta adopted the Jaina faith seems to have won the general approval of scholars interested in the subject.[1] The distinguished Mysore Archæologist Rao Bahadur R. Narasimhācāriar (now retired) who has re-opened the question after Lewis Rice, and has examined it in the light of literary and other evidences, concludes "the evidence may not be quite decisive, but it may be accepted as a working hypothesis until the contrary is proved by future research."[2] This theory is built upon two lines of evidence, one that of Megasthenes and the other that of the literary tradition embodied in the sacred books of the Jainas. The latter version seems to have been based on the inscription No. 1 at Śravaṇa Beḷgoḷa.

It would not be out of place to examine here what is contained in the inscription and what is in the legends. The inscription under notice mentions a Bhadrabāhusvāmin and a Prabhācandra. Lewis Rice ingeniously identified this Prabhācandra with Candragupta Maurya saying that that was the clerical name assumed by him after he became convert to the Jaina faith. Another circumstance in this connection is that this Prabhācandra is called an ācārya or a teacher. This identification of Prabhācandra with Candragupta Maurya is unconvincing, for different reasons.

First Prabhācandra was a Jaina teacher of equal celebrity as the *Śrutakevalin* Bhadrabāhu.

Secondly, a chronological examination of the date of Bhadrabāhu does not fit in with the time

[1] Jayaswal, *J.B.O.R.S.*, III, p. 452; Smith, *Early History*, p. 154; C. J. Shah, *Jainism in North India*, pp. 135-138.

[2] P. 42, *Epigraphia Carnatica*, Vol. II.

of Candragupta Maurya.[1] Dr. Jacobi's researches have led him to assign 170 A.V. as the year of Bhadrabāhu's death.[2] This works up to 297 B.C., which is generally accepted as the last year of Candragupta's rule and death.[3] If this date is accepted and if both Bhadrabāhu and Candragupta died in the same year, no reasonable time would have been assigned to go to the distant Mysore province, and to become a convert and a reputed teacher of the Jaina faith. The legends containing this tradition are those found in the *Bṛhatkathākośa, Bhadrabāhucarita, Munivaṁśābhyudaya,* (a Kaṇṇaḍa work c. 1860), and the *Rājāvaḷikathe* (another Kaṇṇaḍa work of the 18th century). The accounts which find mention in these works do not agree in details. The *Rājāvaḷikathe,* for example, speaks of a Bhadrabāhu and a supposititious grandson of Aśoka, Candragupta by name, and hence the great grandson of Candragupta I Maurya. The son and grandson of this Candragupta, according to this account, are Simhasena and Bhāskara.[4] We are not in possession of any other material to speak of a grandson of Aśoka, Candragupta by name. Whatever this may be, the fact remains that it is impossible to confer credibility on the legends.

Thirdly, not only is there conflicting account between legend and legend, but also between the legends and the inscriptions. If due weight is thrown on the side of the inscriptions, no Mauryan king seems involved in this connection. Apparently some Jaina teacher, a faithful disciple of Bhadrabāhu, is celebrated. The

1 See *Indian Antiquary,* XX, pp. 349-51; XXI, p. 156-ff. *Ep. Ind.* III, p. 171, note; IV, 22.

2 See *Kalpasūtra,* Intro., p. 13.

3 See *C.H.I.,* Vol. I, p. 472.

4 *In. Ant.,* XXI, p. 157.

only possible conclusion is that all the Jaina tradition in regard to Candragupta Maurya is imaginary romance, and does not belong to the province of sober history. But both the inscriptions at Śravaṇa Beḷgoḷa and the legends of the Jaina canon are valuable for their statements as to the outbreak of a continued famine and the consequent migration of the Jaina community from the North to the South of India, as far as the Karṇāṭaka country, to settle permanently, and that the movement was led by Bhadrabāhu and his disciple, one Candra or Prabhācandra.

The evidence of Megasthenes

Fourthly, the other evidence adduced in support of the theory that Candragupta was a Jaina is the *Indika* of Megasthenes and the writings of other Greek writers. The classical writers uniformly speak of Brahmanas and Śramaṇas (also *pravrajitas*). The same is found mentioned in the Edicts of Aśoka.[1] This only demonstrates the esteem and regard which the Brahmana had from the state both as a householder and as an ascetic. This is quite in keeping with the prescription of the *Arthaśāstra* that he was exempted from taxation, confiscation, corporal punishment, death-penalty, etc.[2] This was because he was expected to perform sacrifices and other rites to avert calamities, providential or otherwise, by use of spells, magic, and incantations. He was to read the omens, and fix the auspicious and inauspicious seasons for various undertakings by the state. He was above all a teacher. In return for these services he was allowed to have the

[1] R.E. XIII; Meg. Fg. XLI, 19.

[2] Bk. IV, ch. 8.

privileges of a rare order. There is no incompatibility between the *Kauṭalīya* and the account of Megasthenes in this particular.

Says Megasthenes, "The first is formed by the collective body of the philosophers which in point of number is inferior to the other classes, but in point of dignity is pre-eminent over all. For the philosophers being exempted from all public duties are neither the masters nor the servants of others. They are however engaged by private persons to offer sacrifices due in lifetime and to celebrate the obsequies of the dead; for they are believed to be most dear to the gods and to be the most conversant with matters pertaining to Hades. In requital of such sacrifices they receive valuable gifts and privileges. To the people of India at large they also render great benefits; when gathered together at the beginning of the year, they forewarn the assembled multitudes about droughts and wet weather, and also about propitious winds and diseases, and other topics capable of profiting the hearers. Thus the people and the sovereign learning beforehand what is to happen always make adequate provision against a coming deficiency and never fail to prepare beforehand what will help in time of need. The philosopher who errs in his predictions incurs no other penalty than obloquy and he then observes silence for the rest of his life."[1] From this it is evident that not only was the Brahman a member of the society who fulfilled a sacred function, but a person who was sacred.[2] The same

[1] I ,40-43 cp. Frag. XXXIII, 39; XLI, 59: See also *An. Ind. in Class. Literature,* Sec. IX.

[2] *C.H.I.*, Vol. I, p. 484.

notion more or less prevailed among the Buddhists also.[1] The *Dhammapada* has the following statement:—

"In whom there is truth and righteousness he is blessed, he is a Brahman."[2]

Again it is said "Because a man is rid of evil therefore is he called a Brāhmaṇa. Because he walks quietly he is called a Samaṇa, because he has sent away his own impurities therefore is he called a *Pravrajita.*"[3]

The Śramaṇas of the classical writers

The next question is who these Śramaṇas were, why they were tacked on with the Brahmanas and what public services they rendered to the state to claim special privileges. From what Megasthenes has to say of these Śramaṇas it is certain that he does not mean Buddhists or Jaina by the term. He seems to divide apparently the Brahmana class into two divisions, one purely following the *Śrauta* sacrifices and engaged in study and teaching, and the other adept in *Atharvan* rites serving the state as physicians, diviners and sorcerers. This latter division includes probably those Brahmans of the third and fourth *āśramas.* Elphinstone who has made a study of these classical writings remarks "it is indeed a remarkable circumstance that the religion of the Buddha should never have been expressly noticed by the Greek authors though it had existed for two centuries before Alexander. The only explanation is that the appearance and the manners of

[1] Vide author's article on the *Early History of Buddhism in India, Journal of Bombay Historical Society,* Vol. II, pt. 1.

[2] *S.B.E.,* Vol. X, ch. 26.

[3] *op. cit.*

its followers were not so peculiar as to enable a foreigner to distinguish them from the mass of the people". The Pāli *Sammana* is the Sanskrit Śramaṇa. Lassen sustains the view that from the nature of their functions and their description in the *Indika,* the Śarmanes or Śarmani of Megasthenes, Germanes of Strabo and Samanæans of Porphyrius agree better with the Brahmana *Sannyāsins.*[1]

Views of Colebrooke

We have again the authority of H. T. Colebrooke[2] who is disposed to believe that the word Śramaṇa must refer to Brahman ascetics, and who observes, "It may therefore be confidently inferred, that the followers of the Vedas flourished in India when it was visited by the Greeks under Alexander; and continued to flourish from the time of Megasthenes, who described them in the fourth century before Christ, to that of Porphyrius, who speaks of them on later authority, in the 3rd century after Christ."[3] So the attempt of scholars like Schwanbeck to identify the Śramaṇas of the classical writers with the Buddha teachers is an assumption with no legs to stand on.[4]

Buddhist India, a misnomer

If the inference of Colebrooke is right, then the epoch of earlier Hinduism, *viz.,* the religion and institutions of the orthodox Hindus (the followers of the Veda), continued to flourish with no diminished glory,

1 *Ind. Alter.;* II, pp. 705-ff.

2 See his *observation on the sect of Jains; Miscellaneous Essays.* Vol. II, ch. vii (ed. 1872).

3 *Ibid.,* Vol. II, pp. 204-5.

4 Hultzsch takes this view in his *Corpus.*

at least from the time of Alexander to A.D. 300. In this intervening period it was the Mauryan dynasty that held a vast empire in pre-eminent scale. It would not be therefore proper to entitle this epoch of the History of India as *Buddhist India* as Rhys Davids has done.[1] This was due to the fact that the word *dharma* in the Edicts was sought to connote Buddhist *dharma*, and Aśoka was hence taken to be a Buddhist, and the epoch in which Aśoka flourished was again taken to be the period of Buddhist ascendency, all contributing to a theory of Buddhist India. But the fact is that the *dharma* of the Edicts despite all straining on our part cannot be said to differ from the established ethical code of the orthodox Hinduism. The evidence of Greek writers and the evidence of Sanskrit literature show a continued period of ascendency of the followers of the Vedic school only. Granting for the sake of argument that a single monarch of the dynasty is a Buddhist in his faith, is it reasonable on that account to style the whole dynasty as Buddhist?

Śramaṇas are not Buddhists

There is again the internal evidence of Megasthenes to show that the word 'Śramaṇas' does not denote the Buddhists. In Frag. XLIII he says: "Among the Indians are those philosophers also who follow the precepts of the Buddha whom they honour as a God on account of his extraordinary sanctity." Appropriately to this notion the *Bhāgavata Purāṇa* has accepted the Buddha as an *avatār* of Viṣṇu[2] and has accorded to him a place of honour among the orthodox Gods and deities. By referring to the sect of the followers of the Buddha

[1] *The Story of the Nations Series.*
[2] Book. I. 3-24; II. 7-37.

Megasthenes was certainly able to make the nice distinction between the orthodox ascetics and the Buddhist monks. He has not said much about them like the author of the *Arthaśāstra*. Possibly these authorities did not feel the heavy weight of their influence. The Buddhist sect flourished like many other sects and claimed no ascendency at any period over the established religion of the land.

Again the following description of the Śramaṇas is given to us:

"The shamanas, on the other hand, are, as I said, an elected body. Whoever wishes to be enrolled in their order presents himself to the city or village authorities, and there makes cession of all his property. He then shaves his body, puts on the Shamana robe, and goes to the Shamans, and never returns back to speak or look at his wife and children if he has any, and never thinks of them any more, but leaves his children to the king, and his wife to his relations, who provide them with the necessaries of life. The Shamanas live outside the city, and spend the whole day in discourse upon divine things. They have houses and temples of a royal foundation, and in them stewards receive from the king a certain allowance of food, bread, and vegetables for each convent."[1]

Śramaṇas are sannyāsins

The above description is exactly that of a *parivrājaka* or the orthodox Hindu *sannyāsin*. The phrases, 'elected body,' 'order,' 'royal foundations,' need not detain us here demonstrating particularly to

1. *Ancient India in Class. Liter.*, p. 168.

the Buddhist order and its establishment. This is true of all monastic orders, all being patronised by the monarch of the state whose aim was *der gessellschaftlische culturzweck,* as already pointed out. According to the prescription of the *Kauṭalīya* previous sanction of the authorities of the state was necessary before one could don the robes of the *sannyāsin.* Inasmuch as the state provided for their food and lodging, the state might issue permits to one to embrace asceticism or might not. There seems to be however some confusion as regards the statement that "the Samanæans, again, ... are collected from all classes of the Indians."[1] It may be that the Greek writer has taken the *Pāṣaṇḍas* and other heretics and included them in the orthodox fold. Or it may denote the fact that asceticism was no more confined to the members of the first caste but open to the Kṣatriyas and the Vaiśyas also. Whatever this might be one thing is certain that the expression Śramaṇa with the Greek writers does not mean 'a Buddhist', but does connote 'ascetics' and more likely of the orthodox type.

Yatis and yoga

It must be remembered that the order of *Sannyāsa* either of the orthodox or the heterodox type, did not begin with the Buddha or even Mahāvīra. It was a very ancient institution. The *dhyāna yoga* attributed to the Buddha finds a mention in the *Upaniṣad* and the epics. In fact it is much earlier than we would ordinarily believe. We have archæological evidence to show that this institution of *yoga* can be traced as far back as to

[1] *Ibid.*, p. 170.

the prehistoric culture of the Indus Valley.[1] At Mohenjodäro a group of stone statuettes are found though in a mutilated condition. But the bust which is in a good state of preservation is characterised by the stiff erect posture of the head, the neck, and the chest, and the half-shut eyes looking fixedly at the tip of the nose, in conformity with the description in the *Bhagavad Gītā*.[2] It is undoubtedly the posture of the *yogin*.[3] Rāmaprasād Chanda recognises in these statuettes the images of the *yatis,* first friends and then foes of Indra, as seen from some hymns of the *Ṛg Veda;* and those *yatis* were probably the forerunners of the *vrātyas*.[4] Von Schroeder interprets the expression *yati* as a *shamana* or a diviner, sorcerer.[5] What do these things bear testimony to? They indicate clearly that *yoga* and asceticism were not peculiar to the Mauryan epoch or even to the few centuries before it. But it goes far back into the prehistoric times and it is not possible to determine when exactly such speculation in regard to religion and philosophy commenced.

The practice of *dhyāna-yoga* in the third millennium B.C., bears the test that religion and its institutions were far older than that period. Again the sects of heterodox mendicants are as old as the *Ṛg Veda* when the *yatis* turned inimical to Indra and were reduced in the course of ages to the position of the *vrātyas,* the outcaste

[1] According to Sir John Marshall *yoga* had its origin among the pre-Aryan population. *Mohenjodaro and the Indus Civilisation* (1931) p. 54.

[2] VI, ch. 11-13.

[3] *Memoirs of Ar. Sur. India,* No. 41, p. 25.

[4] *Ibid.,* pp. 32-33.

[5] *Vienna Oriental Journal,* Vol. XXIII, pp. 11-15 (1909).

mendicants of the Vedic literature. If the term *yati* could mean *shamana,* as Von Schroeder would have it,[1] verily is our knowledge of ancient Indian history rapidly changing, partly on account of increasing archæological evidence and partly on account of the scientific interpretation of the technical terms in her ancient literature.

Conclusion

In the light of the above facts it is indeed difficult to believe that Candragutpa either during the period of his reign, or in the evening of his life, became a convert to the Jaina faith. The other possible alternative is that he was a devout follower of the Vedic school of religion, and if the legends have anything to impart, it is, that Candragupta, as was usual with the Kṣatriya monarchs of old abdicated his throne in favour of his son, and betook himself to the third *āśrama* or *vānaprastha,* to lead a life of quiet and ease. Bindusāra was also a follower of the Brahmanical school. This is corroborated even by an accredited Buddhist work, the *Mahāvaṁśa.*[2] What is more remarkable is that another Buddhist work, the *Divyāvadhāna,* speaks of Bindusāra and his son Aśoka as being Kṣatriyas[3] though it is generally believed that the Buddhists did not recognise the institution of caste.

[1] *op. cit.,* pp. 11-15.

[2] P. 15.

[3] P. 370, ed. by Cowell and Neil.

Sec. vi. AŚOKA'S PERSONAL RELIGION

"I intend to make a conscientious study of Aśoka's Dharma and Religion, based only upon contemporary documents. The Buddhist chronicles of the fourth, fifth and sixth centuries have deceived many a scholar. To count so great a monarch as Aśoka among the disciples of Gautama was unquestionably a distinct advantage to the declining Buddhist monachism. Hence their statement is not reliable at all. Centuries after, some Jain authors claimed an analogous honour for themselves as regards Akbar." In this strain the Rev. Fr. Heras, S.J., begins his very interesting paper on *Aśoka's Dharma and Religion.*[1] The theory that Aśoka was a Buddhist is primarily supported by the Buddhist books which were reduced to writing centuries after the Buddha's *nirvāṇa*. Writers who have thrown their weight in this behalf claim that the theory is partially supported by the inscriptions of Aśoka. There is a school of savants who deem that Aśoka was originally a Jaina by faith[2] and was afterwards attracted by the Buddhist ideals and doctrines. There is also another view that Aśoka was neither a Buddhist nor a Jaina, but one who professed the Brahmanical faith.

The Buddhist legends

Years ago Bühler wrote that in his view "a full explanation of Aśoka's Edicts can only be given with the help of the Brahmanical literature and by a careful utilization of the actualities of Hindu life. This conviction has forced me to demur against a specially

[1] *Q.J.M.S., Bangalore,* Vol. XVII, No. 4, p. 255.

[2] See Thomas, *Early Faith of Aśoka*. Also a paper on *Religion of Aśoka* by M. Ghosh in the *Pro. of II Orient. Conf.*, Calcutta.

Buddhistic interpretation of various words and terms."[1] The subject then requires a careful and independent examination. In regard to the theory that Aśoka professed Buddhism, the Buddhist books are claimed to be the chief authority. Here are found stories and chronicles of Aśoka mostly legendary in character. According to V. A. Smith silly fictions "disfigure the Ceylonese chronicles of Aśoka, and disguise their solid merits and hence do not deserve serious criticism."[2] Referring to the story of Māhinda or Māhendra, the younger brother of Aśoka, and his sister, Prof. Oldenberg remarks that "it has been invented for the purpose of possessing a history of the Buddhist institutions in the island, and to connect it with the most distinguished person conceivable —the great Aśoka."[3] A similar view is held by another scholar H. Kern whose special study of the Buddhist works is too well-known to need mention.[4] In the course of his examination of the Buddhist Councils from the traditions of the Pāli Books, and after referring to the absurdities, inconsistencies and dogmatical and sectarian tendencies, imprinted in every page of the works, D. R. Bhandarkar has much justification for the opinion that "very little that is contained in these traditions may be accepted as historical truth."[5]

Notwithstanding these downright and absurd mythological accounts that have gathered round the name of the celebrated Mauryan monarch they are taken

[1] *Ep Ind.,* Vol. II, p. 246.

[2] *Aśoka,* p. 19.

[3] Intro. to the *Vinayapiṭakam,* p. 4 (ii).

[4] *Manual of Indian Buddhism,* p. 110.

[5] *Aśoka,* p. 96.

for granted as a source of information for the history of Aśoka, and theories hardly tenable have been floated in the ever expanding ocean of oriental history. Nothing authentic is on record concerning these legendary chronicles, and any endeavour to utilise them for historical purposes is to get ourselves stranded on the shore of imaginary history.

A calm but deep study of the Pāli Buddhism with its special reference to Aśoka leaves the reader with the impression that the whole thing is marred by glaring inconsistencies, and the views set forth are deeply sectarian and consequently one-sided. Materials culled from these fictions compiled centuries after Aśoka's death can afford no tangible basis to build any historical edifice. Scholars have realised this difficulty though they still believe that these chronicles are materials for scientific history. If it be accepted that the legends do not carry much historical value, the inscriptions of Aśoka can alone be credited with trustworthiness.

Buddhist Inscriptions

What is then the message of the Aśokan Edicts inscribed on rocks and pillars? Do they aid us in settling once for all the vexed question of the king's personal religion? It is rather an intricate task to attempt anything like a definite answer to these questions. Still an humble effort is made here and a decision is arrived it. It may not be out of place to examine here the alleged Buddhist inscriptions of Aśoka. These are the Calcutta-Bairāṭ rock inscription, the Rummindēī and Nigālī Sāgar Pillars, the Kauśāmbī, Sāṁchī and Sārnāth Pillar Edicts. Says D. R. Bhandarkar: "It is no longer permissible to call in question the Buddhist faith of Aśoka. That is now established beyond all doubt by the Bhābru Edict, otherwise called the Second Bairāṭ Edict. It opens with Aśoka expressing his reverence for *Buddha, Dhamma* and *Saṅgha,* exactly in the well-known trinitary formula of Buddhism."[1] Thus this Edict is taken to be a declaration of Aśoka's faith in the Buddhist Trinity. This explanation is largely dependent upon the interpretation of the phrase *aṁ mamayā saghe upayāte* (M.R.E. I).[2] This D. R. Bhandarkar explains: 'I have lived with the Saṅgha,"[3] and R. K. Mookerjee 'I visited the Saṅgha'.[4] If Bhandarkar's interpretation is accepted, the expression must signify that Aśoka became a monk while he continued to rule as emperor. This position is taken by V. A. Smith who remarks: "The fact is undoubted that Aśoka was both monk and monarch at the same time. . . . Throughout his reign he retained the position of the Head of the Church and Defender of the faith."[5] That he became a member of the *Saṅgha* or the order of the Buddhist clergy is also accepted by F. W. Thomas.[6] This position cannot stand a critical test as we shall see presently.

The passage in question simply marks the visit of the emperor to the *Saṅgha*. This is a circumstance which is not incompatible with the active rule of a great and

[1] *Aśoka,* p. 73. See also Vallee-Poussin, *L'Inde Aux Temps Des Mauryas* (1930), pp. 126-133.

[2] Cp. Siddhapura, *upete* (Rūpnāth), *upayāte* (Bairāṭ), *upagate* (Maski).

[3] *Aśoka,* p. 328.

[4] *Aśoka,* p. 109.

[5] *Aśoka,* p. 35. Hultzsch, *Corpus,* Smith, *History of India,* Ch. IX etc.

[6] *C.H.I.*, Vol. I, p. 496.

tolerant emperor. It was one of the several state visits in which Aśoka indulged. Nor were his visits confined to the Buddhist monasteries; they were extended to the Brahmanas, Śramaṇas, Ājivikās and other sects in the empire. Even Bhandarkar feels this inconsistency and seems to reconcile that Aśoka did not become a *bhikṣu* or monk but a *bhikṣu-gaṭika,* a stage higher than that of an *upāsaka* but less than that of a monk.[1] According to the political philosophy of the times the king was an active functionary and there were only two courses open to him. He was either to rule or to abdicate. One cannot eat the cake and have it. There was no third course open to him.

The contention that Aśoka retained the position of the Head of the Church is absolutely baseless. A reference to the constitution of the Buddhist *Saṅgha* as described in the *Vinayapiṭaka*[2] will reveal the fact that the Buddha was the *Satthā* or Head of the *Saṅgha.* After the Buddha it was the Dharma that was the refuge of true disciples as is seen from the interesting discussion in the *Gopaka-Moggallāna Suttanta* of the *Majjihima Nikāya.* Here to a question put by Vassakāra to Ānanda whether the Buddha had elected any to succeed him as the Head, Ānanda answered in the negative; but to a supplementary question put to him how could unity exist among the monks without anybody as refuge, he answered 'the Dhamma'.[3] Sukumar Dutt remarks: "Not only is the idea of the paramount authority of a person—a recognised head, a spiritual dictator or an abbot foreign

1. *Aśoka,* pp. 79-80.
2. *Vinaya Texts,* S.B.E., Pt. I, I, Intro., p. 23.
3. Oldenberg, *Buddha,* p. 198 and p. 341.

to the constitution of a Buddhist Saṅgha, but it is definitely excluded in a number of passages."[1] 'No person however highly placed, could pretend to legislate for the Buddhist Saṅgha and set up as its ecclesiastical ruler.'[2] In the light of the above observations it is impossible for Aśoka to have been a king and a monk at the same time.

If he was not a monk, then it may be contended that Aśoka must have been at least an *upāsaka* (a lay disciple) perhaps of a fervent type. There is not much warrant even to assume this position. According to Dr. Hoernle while the lay adherent formed an integral part of the Jaina organisation, not even a *formal* recognition of him was made in the Buddhist order.[3] In other words the Buddhists were a purely monastic community and took no lay disciples and hence did not interfere with the caste system. The Jains on the other hand admitted lay disciples and accepted the institution of caste.[4] Therefore the *upāsaka* could not be a *de facto* or *de jure* member of the *Saṅgha*. All that is meant by the term is that the house-holder would minister to the needs of the members of the *Saṅgha*. The *Iti Vuttaka* plainly informs us that the Buddhists owed their sustenance to the Brahman householders.[5] To feed them and administer to their needs, and to aid them in the accomplishment of their ends,

[1] See *Early Buddhist Monachism,* pp. 143-45.

[2] *Sir Asutosh Mem. Vol.* (*Patna*), p. 257.

[3] Address (1898) before the *As. Soc. of Bengal.* Cp. Oldenberg, *Buddha,* p. 152 ff; p. 190.

[4] See Author's *Early History of Buddhism in India* in the *Jour. B. His. Society,* Vol. II, pp. 51-74.

[5] P. 125, New York Ed.

were as much the duty of the public as of the state. Aśoka realised this and discharged his responsibility.

A parallel can be drawn from the *Mahābhārata*[1] where among the other duties of a king is mentioned the duty of looking to the comforts of the elders (*upāsitā ca vṛddhānām*) and helping, among others, those who look forward to only one thing, the other world, and *sādhūs* who stand like the mountain steadfast in *dharma.*[2] An *upāsitā* is expected to be *jitatantraḥ,* one who has won over lassitude, and *alolupaḥ,* indifferent to sensual objects. This construction is perhaps warranted by the term occurring in the Buddhist works. It may therefore be safely argued that the inscriptions of Aśoka do not bear the test of a declaration of his Buddhist faith but imply his state visit to the *Saṅgha,* where he learnt to love the monks for their purity and transparent sincerity in having renounced worldly pleasures and subjecting themselves to a life of mortification, which, penance of any kind involves. During his sojourn Aśoka must have also learnt the working of the constitution of the *Saṅgha* and resolved to help it in its accomplishment. Hence the Calcutta Bairāṭ Rock Inscription.

It is significant to note that this Edict is addressed *not* to all his peoples, but only to the *members* of the *Saṅgha.* Even here Aśoka says: 'though whatever has been said has been well said, still he would make a selection which in his opinion would make the *dharma* eternal.'[3] Bhandarkar who has examined the six principles

[1] *Śānti,* 56, 20-ff.
[2] *Ibid.,* 24 and 55.
[3] See *Corpus,* pp. 172-173.

enunciated on behalf of the *dharma* is constrained to remark that this does not reveal any ritualistic or metaphysical element of Buddhism.[1] With regard to the sacred texts quoted in this inscription, and their identification the *Vinaya-samukasa,* the *Aliya-vasas,* the *Anāgata-bhayas,* the *Muni-gāthas,* the *Moneya-sūta,* the *Upatisa-pasina,* and the *Lāghulovāda,* no last word has yet been said. Mookerjee, who has examined this Edict, makes the following statement that "the Bhābru Edict was prior to the main body of the Rock Edicts."[2] If this chronology of the Aśokan Edicts is acceptable, how are we to account for the issuing of the Major Rock Edicts containing his proclamations where there is absolutely no reference to the Buddha or Buddhism? Either the chronological examination is wrong or Aśoka was not a Buddhist. The latter is the more probable. The attempts to prove Aśoka's faith in Buddhism are too far-fetched, conjectural and hence inconclusive.[3]

Visits to the Saṁbodhi and Lummini

Possibly the same interpretation and the same value must be attached to his visits to the Saṁbodhi and Lummini, the latter of which he made tax-free. The inscription on the column at Rummindeī in Nepal is also contended, without much justification, in support of Aśoka's faith in Buddhism.[4] More than 20 years ago this record was subjected to a severe and lengthy examination by that learned indologist J. F. Fleet, and the only possible conclusion to which he could arrive at was

[1] *Aśoka,* p. 88.

[2] *Aśoka,* p. 120*n*.

[3] See Oldenberg, *Buddh. studien, Z.D.M.G.,* Vol. 52 p. 634; Vallee Poussin, *L'Inde Aux Temps Des Mauryas,* p. 127-ff; B. C. Law, *Annals of the Bh. Inst.,* Vol. XII, pp. 171-172.

[4] See for instance D. R. Bhandarkar, *Aśoka,* pp. 82-83.

that it was only a state visit, and the remission of *bali* and *bhāga* was to commemorate his visit to the birth-place of the founder of Buddhism.[1] We need not go into the details once again which Fleet has so critically examined and arrived at the right conclusion. Suffice it to point out here that it could not have been a pious tour, for the sheer reason that a part of this tour was devoted to visit Niglīvā sacred to Konākamana, about thirteen miles north-west of Rummindeī. Thus in the same year and on the occasion of the same tour, Aśoka visited two places, one sacred to the Buddha and the other to the founder of the rival sect. The inscriptions on both these pillars, fortunately preserved to us, demonstrate that the emperor went in person, did worship and left a stone memorial behind. If one could be regarded as a pious tour, the other also must be regarded as such; what is really significant is the mention of the fact that he worshipped in both the places. To-day Aśoka could not be a follower of the Buddha and to-morrow of his rival. Therefore it is reasonable to assume that both were state visits to the holy places of the different cults, and Aśoka left memorials in commemoration of such visits.[2] Any other interpretation seems erroneous and misleading. Even to-day the Hindus regard these as sacred places of pilgrimage and visit them to revere the memory of an ancient saint, the Buddha.

To crown all this comes Aśoka's important public statement: "Thus do I attend to all classes. All sects are also honoured by me with various offerings. But

[1] *J.R.A.S.*, 1908, p. 471-ff; cp. *Ep. Ind.*, Vol. V, p. 162; *Ind. Ant.*, 1905, p. 1-ff: 1914.

[2] See Minor Pillar Inscriptions, *Corpus*, pp. 164-165.

which is one's own approach (or choice) is considered by me as the most essential."[1] His policy was clear. It was non-interference as regards choice of religious belief, but intervention to see that everything was properly accomplished. If the theory that Aśoka fostered the orthodox Buddhist *saṅgha* can be accepted, it is equally acceptable that he showed no less zeal in fostering the rival sect founded by Devadatta, a cousin of the Buddha. The founder of this sect was a mythological saint Konākamana, one of the previous Buddhas, according to the Pāli version of the tradition. He enlarged the *stūpa* dedicated to Konākamana and paid a state visit to it when he had been anointed twenty years.[2]

The following points deserve notice in this connection:—

(1) Aśoka showed equal enthusiasm in honouring the Ājīvikas. These were apparently a heterodox sect of monks whose founder was one Gośāla Maṅkhaliputta, contemporaneous with the founders of the other ascetic sects, Mahāvīra and Gautama. According to the Pāli *sūtras* Gośāla was a prominent rival of Mahavīra and an opponent of the Buddha.[3] In order to support that ascetic community 'which would seem to have, at one time, rivalled in numbers and importance the two still existing great communities of the Buddhists and Jainas' the caves of Barābar Hills were dedicated by

[1] Pillar, E. VI, *Corpus,* pp. 128-129.

[2] Cf. Smith, *Early His.*, p. 33; Nagāli Sāgar Pillar, *Corpus,* p. 165.

[3] See Jacobi, *Kalpa sūtra* Intro., p. 1; Hoernle, *Uvāsaga-Dasāo*, II, Intro.. p. 12; Bühler, *In. Ant.*, Vol. 20, p. 362.

the Emperor[1] in the same spirit with which his successor Daśaratha bestowed rock-hewn caves on Nāgārjuni Hill on the Ājīvikas.[2] One is at a loss to know what weight this testimony carries in the argument about Aśoka's faith in Buddhism. Even Vallee Poussin, the eloquent advocate of the theory that Aśoka was a Buddhist, has to make the following observation in this connection: "On voit mal, en des temps moins anciens, un bouddhiste convaincu favoriser d'aussi mauvaris religieux que les Ajīvīkas, meme pour raison d'Etat."[3]

(2) That the insriptions of Aśoka do not *ipso facto* suggest his proselytism to the Buddhist faith is evidenced by the fact that he equally honoured the Nigaṇṭhas or Nirgranthas who were another dissenting sect of the Hindus.[4] We know from references in the Buddhist *Piṭakas* that the Nigaṇṭhas were a sect hostile to the Buddhists. It would appear that Nigaṇṭha Nātaputta, the founder of the Jaina sect, was an opponent of Gotama the Buddha and hence one of his contemporaries.[5]

According to the Jaina scriptures, the Jaina clergy went by the name of Nigaṇṭhas.[6] In the opinion of Bühler, the term in the inscriptions of Aśoka has reference to the Jaina monks and nuns.[7] If we can

1 See Barābar Hill Inscript. and also Pillar Edict VI-VII. For the use of the term under various designations see B.M. Barua's article *'Ājīvika-what it means'* in *the Annals of Bhandarkar Institute,* Vol. VIII, Part II, pp. 183-188.

2 *In. Ant.,* Vol. XX, p. 361f.

3 *L'Inde Aux Temps Des Mauryas,* p. 126.

4 P.E. VI.

5 *In. Ant.,* Vol. 7, p. 143: also *C.H.I.,* I, p. 160

6 See *Kalpasūtra,* sūtra, 130.

7 *Ep. Ind.,* II, p. 272.

believe the references in Buddhist canons, then there is strong reason for the theory that the Nirgranthas were members of the early Jaina church.[1] This position of extending the royal patronage to the Jaina sect which looked upon Buddhism as a rival faith, and which ignored it by taking no notice of it in any of its old Jaina *sūtras,* is irreconcilable with the theory of Aśoka being a Buddhist.[2]

(3) Professor H. H. Wilson draws our attention to "the total omission of any allusion to Buddha himself by any of his appellations, Sugata, Tathāgata, Gautama, Sākya, or Sākyasinha, all which occur repeatedly in the Buddhist writings, both of Tibet and of Ceylon, and which the Sāranāth Buddhist inscription proves it was not unusual to allude to in the sculptured inscriptions of that religion. Neither is there any allusion to his family, or to any of his early disciples, or to any of the Bodhisatwas, who are sufficiently conspicuous in the Kahgyur and Mahawanso, nor does any hint occur of Stūpas, Vihārs, or Caityas, or of the Bodhi, or Bo tree,—everywhere else so frequently adverted to. Neither do we find anything that can be regarded as peculiarly Buddhist doctrines, for the moral duties inculcated are the same that are enjoyed by Brahmanical writings, and there is at least one duty enforced which it is very difficult to reconcile with the spirit of Buddhism; reverence for, or rather the service of (*suśrusha*) the Brahmans."[3]

(4) The last but not the least were the Brahmans who were the recipients of honour and regard from

[1] *In. Ant.*, Vol. 9, p. 161.
[2] See preface, p. 7 of Jacobi's ed. of the *Āyāraṁga sutta,* P.T.S.
[3] *J.R.A.S.*, XII, pp. 240-1.

Aśoka.[1] Even the *Mahāvaṁśa* which attributes many a Buddhist building to the munificence of Aśoka,[2] states that Aśoka followed his father in bestowing gifts on the Brahmans. The *Rājataraṅgiṇī* places on record many a Brahmanical temple and even Jaina buildings to the credit of the same monarch.[3] Added to this is the evidence of the *Dīpavaṁśa*[4] which clearly makes out that the Buddhism was not his original faith. His interest in the welfare of the other castes and orders like the Ibhyas or Vaiśyas, ascetics and householders is unbounded.[5] His alleged denunciation of rituals said to be contained in the Ninth Rock-Edict is meaningless. For, does he not say '*se katavi cheva kho maṁgale,*' meaning that ceremonies needs be practised. What he drives at here is that mere *karma* will bear little fruit. One must aim at the substance and not at the shadow. So practice of virtues (*śiṣṭācāram*) is more fruitful. From these and other evidences it is impossible to escape the conclusion that Aśoka held catholic views about religion and was an extremely tolerant monarch. His was universal toleration regardless of sects and creeds. In fact he realised that doctrine as one of the proximate ends of the state.[6]

The above examination leads us to the conclusion that he could not have been a Buddhist. The next question that remains to be answered is what was his religion? The following facts which are categorically stated support the theory that Aśoka's personal faith was Brahmanical Hinduism to the very end of his days.

1 P.E. VI, etc. R.E. V.
2 Bk. V, p. 23.
3 Bk. I, ch. 20. Stein, Trans.
4 Bk. VI, ch. 18.
5 R.E. V.
6 Cf. Edmund Hardy, *Konig Aśoka*, pp. 22-23.

(1) Aśoka encouraged exhibitions of representations of the celestials and deities peculiar to Hinduism. These are quite in tune with the recommendations of the *Kauṭalīya*. It may be noted that early Buddhism did not believe in idolatry but actually discarded it.

(2) Aśoka pursued firmly the principle of religious neutrality accompanied with a spirit of universal toleration, an element foreign to the rival sects and especially the dissenting sects.[1]

(3) In more than one place Aśoka has repeatedly mentioned that the reward for the practice of *dharma* was the enjoyment of a life of heavenly bliss. Belief in, and attainment of, heaven are foreign to the Buddhist philosophy.

(4) Non-injury to creatures emphasised by the emperor is as much Brahmanical as the Jaina or even Buddhist. Aśoka's *ahiṁsā* was not of the rigid type peculiar to the Jaina prescriptions. For the practice of slaughtering animals for the royal kitchen was continued. It is more in accord with the epic notions of *ahiṁsā* where it is characterised as *paramo dharmaḥ.* The recognition of this principle is admitted by the *Upaniṣads* and the early *Dharmasūtras* as well.[2]

(5) Aśoka makes no mention whatsoever of the Buddhist notion of *nirvāṇa*[3] and the *nirvāṇic* annihilation which is the fundamental characteristic of the Buddhist faith. In this respect the inscriptions of Aśoka do, not only, not conform to the prescriptions of the *Dhammapada* but differ from them widely. The key-

[1] Cf. Kern, *Op. cit.*, p. 112.
[2] Wilson, *J.R.A.S.*, XII, pp. 238-240.
[3] *C.H.I.*, I, p. 505.

note of the *Dhammapada* is the doctrine of *nirvāṇa.*[1] Hence the remarks of the latest writer on the subject, Vallee Poussin, can hardly be accepted: "Le bouddhisme d'Aśoka, en effect, respire l'atmosphere des textes qui, pour diverses raisons, sont consideres comme les plus archaiques, Dhammapada, Suttanipāta, (dont des mor ceaux sont problement nommes a Bhabra)."[2] As already shown the reference to *svarga* is made in the edicts on more than one occasion. The concept of *nirvāṇa* is such as it does not lead to any enjoyment or happiness after life. . But the concept of heaven does imply all this.

(6) A scholar of the standing of Hultzsch who is disposed to believe Aśoka's faith in Buddhism admits that "the lists of evil passions and dispositions do not tally with the *āsavas* and *kileśas* of the *Buddhists.*"[3] These agree with the Hindu notions and beliefs, 'about the reward of human actions.'

(7) Aśoka makes a significant statement which furnishes a clue as to the profession of his faith. He says that his predecessors engaged themselves in the spreading and propagating of the *dharma* to which he wedded himself.[4] But their efforts did not prove very much of a success in that direction. His predecessors were Candragupta and Bindusāra. There is not even a lengendary record to testify to their attachment to the Buddhism. This more than anything else goes to prove Aśoka's faith in the *sanātana dharma* of the Hindus. At least there is no implication here of any reference to

1 P. 125.

2 See Vallee Poussin, *L'Inde Aux Temps Des Mauryas,* p. 125.

3 *Corpus,* Intro., p. 52.

4 P.E. VII.

the Buddhist *dharma*. According to Fleet it is the ordinary *dharma* of the Hindu kings and he bases his conclusion on the authority of the *Mānavadharma-śāstra*.[1]

(8) According to Bhandarkar, the six constituents of the True Dharma addressed to the *Saṅgha* in the Calcutta Bairāṭ Edict show that "his (Aśoka's) mind was ravished not by the ritualistic or metaphysical elements of Buddhism, but rather by the fundamentals of that religion, or for the matter of that, any religion. He was fascinated not by any specification of rules and regulations to be observed externally and mechanically, but rather what constitutes and conduces to real inner growth."[2]

(9) Next we have to consider the term Devānāmpriya, a title assumed by kings other than Aśoka as well. It was the title of Candragupta Maurya. It is contended that 'Deva' refers to the Jaina deity, and the title 'beloved of the Gods' is taken to be a profession of the Jaina faith. If this were so Aśoka's faith in Buddhism becomes a myth, for, the term occurs in several of the Rock and Pillar Edicts. It is a title borne by Daśaratha, grandson of Aśoka.[3] In fact the R.E. VII (Kālsī and Mānsehrā) shows that Aśoka's predecessors also bore the same title. In the *Dīpavaṁśa* it is an attribute of Tissa King of Ceylon, a contemporary of Aśoka. A century later Patañjali uses it as a honorific and also in the ironical sense of a fool. But in the *Harṣacarita* Bāṇa uses it as an honorific.[4] At the best the title

[1] See *J.R.A.S.*, p. 491.

[2] *Aśoka*, pp. 88-89.

[3] See Nāgarjuni Hill Cave Inscriptions.

[4] See Intro., *Corpus*, p. XXIX.

does not warrant Aśoka's profession of the Buddhist faith.

AŚOKA AND THE THIRD COUNCIL

(10) Similar to the legends which have grown around the three Tamil Academies (*Śaṅgaṁ*) of the Tamil literary tradition, the Buddhist tradition speaks of three councils summoned at different times to settle the disputed points about the *dharma*. There is a tradition that a council (perhaps the fourth) was held under the patronage of king Kaniṣka. The Ceylonese version is silent on this and maintains the council of Aśoka as the third and the last. In a similar manner the Buddhists of Northern India, not to speak of Tibet and China, do not mention anything about the third Council and refer to the Council of Kaniṣka as the third and the last. Thus there is a conflict of opinion among the Buddhists themselves as regards the so-called Third and Fourth councils. Examining the historical character of the First council Prof. Oldenberg has made the remark that it was pure invention and not history.[1] Considering the disagreement of the varying accounts with regard to the Second Council Kern held that it was dogmatic fiction.[2] Judged by the modern critical standards we have to conclude that whenever a dispute arose as to the discipline or the doctrine, the leading monks met together and came to some agreement. Not only three or four but a good number might have been held and "later traditions have jumbled them all up into one story", and

[1] *Vinaya Texts*, Vol. I, p. 26.
[2] *Histoire du Bouddhisme,* Vol. II, p. 290.

fathered every one of them invariably to a great monarch like Aśoka or Kaniṣka. Confining ourselves to the Third Council, it is mentioned by the *Dīpavaṁśa* and the *Mahāvaṁśa* and referred to by *Buddhaghoṣa* in his Introduction to *Samantapāsādika*.[1]

The *Ceylonese Chronicles* which are the primary authority or rather the sole authority for this tradition, with the exception of a single reference in Buddhaghoṣa's writings, have it that a great Council was held under the patronage of Aśoka in his capital city. Briefly the story is as follows:—The Buddhist monasteries were flooded by a large number of people belonging to different heretical sects who practised their own doctrines in the name of the Buddha. Consequently the Buddhist monks had to discontinue for seven years the *Uposatha* and *Pavārana* ceremonies. On a representation to the king, who was then Aśoka, he sent on the advice of the Bhikkus, for Tissa Moggaliputta, an eminent Bhikku of the time. With him in an open assembly summoned by Aśoka it was resolved that the Vibhajja doctrine was not unacceptable to the teachings of the Buddha.

The latest writer on the subject Dr. R. C. Majumdar justly remarks[2]: "The story stands self-condemned. It is impossible to hold that thousands of heretics entered into the *Saṅgha* and were not detected for years; that the *Uposatha* ceremony was stopped for seven years even in his own *ārāma* in Pāṭaliputra and Aśoka did not know anything of it till at the end of that long period; and lastly that the name and fame

[1] *Dīp.* VII, p. 34-ff; *Mahā.*, Ch. V; *Vinaya Texts,* Ed. Oldenberg, Vol. III, p. 306-f.

[2] *Buddhistic Studies,* pp. 26-72, ed. B. C. Law (Cal. 1931).

of such a great Arhat as Tissa Moggaliputta is represented to be, could possibly remain unknown to Aśoka till the 18th year of his coronation."[1]

In addition to the above, other arguments which go to disprove the authenticity of this tradition can be categorically stated.[2]

1. The accounts are a jumble of myth, the miraculous elements predominating.

2. If the tradition has any basis the original canon must have been in Māgadhī, the vernacular of Aśoka's capital. What we have on the other hand is the Ceylonese Pāli canon which was reduced to writing some centuries after Aśoka. Whether the rendering in Pāli was from the original Māgadhī we cannot say for certain.

3. According to Professor Poussin 'the apostolic or conciliar origin of the *abhidharma* is a pious fraud'. For, all the schools except these of the Vibhajjavādins and of the Sarvāstivādins, approve of two baskets—*vinaya* and *sutta piṭakas.*

4. The Council was at the most a sectarian assembly of the Vibhajjavādins, perhaps to get their doctrines approved.

5. There is no reference to it in the *Chullavagga.*

6. Hiuen Tsiang who records many a tradition about Aśoka does not say anything about this council.

[1] *Buddhistic Studies,* p. 67.

[2] See J. N. Farquhar, *Outline of the Religious Literature of India,* pp. 68-69; R.C. Mazumdar, *Buddhists and Councils,* in *Buddhistic Studies,* pp. 64-69.

7. Last but not least is that a Council held under the patronage of Aśoka, it is reasonable to assume, will be mentioned in his inscriptions. According to Farquhar 'his silence thus suggests a serious doubt about the whole tradition.'

THE EVIDENCE OF ARCHAEOLOGY

(11) Literary and inscriptional evidence has led us to the conclusion that Aśoka's faith was not Buddhism as is the current view. This is further supported by the testimony of archæology. As this has been examined fully elsewhere,[1] it is enough to point out here the main lines of argument adduced in support of our theory. Tradition records that Aśoka was a great builder of cities, stūpas and pillars. This is corroborated by the records of the Chinese travellers Fa-hien and Yuan Chwang. While Fa-hien noticed six pillars[2] of Aśoka, Yuan Chwang saw as many as fifteen.[3] But of these only five can be identified with the existing monuments. But pillars which find no mention in these records are now discovered, as for example, the Lauṛiyā-Ararāj pillar with no capital and the Lauṛiyā-Nandangaṛh pillar, its capital being bell shaped "with a circular abacus supporting the statue of a lion facing the north."[4] Even among the few identified with those mentioned by the Chinese travellers, there is some discrepancy. For instance, the pillar at Sārnāth measures in height just half of what has been attributed to it by Yuan Chwang.[5]

1. See for a full discussion of the subject author's paper in the *Journal of Oriental Research,* Madras, Vol. V, Pt. III, pp. 267-281.
2. Legge's trans., p. 80.
3. Watters I. 344 and 383, II 5, 6, 28 ch.
4. Ar. Rep. Vol. I, pp. 67-73.
5. See Ar. Sur. Rep. 1904-5, p. 69: Watters, II 50; Beal, *Buddhist Records,* Vol. II, p. 46.

Most of the monuments pre-Aśokan

It would appear further untenable to assume that Aśoka set up pillars at different places for inscribing his edicts. It would be more reasonable to hold that these monuments stood long before Aśoka, and served convenient material for the emperor to record his inscriptions so as to give an element of permanence to the record of his achievements. This is evident from his own words. He says that he enlarged to twice its size the stūpa of Konākamana.[1] In another place he says that he caused his records to be inscribed wherever pillars of stone existed in his empire.[2]

Aśoka's monuments

In brief, the following monuments are attributed to Aśoka by modern archæological research:—

(1) The stūpa at Sāñci.

(2) The stūpa at Bhārhut.

(3) The enlarging of the stūpa of Konākamana.

(4) Erecting three sets of caves in the Barābar Hills.

(5) Four uninscribed pillars—those at Rāmpūrva with bull capital, Saṅkisa with elephant capital, Bakhra (Vaiśāli) with lion capital, and Kośam (Kauśāmbi) with no capital.

(6) Other so-called Aśokan pillars containing his inscriptions are those discovered at Topra, Meerut, Allahabad, Lauṛiyā-Ararāj, Lauṛiyā-Nandangaṛh, Rāmpūrva, Sānchi, Sārnāth, Rummindeī, and Niglīva.

[1] Nigāli Sāgar Pillar, *Corpus*, p. 165.

[2] Minor R. Edict (Rūpnāth text) and Pillar Edict VII, *Corpus*, pp. 116-131.

Animal capitals

To a student of Aśoka's religion the animal capitals are far more important than the pillars themselves. Discussing this, V. A. Smith arrives at the following results:

9 examples of lion.
2 „ of elephant.
2 „ of bull.
1 „ of horse.
1 „ of wheel.
1 „ of Garuḍa.
1 „ of man.
2 „ of four lions back to back.

Of these the lion, the elephant, the bull and the horse are explained as the riding animals of the guardian deities of the four quarters. These are Vaiśravaṇa, or Kubera with the lion on the north; Dhṛtarāṣtra with the elephant on the east, Vīrūḍha with horse on the south and Virūpākṣa with the bull on the west.[1]

From these Mr. Smith formulates the theory of the universality of the church, 'the congregation from the four quarters, present and absent', adding that the number four has some mystic significance, and that the selection of the symbol was influenced in some cases by the origin of monks. There is nothing impossible in that some of these animals are the *vāhanas* of the guardians of the four quarters, or the *dikpālas* of Sanskrit literature.[2] There is no mystic significance about the number four, as more than four riding animals crown the various capitals of these pillars. In the light of the refer-

[1] *Z.D.M.G.*, Vol. LXV, pp. 221-240.
[2] *Śabdakalpadruma*, p. 709, and *Mānasāra*, Ch. LXII and LXIII.

ences occurring in the Vedic literature about these animals, it was argued that there is no foundation for the theory of the universality of the church as V. A. Smith would have it.[1] These pre-Aśokan pillars with animal capitals were pillars of victory, planted as memorials by the ancient kings of India of whom we have unfortunately no record, the images of the capital representing the emblem of their ensign, symbolical of the object of their worship.

Mr. R. P. Chanda points out that the Mauryan pillars were primarily intended for worship.[2] Perhaps the pillar cult is as old as the chalcolithic period in the Indus valley.[3] That the choice of the symbol was due to the influence exerted by the origin or nationality of the monks of an adjoining monastery, has no basis in fact. According to this assumption all the pillars in the north must possess the lion on their tops, in the east the elephant, in the south the horse, and in the west the bull. But the extant pillars do not conform to any such system. It is a historical fact that Aśoka did not erect most of them and hence was not responsible for the arrangement which we attribute to-day to him. It is therefore far from correct to say that these monuments were intended by the emperor to perpetuate the memory of the Buddha. An attempt has been made without much success to explain the symbols of the figure of a man on one of the monuments, of the Brāhmaṇi geese on the Lauṛiyā-Nandangaṛh pillar, and of the bell capital.[4]

[1] *Śabdakalpadruma,* pp. 276-7.

[2] *Memoirs of Ar. Sur. of India,* No. 34, pp. 31-33.

[3] *Ibid.*, No. 41, p. 35.

[4] See A. K. Coomaraswami's article on the *Origin of the Lotus (so-called Bell) capital in Ind. His. Q.*, Vol. VI, No. II.

To conclude, the fact that Aśoka enlarged the stūpa sacred to Konākamana whom orthodox Buddhism would style as heretic, and also the fact that three caves were erected in the Barābar Hills for the Ājīvikas, the rival sect of the Buddhists, are sufficient to tell the true tale, *viz.*, that the emperor had the same amount of sympathy which he had for Buddhism, for other sects as well, which were to all intents and purposes its rivals. It is quite obvious that the extant monuments eloquently voice forth the catholicity of his religious views, the most wonderful and the best relieving feature of the Hindu religion. It is not easy to believe that such ferocious animals as the lion and elephant symbolise the Buddha himself, the enlightened sage of Kapilavastu. Neither the monuments nor the animal symbolism can carry home the conviction and decide the religious leaning of this emperor to Buddhism.

Conclusion

These are some of the weighty arguments which tend to negative the position of Aśoka's personal faith in Buddhism. They are positive in establishing the indisputable fact that Aśoka was a follower of the *dharma* of his predecessors. In the face of the inscriptions of the period and the monuments of the age which throw great light on the question there is no use in depending merely on the Buddhist chronicles. An intelligent and impartial interpretation of the Edicts cannot but prove conclusively the fact that Aśoka "remained Hindu and Brahmanical till the end of his days."[1]

[1] H. Heras, *Q.J.M.S.*, Vol. 17, 276.

APPENDIX I

THE AUTHENTICITY OF THE KAUṬALĪYA

As the authenticity of the *Arthaśāstra* has been questioned by scholars of standing like Professors Keith[1] and Winternitz,[2] we propose to examine some of the arguments advanced by them in support of their theory with a view to demonstrate their inconclusiveness.

(1) Dr. Winternitz refers[3] to the verse in which Kauṭalya says that he had taken the kingdom from the Nandas and remarks that the real minister in a book written by the order of or intended for his king would not have written such words, for, it could not have been very pleasing to the king. The verse under reference is a piece of internal evidence which goes to confirm the traditional story in the Purāṇas of Kauṭalya's part in the revolution which resulted in the overthrow of the ruling Nanda dynasty of Magadha and the establishment of the Mauryan dynasty.

This verse is, therefore, valuable as it demonstrates beyond all doubt that the writer of the extant work of the *Arthaśāstra* is the same Kauṭalya who had contributed not a little to the overthrowing of the old dynasty and to the founding of the new dynasty. Without this verse which is indeed significant the work will not appeal

[1] *A History of Sanskrit Literature*, p. 458-f.

[2] *Some Problems of Indian Literature*, p. 82-ff. (Cal. Uni., 1925).

[3] *Ibid.*, p. 96.

yena śāstram ca śastram ca nandarāja gatā ca bhūḥ|
amarṣeṇoddhṛtānyāśu tena śāstramidam kṛtam||

to us as the accredited writing of the first Mauryan Chancellor. The objection that it is a thing not likely to have been pleasing to the king is no argument. Kauṭalya will not stand to lose by writing thus. There is a baseless version that Candragupta was not a Kṣatriya but of a mixed caste. Granting that he was a Kṣatriya, a true Kṣatriya monarch of ancient days would not unduly take on himself the credit which legitimately belonged to others. And if it were a fact that Kauṭalya took up arms openly against the reigning dynasty and helped the succeeding dynasty in securing the throne there is no reason for the king to feel displeased at such a statement.

Dr. Winternitz translates the verse as follows:—

"This text-book has been composed by him, who quickly and impatiently raised the *Arthaśāstra* (from former imperfect text-books) passed his sword and took the earth that had passed to the Nandas[1] (out of their hands)." We can have it translated thus: "This treatise was written by him by whom the Śāstras (not necessarily the Arthaśāstra), the science of weapons and the earth that had passed to the Nanda kings were soon and in jealous anger raised aloft." According to V. A. Smith the Nanda king who was deposed and slain by Candragupta was of low caste and a heretic hostile to the Brahmanas and the Kṣatriyas.[2] He further remarks that "the nine Nandas were considered to be unholy persons unworthy of inclusion in orthodox Hindu annals". Then it is clear that during the period of the Nandas that both the *śāstras* of the Brahmanical science and the *śastra* or the Kṣatriya science, were in a

1 *Op. cit.*, p. 96.

2 *Oxford Hist.*, p. 57.

neglected and decadent condition. This receives corroboration from the Aśokan Edicts where Aśoka expresses in certain places the neglect of certain institutions and the practice of some aspects of *dharma* by his predecessors. The elevation to the throne of an orthodox King like Candragupta led automatically to the elevation of both the *śāstra* and the *śastra.* Kauṭalya who could have played no mean part in bringing about this happy consummation, has expressed in this verse his contempt for the Nandas and his relief at the succession of Candragupta. As I have said elsewhere he compliments the king by complimenting himself. The verse is then a visible demonstration, by Kauṭalya, of his satisfaction at the new state of affairs of the kingdom with Candragupta at its head. And rightly Professor Jacobi reads into these lines "the proud self-consciousness of a great statesman of the Indian Bismarck"[1] as he calls Kauṭalya.

(2) There is another statement[2] as explicit as this which mentions that the work was mainly intended for his king (Narendra). Why he felt called upon to undertake this arduous task can be easily explained. Previous to the epoch of the Nandas and the Mauryas we have not definitely alighted upon any historical ground. If we are going to believe tradition once again, there were a number of short-lived dynasties coming and going, commencing with Parikṣit. In these centuries apparently a number of *Arthaśāstra* teachers and also schools sprang up in the land, and each teacher or fol-

[1] See *J.I.H.*, IV, Pt. II, pp. 111-12: Meyer, *Kau. Artha.* Einleitung, pp. 23-24. *Contra* E. H. Johnston: *Studies in the Arthaśāstra of Kauṭilya, J.R.A.S.*, Jan. 1929.

[2] Kauṭilyena Narendrārthe Śāsanasya Vidhihkṛtaḥ||

lower of a certain school was pushing forward his or its own theory of the state and administration. Kauṭalya mentions twelve writers on polity who were all his predecessors. He could not afford to neglect them. He often refers to their views either to refute, or to accept them. Kauṭalya's mission was, it would appear, to critically examine the floating theories on polity as befits the statesman at the helm of affairs of a great empire, and strike at some definite proposals conducive to the good government of the state, and yet in accordance with the traditions of the land.[1] The Narendra who was no other than Candragupta Maurya must have been pleased with the work, for something definite was presented to him to follow, and by following which he could have the supreme satisfaction of being able to administer the land on right lines.

(3) Another argument is that the contents of the *Arthaśāstra* do not justify the assumption that it is the work of a statesman but only of a Pandit.[2]

From the contents of the work it is unthinkable that the hand of the statesman is not present in it. Dr. Winternitz has taken pains to select one or two passages wherein Kauṭalya has loosely expressed his views, and on the strength of such slender basis, he dismisses the author as a mere Pandit.[3] No one can deny for a moment that there are some places where Kauṭalya is not definite or assertive. It is probable that in these particulars he was not quite convinced of the prevailing opinions; still expediency might have dictated such a

[1] *In. Ant.* (1918), p. 55.
[2] Jolly ed., Intro., p. 44.
[3] *Op. cit.*, p. 97.

policy under certain circumstances. In such places he could have subordinated his opinion to that of the others. Apart from this construction any other cannot be placed on the so-called weak points in the treatise. But at the same time it is pertinent to remark that there is much truth in the statement that it is the work of a Pandit. And who is a Pandit? He who is deeply versed in a science or sciences is a Pandit. If Kauṭalya had not established his reputation as a great author on administrative science, *viz.*, statecraft, no one would seriously think of his work or attach any value to it. The king would not have ordered a layman to write for him a manual on statecraft.

Further only the highly learned Pandits occupied superior positions in the government as ministers, councillors, judges, etc. If Kauṭalya had not been a Pandit he would have been unworthy to hold the Chancellorship of a new government which indeed involved serious responsibilities. The fact was that in ancient times the high class Pandits (the *śiṣṭas* and *viśiṣṭas* of the *Dharmaśāstra* literature) carried on the civil administration of the realm while the military administration was exercised by the Kṣatriya monarch. This does not mean that there was a cut and dried military or civil department which only this class or that class could monopolise. The departments were interdependent and by co-operation everything went on smoothly. Examples of Pandits who had been the soul of administration from both traditional and historical accounts are not wanting. There is the tradition of Vasiṣṭha, the Purohita of king Daśaratha. Here the king did not take the initiative in any affair without previous consultation with and advice of his Guru and friend Vasiṣṭha.

In mediaeval times we know of Vidyāraṇya, the minister of the Vijayanagar emperor, Bukka. He was also known as Madhvācārya, the worthy brother of the worthy Śāyana, the celebrated commentator of the Vedas. As there was another minister by name Mādhava we can appropriately call him Mādhava Vidyāraṇya.[1] This Vidyāraṇya was both a Pandit and statesman. The *Bṛhat-Katha* informs us that Kātyāyana, the famous jurist, was a minister of the Nanda kings. At a period so late as the 17th century we find a Pandit Govinda Dīkṣita as the minister of the Tanjore kings. These were Pandit-statesmen, or statesmen-pandits who have gloriously adorned many an enviable station in every Hindu state.

Under this category comes Kauṭalya. He was a Pandit of a rare order as also a keen statesman. If he were a mere Pandit he would not have cared for the opinions or the theories of his predecessors. He would give us a new work completely original wherein controversial theories would have been rigidly excluded. For example treatises on similar subjects like the *Śukranītisāra* or *Bārhaspatyaśāstra* do not at all discuss the opinions of their predecessors, much less contemporary views. Rarely do they mention even the names of such treatises. But by discussing other views with care and attention which they deserve, Kauṭalya shows himself more than a Pandit, and having been acquainted with the practical administration of the land we can call him a Pandit-statesman. If in a few places he

[1] S. K. Aiyengar, *Sources of Vijayanagar History*, pp. 2-3.

has shown himself a Pandit, in many places he shows himself a statesman.

There is no need to call attention to these special passages. But a reference may be made to a statement of Dr. Jolly himself who remarks that Kauṭalya must have been "an official in a state of medium size where he had obtained insight into the working of the administration."[1] This means that the German scholar is prepared to grant that Kauṭalya possessed an intimate or first hand knowledge as regards the different methods of working an administration. If it could be conceded that he was an official, it strengthens the position which we have taken that he was more than a mere Pandit. Tradition affirms that he was an official of much more importance, viz., the Chief Minister. No purpose is served by denying a fact, and the fact was that Kauṭalya was the Chancellor of Candragupta. E. H. Johnston remarks: "If it is wrong on the one hand to read into it (the *Arthaśāstra*) the ideas of a great statesman or a deep political thinker, on the other hand half its value is missed by treating it as the pedantic theorisings of a Pandit."[2] Later on[3] Johnston shows how Kauṭalya is profoundly practical in his prescriptions. Suffice it to say here that statesmen in ancient India were generally from the Pandit's class though particular instances of statesmen from other classes are not lacking.

(4) It is argued again that the discussions in the *Arthaśāstra* generally end by stating the author's

[1] *Op. cit.*, p. 47.

[2] *J.R.A.S.*, 1929, p. 89.

[3] *Ibid.*, p. 101.

opinion with the words: "Iti Kauṭalyaḥ . . . ."[4] We generally find this mention of the name of the teacher in texts emanating from schools, *e.g.*, Jaimini in the *Pūrvamīmāmsa Sūtra,* Bādarāyana in the *Vedānta Sūtra,* Baudhāyana in the *Baudhāyana-Dharmaśāstra.* But Patañjali does not state his opinion by saying "Iti Patañjali." Much is made of the expressions "Iti Kauṭalyaḥ" and "neti Kauṭalyaḥ" which occur as many as 72 times in the work. To an ordinary Sanskrit Pandit in India the phrase connotes no special significance. It is always taken for granted that such works, where expressions like "Iti Kauṭalyaḥ," "Iti Baudhāyanaḥ," etc. occur, are the works ascribed to these authors. The attribution to schools will not find favour with an orthodox Pandit. One could not divine reasons for supposing that Jaimini's *Pūrvamīmāmsa Sūtra,* Bādarāyana's *Vedānta Sūtra* or Baudhāyana's *Dharmasūtra* belong to schools and not to individual authors. Not that we do not accept any school as such. But it is more reasonable to assume that originally a certain Jaimini or Bādarāyana flourished and propounded certain doctrines which were accepted and followed by their devoted disciples. To-day while one Hindu follows Āpastamba his neighbour follows Baudhāyana. This means that the former belongs to the Āpastamba school while the latter is of the Baudhāyana school.

What is the underlying idea? Originally when Āpastamba propounded his theory it appealed to certain

[1] *J.R.A.S.*, 1916, p. 131-33. See Keith, *History of Sans. Literature,* p. 458; Hillebrandt, *Uber das Kauṭ. studien,* p. 10. Also Hillebrandt, *uber die Aufauge de indischen dramas,* p. 17 (Munchen, 1914), *contra* Jacobi, *Ind. Ant.,* 1918, p. 157-f.

members of the community. They followed them and then their descendants. Thus the school automatically came into being. But it may be asked, how could we explain the peculiar use of "Iti Kauṭalyaḥ," "Iti Baudhāyanaḥ" in certain works, and its absence in other books like Patañjali's *Mahābhāṣya?* The answer is simple. In India literature is broadly classified into two heads, the *sūtra* and the *bhāṣya.* The *sūtra* is an original work composed by master minds on a certain subject or subjects. It may be philosophy, theology, or any secular science. The *sūtras* (सूचनात्सूत्र) in themselves are a strenuous reading and especially so, when they deal with abstruse and technical sciences. It was not possible for all persons to grasp them. Hence interpreters came into being. Their works were *bhāṣyas* or interpretations of the *sūtras* in popular style. The *sūtrakāras* generally—there are also exceptions,—used the phrase "Iti Baudhāyanaḥ", etc., meaning thereby that that was their final conclusion. On the other hand a *bhāṣyakāra* could not speak with such definiteness. For, oftentimes, more than one interpretation may be placed upon a certain phrase or passage. It depends to a large extent on the ingenuity of the writer. Some interpretations might be ingenious but could not win general approval. Therefore, the *bhāṣyakāras* are justified in omitting their names.

In the light of this can we still maintain that *Iti Kauṭalyaḥ* is a serious argument against the authenticity of the work? We cannot follow Prof. Keith when he advances the argument that under the explanation of the term *apadeśa* in the last book of the *Arthaśāstra* is cited one of Kauṭalya's sentences from which the *prima facie* conclusion is that Kauṭalya is cited as an authority and not as the author.[1] The passage is as follows:—

> sukha grahaṇavijñeyam tatvārtha padaniścitam|
> Kauṭalyena kṛtam śāstram vimuktagranthavistaram||

This science has been composed by Kauṭalya, easily understandable, correct in the exposition of truth and in the use of words, and all free from errors. J. J. Meyer in his translation of the *Arthaśāstra* furnishes a convincing reply.[2] Based as it is on old works 'every sūtra having original opinion of the author necessarily became *apadeśa'*. It is a commonplace practice in India to give the author's name in his works.[3] Jacobi's observations are to the point: "The agreement obtaining between the words of Kauṭalya and the character of his work, and the personality that characterises them would be difficult to understand, if those were not the very words of the author. A later writer who wanted to palm off his own lucubration of that of his school on the name of the famous statesman, would surely have faltered somewhere. From this view-point the higher criticism must acknowledge the authenticity of the Kauṭalīya."[4]

(5) 'The very name Kauṭilya—never called Cāṇakya and only once Viṣṇugupta raises great doubts.' For, Kauṭilya means 'crookedness', 'falsehood', etc. It is unlikely that a minister should style himself 'Mr. Crooked' or 'Crookedness personified'.[5]

1 *History of Sanskrit Literature,* p. 459.
2 P. 665, *n.*
3 *Hindu Polity,* p. 211.
4 *Ind. Ant.,* 1918, p. 194.
5 Winternitz, *op. cit.,* pp. 98 and 99.

There has been a war of words about the name Kauṭalya. Some manuscripts contain the word Kauṭilya while others Kauṭalya. The *edito princeps* Shāma Shāstri and Jolly[1] used Kauṭilya, while the editor of the Trivandrum edition, Gaṇapati Śāstri used Kauṭalya. It is asked whether a minister would style himself Kauṭilya meaning "Mr. Crooked" or "Crookedness personified". Granting that it is Kauṭilya, such nicknames are not uncommon in ancient India. Mention may be made of a few; Vātavyādhi (the wind-diseased) is no other than Uddhava, a relative of Kṛṣṇa according to the Purāṇas. Piśuna (tale-bearer) is another name for the sage Nārada; this is also the name of the Brahman minister of king Duṣyanta according to Kālidāsa's *Śakuntalā*. Kaunapadanta (the teeth of the Rākṣasas) is identified with Indra, the God of Heaven. When one minister can style himself as Piśuna, why not another as Kauṭilya? What we wish to point out for the sake of argument is that after all there is nothing in the name. To advance such feeble arguments with regard to the name of the author, demonstrates their weakness in all nakedness.

There is, however, another reading Kauṭalya which may be adopted with advantage and which may silence all controversy so far as this particular topic goes. Not only is there the authority of the manuscripts for this but also there is inscriptional evidence besides lexicographical. Gaṇapati Śāstri says that the term Kauṭilya is certainly a misnomer. For, neither the term Kauṭilya nor its root Kuṭila as explained in the *Nighaṇ-*

[1] We hear to-day names like Stone, Fox, etc., in the western countries. Suppose there is a Lord Stone, or a Baron Fox referred to in literature, could a future generation ask a baron or noble style himself Stone and Fox?

ṭus as Gotrarṣi and crooked. On the other hand the word Kuṭala is mentioned by Keśavasvāmin in his *Nānārthārṇavasamkṣepa* as meaning both Gotrarṣi and an ornament.

"अथस्यात् कुटलो गोत्रकृत्यृषौ पुंसि नपू पुनः ।
विद्यादाभरणेऽथत्रिः कुटिलं कुञ्चिते भवेत् ।
तगरेतुक्ली तगरपादिकायां स्त्रियामिति ॥"

It is then obvious that the name is derived from the root Kuṭala. If it is granted that the patronymic is Kuṭala then we cannot grammatically derive Kauṭilya but only Kauṭalya.[1] Secondly, there is the testimony which bears to the fact that all the manuscripts of the text and the commentaries relating to the same invariably contain the expression Kauṭalya and not Kauṭilya. It is difficult to understand how Indian and European scholars have failed to notice this in handling

[1] In the *Gotrapravaranibandhakadamba* (Mysore Govt. Orient. Series, 1900, pp. 32 and 161) the term Kauṭalya occurs as a *gotra* name in two different places. The *pravaras* mentioned in the first reference are Bhārgava, Vītahavya and Savedasa, and the *pravaras* mentioned in the second reference are Gautama, Bhāradvāja and Aṅgirasa. Thus the *pravaras* for the two Kauṭalyas occurring in different places are different; and it is impossible to decide whether these two Kauṭalyas are one and the same person. If there is any force in the argument of the late Gaṇapati Śāstri and if from Kuṭala—not found mentioned in the Mysore publication and hence an insignificant *gotra*—the name Kauṭalya is to be traced, then we have to take that Viṣṇugupta must have been a *putrikā-putra* or *dvyāmuṣyāyana* for whom, two *gotras* are generally mentioned, one that of his mother's father and the other that of his own father (*Janaka-pita*). If this position were granted, both Kuṭala and Vatsa must be his *gotras*. This will explain the identification of Kauṭalya and Vātsyāyana by the well-known *nighaṇṭus* like the *Vaijayanti* and *Abhidhānacintāmani*. These writers did not invent anything. Neither did they confound the one with the other as Haraprasad Śāstri would have it. They simply put into writing what was traditionally current in their times. Literary tradition, being one fruitful source of information for the early epoch of Indian History, cannot be easily discarded. There is much to say for the identification of the author of the *Arthaśāstra* with that of the *Kāmasūtra*.

the manuscripts when editing and publishing them. Apparently some have noted it but have not utilised it. For example in page 3 of Volume II of Jolly's edition (*Punjab Sanskrit Series*) it is mentioned thus: Title B. M. generally read: कौटलीयम् for कौटिलीयम् and कौटल्य: for कौटिल्य:. Evidently Jolly discarded the correct reading Kauṭalya. It may be that in his opinion it was a wrong reading.[1]

That Kauṭalya is the correct reading is attested to by another literary evidence. In the *Jayamaṅgalā* commentary of the *Kāmandakanītisāra,* Śaṅkarārya the commentator remarks:

कौटल्य इति गोत्रनिबन्धना विष्णुगुप्तस्य संज्ञा।

It appears that Kauṭalya is the family name of Viṣṇugupta, the family name being derived from the patron saint or ṛṣi Kuṭala by the addition of derivative suffix 'yañ'.[2] Last but not the least is the invaluable inscriptional evidence supplied to us by D. B. Diskalkar. He writes: "I have found an inscription of V. S. 1291 (Vaiśākha Śudi 14 Guran) from the village Gaṇeṣar near Dholkā in Gujarat which in *l.* 9 clearly reads Kauṭalya. It records that Vastupāla, the famous Jain minister of the Vāghela king Viradhavala, who built a temple of Gaṇeśvara in V. S. 1291, was equal to Kauṭalya in statesmanship."[3] This inscription is valuable to us in more than one respect. Not only does it show that the name *Kauṭilya* is the misspelling of the name Kauṭalya but also it bears witness to the fact that Kauṭalya is acknowledged to be a statesman and not a

[1] J.I.H. IV, Pt. II, pp. 107-8, *Ar. śās.* (Trivandrum ed.) Vol. I, Intro.

[2] See V. Venkatarama Sharma, *A Note on the word Kauṭalya, I.H.Q.*,, I, pp. 569-70.

[3] *Ibid.*, p. 786.

mere Pandit. It silences two important arguments in regard to the name of the author and the authenticity of the work. But it may be asked why the name *Kauṭilya* also sticks on in some Indian literature. Only one explanation can be offered and that is due to the ingenuity with which Viśākhadatta invested his character Kauṭalya in his famous play *Mudrārākṣasa.* For the purpose of his play he perhaps drew from his imagination a name which, being a twisting of the original name, answered his purpose well. Dramatic literature always being a popular branch of literature the wrong name might have caught the fancy of the masses and might have eventually become a bye-word for 'crookedness' or 'crooked policy'.

Kauṭalya is known not by one or two names, but by a number of names. These are Vātsyāyana, Mallanāga, Kauṭalya, Cāṇakya, Dramila, Pakṣila, Svāmi, Viṣṇugupta, Aṅgula.[1] The *Vaijayantī* of Yādavaprakāśa (cir 1100 A.D.), a contemporary of Hemacandra, mentions Vārāṇaka and omits Cāṇakya.[2] The name Cāṇakya is unmistakably a patronymic, for, Hemacandra distinctly says: चणकात्मजः or son of Caṇaka. This falsifies the story contained in Viśākhadatta's *Mudrārākṣasa,* namely, that the Nanda king imprisoned Kauṭalya who consequently had to take gram (*caṇaka*) for his food, and hence the name Cāṇakya.

[1] *Abhidhānachintāmani* of Hemacandra, 12th century.

वात्स्यायने मल्लनागः कौटिल्यश्चणकात्मजः ।

द्रामिलः पक्षिलस्वामी विष्णुगुप्तोऽङ्गुलश्च सः ॥

[2] Bhūmikāṇḍa, *Brahmanadhyaya,* verse 159, ed. by Oppert, p. 96 (1893) Madras.

वात्स्यायनेस्तु कौटिल्यो विष्णुगुप्तो वराणकः ।

द्रामिलः पक्षिलस्वामी मल्लनागोऽङ्गुलोऽपि च ॥

This story is nothing but a product of the dramatist's imagination and is valuable so far as it shows the author's ingenuity.[1] The same value should be attached to the other interpretation of Viśākhadatta in regard to the name Kauṭilya:

कौटिल्यः कुटिलमतिः स एष येन क्रोधाग्नौ प्रसभमदाहि नन्दवंशः ॥

Because he had perverted and crooked views, people called him Kauṭilya though his name was really Kauṭalya. Even a Pandit of a lower order could not style himself 'Mr. Crooked,' speaking of himself *'iti Kauṭalya'* or *'ne iti Kauṭalya'* as many as 72 times in the text. To add to this is the fact that Kāmandaka speaks of him as **'वेधस्'** a term of great respect generally used when speaking of sages. Kāmandaka adds that he belonged to an eminent family renowned for culture, a past master of all the four Vedas, who, by force of intelligence and skill, deposed the powerful

[1] See *J.A.S.B.*, Vol. 52 (1838), R. L. Mitra's article especially p. 268. The reference that traces to a tradition from Baṭṭotpala's commentary to the *Bṛhat-jātaka* to the effect that Cāṇakya and Viṣṇugupta Kauṭalya were different persons, is not convincing. (*J.R.A.S.*, 1929, p. 88.)

वंशे विशालवंशानाम् ऋषीणामिव भूयसाम् ।
अप्रतिग्राहकाणां यो बभूव भुवि विश्रुतः ॥
जातवेदा इवार्चिष्मान् वेदान् वेदविदां वरः ।
योऽधीतवान् सुचतुरश्चतुरोऽप्येकवेदवत् ।
यस्याभिचारवज्रेण वज्रज्वलनतेजसः ॥
पपातमूलतः श्रीमान् सुपर्वा नन्दपर्वतः ।
एकाकी मन्त्रशक्त्या यः शक्त्या शक्तिधरोपमः ॥
आजह्रार नृचन्द्राय चन्द्रगुप्ताय मेदिनीम् ।
नीतिशास्त्रामृतं धीमान् अर्थशास्त्रमहोदधेः ॥
यमुद्दध्रे नमस्तस्मै विष्णुगुप्ताय वेधसे ।
दर्शनात्तस्य सुदृशो विद्यानां पारदृश्वनः ।
राजविद्याप्रियतया संक्षिप्तग्रन्थमर्थवत् I. 2:8.

Nanda king and crowned Candragupta, the moon among the people (नृचन्द्र), king. Kāmandaka does not stop there but concludes that section by saying that it was the same politician who was the author of the well-known *Arthaśāstra,* the very cream of political science.

It is significant to note that Kauṭalya's another name is Vātsyāyana. Vātsyāyana is the author of the extant *Kāmasūtra.*[1] There is another Vātsyāyana, the commentator of the *Nyāyasūtra* of Gautama. Both the Vātsyāyanas may be the same as Prof. Rangaswami Aiyangar seems to think.[2] But the really interesting feature is the identification of Kauṭalya with Vātsyāyana.[3] Kauṭalya's reputation for versatile genius and all-round knowledge should be acknowledged on all hands. His aim, even according to the *Arthaśāstra,* was not mere policing of the state which would amount to the safeguarding of the security of life and property. It extended beyond and looked to the common good and welfare of the citizens at large. These are indeed the primary functions even of the modern state in spite of all our vaunted constitutional progress. This narrow outlook on politics did not appeal to a versatile mind like that of Kauṭalya. He wanted the state to rest on an economic foundation. In other words Kauṭalya devoted more to analysing a man's aims in life and endeavouring how best to promote individual interests with those of the social group as a whole. His aim was the ultimate realisation by the people of the state of the four objects of human existence (*caturvarga*).

[1] See H. C. Chakladar, *Studies in the Jour. of Dept. of Letters,* (Cal.) IV, pp. 85-122; *Modern Review,* March, 1928, p. 274; *Journal of the Mythic Society,* Vol. VI, pp. 210-16; *Ind. Ant.,* 1915, p. 82.

[2] P. 90. *Aspects of Indian Polity.*

[3] Vātsyāyana is not a generic term but "is generally used as an individual personal name, a proper noun."—*J.A.S.B.,* Vol. LII, p. 267.

If this were his policy, it may not be far wrong to state that he could have been the author of a Dharmaśāstra, Arthaśāstra, Kamaśāstra, and Mokṣaśāstra as well. There is therefore some justification for the assumption that Kauṭalya was no other than Vātsyāyana, the author of the *Kāmasūtra*. The following coincidences endorse our statement:—

(1) The style followed and the method adopted in the *Kāmasūtra* are exactly the same as are met with in the extant *Arthaśāstra*. (2) The style is didactic, mid-way between that of the *sūtra* and the *bhāṣya*. (3) The sections end invariably with verses in the manner of the *Arthaśāstra*.[1] Vātsyāyana like Kauṭalya seems to have composed aphorisms (*sūtra*) and comments (*bhāṣya*). (4) Both authors claim to base their teachings on experience or usage.[2] (5) Of the previous writers quoted by Kauṭalya, Gotamukha and Cārāyana find mention in the *Kāmasūtra*. (6) Both refer to *Vaiśika*, apparently the work of Dattaka of Pāṭaliputra, written according to Jacobi, at the earliest in the second half of the 5th century B.C.[3] (7) The aim of both seems to be the realisation of the three objects of human pursuit, *dharma, artha* and *kāma*. (8) The *Kāmasūtra* ends with a secret chapter as in the *Arthaśāstra*.[4] (9) The morality of the *Kāmasūtra* is that of the *Arthaśāstra* "all is fair in love and war."[5] (10) As Kauṭalya often refers to an ācārya so also Vātsyāyana refers to an ācārya. (11) Both refer to a work of Parāśara as an authority.

[1] Keith, *Sans. Lit.*, p. 468; *In. Ant.*, p. 192.
[2] Prayoga, *Aspects*, p. 99.
[3] *Ind. Ant.*, 1918, p. 189.
[4] Keith: op. cit., p. 467.
[5] Keith, *Sans. Lit.*, p. 467.

As against these remarkable coincidences, the differences are only few and far between. One mentioned by Jacobi is Vātsyāyana's prescription of abstention from meat, and Kauṭalya's rules regulating the sale of meat.[1] Even here the *Arthaśāstra* is a practical manual of administration and hence must formulate regulations of a comprehensive character. It does not mean a recommendation or acceptance of the principle. The *Kāmasūtra* discusses the question from an entirely different aspect.

It is indeed difficult to explain why Kauṭalya has been known by so many names. One explanation is that due to his popularity as well as his rare skill and policy, different people endowed him with different titles. Mallanāga is another name. It means Indra's Elephant and this implies that he possessed the great energy and prowess of the Irāvada, the state elephant of the Lord of Heaven. This seems to fit in especially in view of the fact that Sakara, in the first Act of *Mṛcchakaṭikā,* who thinks too much of his valour, takes pride in comparing himself to Cāṇakya. It may be again that Malla is the name of a country[2] and perhaps Kauṭalya is a native of that Malla country. He was styled an elephant among the Mallas who were the people of the Malla country. If this interpretation be established Dramila may not mean a native of Dramila or Tamil country as is rendered by the *Vācaspatya* of Tāranātha. The view that Kauṭalya must have been a native of South India is gain-

1 *Ind. Ant.*, 1918, p. 189 (*note*).

2 Mallabhoom or the Malla country is identified with Bishnupur, modern Bankura being a portion of the ancient kingdom.

ing currency among the scholars.[1] J. J. Meyer, the latest writer on the subject, seems to favour this view[2] from the fact that Kauṭalya's *paṇa* was of silver and was equal to 16 *māṣa* as against 20 in the *Smṛtis.* But R. L. Mitra speaks of a poet known as Dramila. He also explains the term Pakṣilasvāmi thus: "As a student of Nyāya his memory was strong that he could remember for a fortnight (*pakṣa*) a thesis once told him and hence the name."[3] That this interpretation is not impossible is seen from the fact that it is said of a much later writer by name Pakṣadhara Miśra. His other name was Aṅgula as is seen from the *Nānārthārṇava Saṃkṣepa.*[4] Pakṣilasvāmi is a well-known name for the celebrated Vātsyāyana. R. L. Mitra suggests that the epithet shows that Kauṭalya became an ascetic-preceptor in the evening of his life. Or as the teacher of teachers he could have been regarded master by his successors who were authors of Nīti texts. For example, Kāmandaka calls him as his Ācārya. Daṇḍi calls him as Ācārya Viṣṇugupta.

To repeat the remark of Dr. Winternitz again "the very name Kauṭilya never called Cāṇakya and only once Viṣṇugupta raises great doubts."[5] There seems to be no necessity for a doubt for obvious reasons. It has been already shown that Kauṭilya with vowel 'i' in the middle is a misspelling and Kauṭalya with vowel 'a' is the right spelling. Viṣṇugupta is his own name perhaps given by

[1] Jolly, *Intro.*, pp. 43-44.
[2] Einleitung, p. liv.
[3] *J.B.A.S.*, 52 (1833), p. 268.
[4] *T.S.S.*, 29, p. 53.

अङ्गुलोऽस्त्री तिर्यगष्टयवमाने पुमांस्तु सः ।
पक्षिलस्वामिसंज्ञर्षावङ्गुष्ठेऽस्त्रत्थपादपे ॥

[5] See above, p. 310.

his parents. And the name, according to Mitra, "is a fair index to the religion which his father professed."[1] As a true Hindu he took a legitimate pride in his ancestry and styled himself after his far-famed ancestor Kuṭala ṛṣi. He could not be using different names of his in one and the same work. If it had been done it would give rise to grave doubts that different hands had been at the work. Probably to avoid such a mistake, towards the end of the book he made it clear that Kauṭalya of the extant book is the Viṣṇugupta of the family of Kuṭala. Excepting the name Viṣṇugupta, other names are the titles earned by him from the public and not taken by himself. It may, however, be asked that Cāṇakya is not a title and still he has not used it. It is the peculiar custom in India even in modern days to venerate the father and the teacher to the end of their lives. One mode of veneration is not to utter the name of either the father or even the teacher. It may amount to an insult if not to an offence. Kauṭalya was Cāṇakya because he was the son of his father Caṇaka. A man like Kauṭalya who had profound respect for orthodox tradition could not go against it. In the light of the above observation we are led to think that scholars will do justice to a name and a personality, the type of which is indeed rare in the history at least of the ancient world.

(6) The Purāṇas or other literature never mention a single word about his authorship or writings.[2] This is not entirely true. References to his authorship are so many that by themselves it will make a thesis. We shall therefore rest content with merely mentioning the

[1] *A.S.B.*, lii p. 268.
[2] Keith, *Sans. Lit.*, p. 459.

names of the literary works where unmistakable references are made to our celebrated writer on Polity.

(*i*) That *Kāmandaki*[1] already quoted attaches a high value to his work on *rājanīti* identifying him at the same time with the minister of Candragupta.[2]

(*ii*) The *Upādhyāyanirapekṣaṭīka* on the *Kāmandakinītisāra*[3] designates the *Arthaśāstra* as *Kauṭalyabhāṣya*[4]; and what is more remarkable, it calls the author of the *Kāmasūtra, asmadguru,* identifying thus Vātsyāyana with Kauṭalya.

(*iii*) The *Tantrākhyāyika,* the oldest recension of the *Pañcatantra* has the following in the opening page of the book[5]:—

मनवे वाचस्पतये शुक्राय पराशराय समुताय ।
चाणक्याय च महते नमोऽस्तु नृपशास्त्रकर्तृरयः ॥

(*iv*) The *Pañcatantra,* whose date is still a bone of contention, has significant references in more than one place to the work and the policy of Kauṭalya.

(a) ततो धर्मशास्त्राणि मन्वादीन्यर्थशास्त्राणि
चाणक्यादीनि कामशास्त्राणि वात्स्यायनादीनि

(b) कूटलेख्यैर्धनोत्सर्गैर्दूषयेच्छत्रुपक्षजम् ।
प्रधानपुरुषं यद्वद्विष्णुगुप्तेन राक्षसः ॥

Here the author shows how he follows the principles of diplomacy enunciated by the master-politician. This verse is again instructive in the sense that it refers

[1] Probably 3rd century A.D according to Jacobi, *Ind. Ant.* (1918), p. 159.

[2] I, 2-8; cp. V, 2-8.

[3] *Bibl. Ind., New Series,* No. 511, Fasc. V, pp. 136 and 138.

[4] *Ind. Ant.* (1918), p. 190.

[5] H.O.S., XIV, p. 1.

to Rākṣasa, a prominent character of the *Mudrārākṣasa.* Professor Tawney's[1] view that the *Mudrārākṣasa* is anterior to the *Pañcatantra* seems to be the correct hypothesis.

In the last book again the author of the *Pañcatantra* refers with approval to the unimpeachable policy of Cāṇakya. Says he:

(c) बुद्धेर्बुद्धिमतां लोके नास्य गम्यं हि कंचन ।
बुद्धया यतो हता नन्दाश्चाणाक्येनासिपाणयः ॥

A repeated mention of the acceptance of the Kauṭalīyan policy is seen from the statement

(d) सः औशनसबार्हस्पत्यचाणक्यमतवित्तदनुष्ठाता ।

(*v*) In the *Mudrārākṣasa* of Viśākhadatta (Act VII) Rākṣasa compliments Cāṇakya thus: —

आकारः सर्वशास्त्राणां रत्नानामिव सागरः ।

(*vi*) The *Jātakamāla* of Āryasūra, probably 4th century A.D. (for the work was translated into Chinese in A.D. 434) definitely refers to the *Arthaśāstra.*[2]

नीतिकौटिल्यप्रसङ्ग

(*vii*) The *Laṅkāvatārasūtra* probably 4th century A.D. of Āryasūra (this work was first translated into Chinese in A.D. 443, and again in A.D. 513, now with an appendix of 884 ślokas) mentions Kauṭalya as a ṛṣi.[3] On this, Johnston, according to whom the lower limit of the *Arthaśāstra* is not later than A.D. 250, is obliged to make the following observation: "Evidently therefore at the end of the fifth century

[1] *J.R.A.S.* (1908), p. 910.
[2] XXXI, 54; cp. IX, 55-64.
[3] See verse. 816.

A.D. Kauṭalya was placed on a level with the ancient ṛṣis in point of age and the work which earned him this position must be at least several centuries earlier than that date."[1] Certainly the period from the third to the fifth century cannot be counted as 'several centuries earlier'.

(*viii*) Daṇḍi regards Kauṭalya as the veritable master of the science of politics.[2]

अधीष्व तावद्दण्डनीतिम् । इयम् इदानीमाचार्यविष्णु-
गुप्तेन मौर्यार्थे षड्भिः श्लोकसहस्रैः संक्षिप्ता । सैवेय-
मधीत्य सम्यगनुष्ठीयमाना यथोक्तकार्यक्षमेति ॥

A reference to the introduction of Shāma Śāstri's translation of the *Arthaśāstra* (pp. x and xi, 2nd ed.) shows parallel passages from Daṇḍi.

(*ix*) Bāṇa, the reputed author of the *Harṣacarita* and of the more celebrated romance *Kādambari,* refers to Kauṭalya's work though he adversely criticises it. But what is to our point here is an authentic reference to his writings. Says Bāṇa:

किं वा तेषां सांप्रतम् । येषामतिनृशंसप्रायोपदेशनिर्घृणं कौटिल्यशास्त्रं प्रमाणं[3] ....

(*x*) Somadevasūri in his *Nītivākyāmṛta* quotes often the very words of Kauṭalya and makes an explicit reference to the incidents connected with the Cāṇakya story. He notes especially Kauṭalya's unquestioned help to Candragupta.

[1] *J.R.A.S.,* 1929, p. 87.

[2] *Daśakumāracarita,* Part II, ucc l. 8.

[3] See also *Kādambari,* Vol. I, p. 109 (ed. by Peterson).

(*xi*) There is again a reference to his work in the Jain *Nandi Sūtra* स्वमये अमग्वपुत्रे चाणक्के थूलबदेय though the Jain canonical writer treats his work as one among the false sciences.[1]

(*xii*) Mallinātha (14th century) in his commentary on the *Raghuvaṁśa*[2] of Kālidāsa quotes the *Kauṭalīya.*[3]

(*xiii*) Nārāyaṇa Paṇḍita refers to it in his commentary on Aruṇācala's gloss on the *Kumārasambhava* of Kālidāsa.[4]

(*xiv*) Medhātithi (8th century A.D.) an earlier commentator on *Mānavadharmaśāstra* makes a reference in his gloss on VII, 43, to Kauṭalya as the desirable type of teachers.[5]

(*xv*) Kṣīrasvāmin, an old commentator on *Amara Kośa* (about 11th century) in commenting on V, 21 (Canto 11) says[6]:

यत्कौटिल्यः—उपधाभिः शौचाशौचज्ञानम् अमात्यानाम्

(*xvi*) In his commentary on the sixty-four *kalas* of Vātsyāyana's *Kāmasūtra,* Yaśodhara attributes the device of one variety to Kauṭalya.[7]

(*xvii*) Dinakara Miśra (1385 A.D.) a commentator on Kālidāsa's *Raghuvaṁśa* quotes the *Kauṭalīya* in commenting on the verse 12 of Canto III.[8]

[1] N. C. Bandyopādhyaya, *Kauṭilya,* Part I, p. 3.

[2] IV, 35; VIII, 21 and XV, 29; XVII, 49, 55-6, 76 and 81; XVIII, 49.

[3] See also *Aspects of Polity,* p. 90.

[4] *Ibid.,* I.29; II.31.

[5] *Ibid.,* p. 96.

[6] *Ibid.,* p. 97.

[7] *Mysore Ar. Dpt. An. Rep.,* 1927, p. 20.

[8] See *Aspects of Polity,* p. 97.

(*xviii*) Caritravardhana, another commentator older than Dinakara and quoted by the latter. refers to Kauṭalya in his gloss on the *Raghuvaṁśa.*[1]

(*xix*) Jīmūtavāhana's *Vyavahāra-mayūka* (fourteenth century A.D.) has a quotation from the *Kauṭalīya* besides passages identical in substance.[2]

(*xx*) The *Śivatatvaratnākara* (17th century A.D.) refers to Bṛhaspati, Śukra, and Cāṇakya, as authorities on Political Science.

(7) Yet another argument is that the contents of the work itself deal with not only politics but a great many subjects under administration which require a knowledge of the specialists in architecture, in agriculture, in mining, in military organisation, etc. It is impossible that one man should have been a specialist in all the branches of knowledge. Against this it may be remarked at the outset that this is not impossible in India and especially in Ancient India where we know of the versatile knowledge possessed by many a Pandit in those days. They became sages and seers because of their knowledge in all branches of arts and sciences. The specialisation of education is a modern cry and the evils of such specialisation are patent enough. It makes the specialist devote all his time in his own subject oftentimes to the utter neglect of the other subjects. Specialisation may make one learned but not cultured. Ancient Indians took legitimate pride in their culture, nurtured it with great care and attention, and promoted its growth themselves being the custodians of that world-wide

[1] III, 13; IV, 21; XVII, 56.

[2] Published 1912, p. 174, p. 148, etc.

culture. For instance, Bhīṣma can speak with authority on any question submitted to him, whatever branch of science it might refer to. Vasiṣṭha the Purohita could assert with first-hand knowledge his opinion on any subject. Indeed the Purohita was Purohita because he was thoroughly versed in all branches of knowledge. For the conduct of sacrifices and rituals which belonged to his department he ought to have mastered the Saṁhitās; for propitiating rites and ceremonies he must have learnt the Atharva Veda; for fixing auspicious times, he had a full knowledge of the sciences of astronomy and astrology; for encouraging soldiers fighting in the field of battle, he taught himself the Dhanur Veda; to sit in judgment over the king's discussions and lead him in the right path, he was a veritable master of the *Dharmaśāstras* and the *Arthaśāstras*.

Thus it was common in ancient India that he was deemed a *śiṣṭa* or a cultured person who had at his finger's end knowledge of all branches. There is nothing wonderful about this fact. Again the authors of law-books, epics and the Purāṇas must have been specialists in all branches of knowledge, for, they had to handle directly or indirectly all different arts and sciences. As for Kauṭalya there is a tradition that he must have been the author of a Dharmaśāstra, an Arthaśāstra, a Kāmaśāstra and a Mokṣaśāstra. If Vātsyāyana is a synonym for Kauṭalya, and if Cāṇakya be established an authority in astrology according to *Bṛhat-Saṁhitā*, and again if the commentator of the *Nyāyasūtra* be the same as the author of the *Kāmasūtra*, is it not incorrect to say that one cannot have a specialised knowledge in everything? Parāśara is quoted as an authority on the *Arthaśāstra* by Kauṭalya and on the *Kāmaśāstra* by Vātsyāyana; while the extant works by Parāśara are a *Dharmaśāstra* and another on astrology. These, then, would tend to show "that the schools of the age did not confine themselves to certain subjects only to the exclusion of others but attempted to deal comprehensively with all or most of the sciences or subjects of interest in the period."[1]

(8) The other argument is that Candragupta possessed a great empire and that what the *Arthaśāstra* postulates is only a small state of medium size. This simply means that the political horizon of the *Kauṭalīyan* world was narrow and limited to a state of medium size, and that Kauṭalya had no imperial outlook. This is again far from the truth.[2] The description of the *maṇḍala* or Circle of States and the policy of the states towards one another have been to a large extent responsible for this theory. Jayaswal conclusively shows the hollowness of this theory. He writes: "The supposition is contradicted by fact. Kauṭalya says that the Imperial tract (Cakravarti-kṣetra)[3] lies between the Himālayas and the Ocean, ninety-two thousand *yojanas* in the straight line (as the crow flies). It is hardly possible to imagine a state without neighbours. A policy towards neighbours will have to be postulated by any statesman however large his empire may be. Then we know that there were a number of neighbours in the south who were reduced in the next reign, *i.e.*, Bindusāra. When Candragupta took the territories now called the N. W. Provinces from the Greeks it does not

[1] *Aspects of Ancient Indian Polity*, p. 90.

[2] See above, pp. 74 and 76.

[3] Bk. IX, ch. 1.

follow that he took the land without its rulers, republics generally, who were existing under the system of Alexander. The *Sanghavṛitta* lays down a policy towards the republics which it assumes to be under the king's sphere of influence, be they in (1) the Punjab, (2) Áfghanistan (Kamboja), (3) Western India, or (4) North Bīhar. There were therein parties in favour of the suzerain and parties against him. He was to sow the seed of dissension, patronise some, instal or depose one of the leaders.. Now we know that in no other than the early Maurya time, Afghanistan, the Punjab, Western India, and North Bīhar were at one and the same time under the sphere of one Indian king. The fact that Kauṭalya hardly tolerates sub-kings is one which is only compatible with the Mauryan times."[1] In addition to this it may be noted that in the fifteenth and the sixteenth chapters of the seventh *adhikaraṇa*, Kauṭalya lays down interstate, if not, international, relations which ought to exist between an emperor and his subjects or allied kings. A reading of these two chapters bears testimony to the prevailing imperial ideas which swayed the master-mind of Kauṭalya. He certainly enunciated an imperial policy as is seen from the laws prescribed on the treatment to be accorded to the conquered king by the conqueror.[2]

[1] *Hindu Polity*, Pt. I, p. 204.

[2] See Law, *Interstate Relations in Ancient India;* S. V. Visvanatha, *International Law in Ancient India.*

APPENDIX II

MEGASTHENES AND KAUṬALYA

An endeavour is made here to examine briefly the differences and the similarities between Megasthenes' *Fragments* and the *Kauṭalīya* and see how the differences so called are really minor and mostly imaginative. A comparison is instituted here as it falls within the scope of the present work. In this particular the plan followed is to a large extent that of Otto Stein in his *Megasthenes und Kauṭilya*[1] where he has exhaustively dealt with this question.

1. *Roads*

Among the public institutions examined by Stein are first the roads. According to Megasthenes,[2] "The length from west to east as far as Palibothra can be stated with greater certainty, for the royal road is measured by schoni, and is in length 10,000 stadia." The Greek expression in the *Indika* means the Indian *rāja mārga* or royal road. And it is argued that in the *Kauṭalīya* the road which goes from west to east is not the royal road but the high road which is a trade route (*vaṇik-patha*).[3] This is an *argumentum ex silentio,* and it may be that Kauṭalya was aware of it and he had no occasion to mention it.

[1] Wien. 1921.

[2] Fg. 4.

[3] *Megasthenes und Kauṭilya,* pp. 17 and 18. Cp. *Ar. Śās.,* Bk. 7, ch. 2.

2. *Milestones*

Secondly, the following are the remarks of Megasthenes on the milestones[1]: "They (Agoranomen) construct roads, and at every ten stadia set up a pillar to show the bye-roads and distances." In the opinion of Schwanbeck,[2] the *schoenus* which with Eratosthenes coincides with the Indian measurement of distance, *yojana,* is a measure of 40 stadia of four *krośas.* While we do not meet with the term *krośa* as an official measurement in the *Arthaśāstra,* the term is not unknown to Aśokan inscriptions. According to the seventh Pillar Edict of Aśoka at intervals of eight *kos* the roads were marked by trees and fountains of water.[3] Mile-stones might have been used or might not have been used. It may be as Stein suggests that Megasthenes has imported the Persian or Egyptian idea into India.[4] If this were established it would not detract the value of the *Arthaśāstra* which portrays a state of affairs actually obtaining in the land. It, on the other hand, tends to reduce the intrinsic value of Megasthenes' writings on India.[5]

3. *Measurement of land*

With regard to the measurement of land, Megasthenes has the following observation[6]:—"Some (Officials) superintend the rivers, (and) measure the land as is done in Egypt." It is argued that whereas the *Arthaśāstra* mentions measurements of landed pro-

[1] Fr. 34.3.
[2] P. 48, Cal. ed.
[3] Fleet, *J.R.A.S.*, 1906, p. 401 ff.
[4] *Op. cit.*, p. 21; Barnett, *Ind. Ant.*, p. 107; and Smith, *Early History*, p. 135.
[5] Cp. *Glories of Magadha*, p. 61.
[6] Fg. 34.

perty of the village perhaps for purposes of taxation, Megasthenes seems to refer to a general measurement of lands in vogue. Scholars like Law[1] and Mookerjee[2] have accepted the theory that the measurement of land was in practice in Ancient India. It is true that the measurement in the *Arthaśāstra* refers only to the village and its borders, and at the same time one cannot agree with Prof. Stein that Megasthenes refers to a general measurement of lands. That this is only a supposition of Dr. Stein, and that Megasthenes must have meant only the village measurement is evident from Strabo whom the learned scholar himself has quoted. "Strabo speaks about the land measurement of Egypt in order to fix the limits of the property which were damaged by the floods of the Nile."[3] Fixing the borders of the property must necessarily refer to the landed property of every village and not to a general land measurement though Strabo has not mentioned the particular expression 'village'. One of the functions of officials like the Gopa and the Sthānika in the *Kauṭalīya* is the survey and the measurement of lands.[4]

4. *Irrigation canals*

Speaking on irrigation, Megasthenes observes[5] that the officials supervise waterways (McCrindle, sluices) which can be closed, and out of which water is let out slowly so that all may have access to it. Prof. Stein would not accept the rendering by McCrindle[6] of the

[1] *Studies in Ancient Hindu Polity*, p. 112.

[2] *Ibid.*, Int., p. 36.

[3] Stein, p. 22.

[4] See Mookerjee, Int., p. 36.

[5] Fg. 34.

[6] *Meg. und Kauṭilya*, pp. 22-27. See also Barnett, *Antiquities of India*, p. 107.

Greek expression in the *Indika* as sluices. He interprets it as any waterway that could be shut up. We can accept Stein's interpretation as it well fits in with the use of the term in the *Arthaśāstra,—Setubandha.*[1] The term is also used in another sense, *viz.,* connection by iron railings. With this we are not concerned now. *Setubandha* is a construction of a dam or bridge to shut out or let in water. This is the generally accepted interpretation and no purpose is served by twisting it and interpreting it in other ways. It has been accepted on all hands that one of the means of India's irrigation was by means of canals and channels and this finds an unmistakable expression in the extant *Arthaśāstra.*[2]

5. *Two harvest seasons*

Dr. Stein next examines the mention of the two crops in the course of the year by Megasthenes who speaks also of the fertility of the soil and a double rainfall, one in the winter season and the other in summer.[3] Wheat, rice, *bospore,* sesamum and millet are mentioned. Megasthenes who had heard of the agricultural industry from report—because there is no statement that he went into the country-parts outside the Capital —could not furnish more details than these. Kauṭalya mentions the crops of the rainy season and crops which could be raised in other seasons also. The fertility of the soil and the raising of two crops, summer and winter, can be easily proved from the *Arthaśāstra* and especially the chapter entitled *sītādhyakṣa.*[4]

1 Bk. II, ch. 1; Bk. VII, ch. 14.

2 Bk. II, ch. 24.

3 Fg. I and II.

4 Bk. II, ch. 24; cp. *Meg. und Kauṭ,* pp. 27-28.

6. *Fortress at Pāṭaliputra*

On the fortification of Pāṭaliputra says Otto Stein:—"The fragments of Megasthenes refer to Pāṭaliputra and its fortification. In the *Arthaśāstra* however there is no mention of Pāṭaliputra."[1] Megasthenes also speaks of several cities situated on the banks of rivers or on the sea-coast built of wood instead of brick and of cities on other commanding situations built of brick and mud.[2] Strabo on the other hand mentions wooden buildings all round, which is not a fact. Rhys Davids[3] speaks of fortifications in India built of stone walls in the 6th century B.C. Kauṭalya refers unmistakably to walls of stone. Therefore Strabo could not be credited with full knowledge of facts about India. There were certainly wooden portions in the buildings. This is true even of houses built to-day. N. N. Law has shown that houses of wood were indeed common in the fourth century B.C. side by side with stone.

An attempt has been made by Stein to compare the description of Pāṭaliputra with that found in the *Kauṭalīya*.[4] It may be that Kauṭalya describes the fortress, its construction and plan from actual conditions, and not as mere theory. On that account it does not stand to reason that Kauṭalya has purely drawn his materials for the construction of a fortress from Pāṭaliputra. It may be that Pāṭaliputra served him as the basis for constructing his theory of a fortress. But we cannot expect Kauṭalya who writes a general treatise

[1] P. 28.
[2] Fg. 26.
[3] *Buddhist India*, p. 96.
[4] *Meg. und Kauṭ.*, p. 30 ff.

on statecraft to follow the details and measurements of Pāṭaliputra. Though the *Arthaśāstra* was for the time being intended for Candragupta, it was a textbook on Polity for all time, and for all kings, and for all places. Therefore Kauṭalya could not have prescribed only one standard,—the model of the fortress at Pāṭaliputra. On the other hand he mentions different kinds of fortresses such as *nadīdurga, vanadurga* with respective measurements in details. Some may have four gates and some twelve gates. Some may have one trench around and others three trenches. It all depends on the environs and eminence where such fortress is erected. For the construction of a fortress is purely dependent on topographical and geographical circumstances. By sheer accident, some measurements or details of Megasthenes may coincide with the *Kauṭalīyan* description, as for example, Pāṭaliputra in the form of a square, the wall of Arrian to the *prākāra* of the *Kauṭalīya,* etc. On this account we cannot proceed to compare the two because Kauṭalya is certainly not describing the fort at Pāṭaliputra but is describing how and in what manner a fort could be erected at such and such a place.

Connected with this is the theory that as Kauṭalya does not mention Pāṭaliputra he could not have been the Minister of Candragupta. It is very probable that there was no occasion for Kauṭalya to mention his Capital city by this name. It may be repeated again that Kauṭalya's mission was not to sketch Candragupta's administration, though Candragupta seems to have based his administration on the model suggested. His purpose was to write a scientific treatise on administration which his King Candragupta and his successors as well might use with profit and advantage to themselves. In such a treatise there would certainly be no occasion for mentioning the city of Pāṭali, and the mere omission of this fact cannot be seriously advanced as an argument for or against establishing the authenticity of the work.

7. *Houses and property*

Megasthenes says[1] that the houses and property of Indians were left generally unguarded. This observation is the outcome of the idealistic tendency of Megasthenes to establish the honesty of Indians. This does not mean that there was no theft of any kind or robbers of any sort. Human nature being what it is, it is impossible to think of a state of affairs at any time and in any clime, where robbery was totally absent and where transparent honesty prevailed. What Megasthenes evidently means is that the administration of the land was under such powerful hands that none dared to commit crime of any sort. Nothing more can be deduced from this statement.

8. *On Elephants*

Dr. Stein has examined at length the passages of the *Kauṭalīya*[2] on elephants with the relevant statements of the *Indika* under different headings: (*a*) places where they are caught, (*b*) their height, (*c*) age, (*d*) hunting, (*e*) stalls, (*f*) size, (*g*) feeding, (*h*) training, (*i*) diseases and their remedy. It is gratifying to note that under almost all these items he finds more

[1] Fg. 27; Stein, p. 41; cp. Bk. III, ch. 8.
[2] *Op. cit.*, p. 47-ff.

points of resemblance between the Greek account and the *Arthaśāstra*. The minor differences under this section are with regard to age. According to Kauṭalya elephants which are 40 years old are the largest, those of 30 medium size, and those of 5 and 20 of the lowest class.[1] But the Greek accounts refer to elephants aged 200 and 300 years. Commonsense tells us that this portion of the account must be an exaggeration, perhaps to glorify the importance of those animals for the state in respect of war, traffic, etc. It is unfortunate that such incorrect statements have found a place in their documents. In regard to particulars about hunting, it is only a question of details which do not legitimately belong to the province of a work on polity.

9. *On Horses*

The fragments available do not furnish details in respect of the training, feeding, and housing of horses. Dr. Stein remarks: "What Megasthenes has given is hardly worth comparing, nor very much has he left to speak with definiteness." The statement that no bridles were used for horses is contradicted by himself. In Fg. 35 it is said that "the professional trainers break them in by forcing them to gallop round and round in a ring"—a kind of training that is mentioned with certain modifications by Kauṭalya.[2] In this connection it may be pointed out that the statement of Megasthenes that the elephants and horses were the monopoly of the king and that no private person had the right to enjoy them has been contradicted by other Greek writers. Strabo and Arrian definitely state that these animals were as much private

[1] Arrian, Fg. XVII.

[2] *Meg. und Kauṭ.*, pp. 58-60.

property as that of the state.[1] The *Kauṭalīya* on the other hand nowhere commits itself to a statement that these animals were the sole property of the king. A perusal of the several connected chapters shows that these animals were used also as private property though preference was certainly given to the king who required their frequent use especially for purposes of war. Thus under these heads there is little or nothing worth comparison and the points of coincidences outweigh those of differences.[2]

10. *On metals and mines*

Prof. Stein agrees with Jolly when he says that Megasthenes mentions only silver, gold, bronze, iron, and tin, whilst the list of Kauṭalya includes more metals like copper, lead, *vaikarantaka,* mercury, and brass, and shows that that period must have been an infant stage of knowledge with regard to metals whilst that of the *Kauṭalīya* shows a highly developed knowledge in both chemical and technical sciences. Stein concludes thus[4]:—"The enumeration of these metals with details as to shape, colour, and quality, ability to work upon the metals, and finally, the many kinds of officials for almost every branch of the mining industry, overseers and inspectors of mines, of useful metals (lohādhyakṣa), of coinage, of salt, of gold, of goldsmith, and legal regulations with regard to private management,—all these demonstrate that in this field there is a higher culture than in the Greek reports commencing with Megasthenes. Undoubtedly here we

1. Arrian, Fg. XVII.
2. *Meg. und. Kauṭ.*, pp. 58-60.
3. *Op. cit.*, p. 61.
4. Pp. 63-64.

find a more recent epoch." The above conclusions are untenable for the following reasons:—

(*a*) The report of Megasthenes does not simply mention only these five metals and does not say that India knows only of these and no other. We shall quote Megasthenes[1]: "And while the soil bears on its surface all kinds of fruits which are known to cultivation, it has also under ground numerous veins of all sorts of metals, for it contains much gold and silver, and copper and iron in no small quantity, and even tin and other metals are employed in making articles of use and ornament, as will be the implements and accoutrements of war."[2] Thus Megasthenes mentions by name five metals but is careful to speak also of "other metals." It is a significant phrase. It shows that other metals and their use were well known. Apparently he did not seem called upon to give a complete list of metals known. In fact they were so many that he used the term "other metals" advisedly.

(*b*) It is also evident from the above passage that these metals were put to different uses, jewellery, arms of war, etc. This means that there were different flourishing industries and the work was done by skilled labourers. It seems that these industries were under the supervision of the state and its officials. Nevertheless private enterprise was not discouraged. Private people could take to these manufactures after obtaining the necessary licence. Even mines were exploited by private people with licences previously

[1] Fg. 1.

[2] Cf. Jolly, *Intro.*, p. 35; Keith, *Sanskrit Lit.*, p. 460.

obtained. To turn the metals into articles of utility requires naturally a sound knowledge of melting, smelting, moulding, and other chemical and technical processes.

(*c*) Metallurgy and alchemy are not recent growths in India as the learned German scholar would have it. It has been already shown[1] that there were ancient works on metallurgy and alchemy as is evidenced by the *Kauṭalīya* itself. It is a wrong reading of Indian history, to repeat what has been already said, that Indian culture began with or after Alexandar's invasion to India. The *Buddhist Jātakas,*[2] the *Rāmāyana,*[3] and other ancient works, composed before Alexander invaded India, knew of different arts and crafts connected with metals.[4]

(*d*) To say that Megasthenes' account betrays an infant stage of India's technical sciences is a contradiction in terms. His mention of other metals as well as their different uses show as much an advanced stage as that portrayed in the *Arthaśāstra.* We are not able to find any difference between the two versions except the fact that Megasthenes does not mention much by way of workmanship in metals. If we rely on literary tradition, advancement of metal culture has reached a great stage before Kauṭalya's time. It continued to keep its level and maintain its prestige with greater glory and success

[1] See above, pp. 16-17.

[2] G. Bühler: *Indische Palaeographie,* p. 17; Fick's *Social Organisation,* translated by S. K. Maitra, (1920) *Intro.,* pp. ix-x.

[3] According to Prof. Jacobi, *Das Rāmāyana, Geschichte und inhalt,* (Bonn, 1893), the date suggested is before 500 B.C. Prof. Keith suggests the fourth century B.C. (*J.R.A.S.,* 1915, pp. 38 ff).

[4] J. J. Meyer, *Intro.,* pp. 45-47.

under the Mauryas, because the Mauryas gave the country tranquillity and peace which are so essential for the progress of any business or industry. It may be however surmised that it had become decadent under the Nandas and revived under the Mauryas with greater vigour and fresh enthusiasm. Whatever may be the truth, the fact remains that there is no warrant to call the statement in Megasthenes' records as infantine and that in the *Arthaśāstra* as progressive culture. It is something like the proverb "Give the dog a bad name and hang it".[1]

11. *Institution of Marriage*

Discussion then centres around the forms and the institution of marriage.[2] Megasthenes says[3]: "They marry many wives, whom they buy from their parents, giving in exchange a yoke of oxen. Some they marry hoping to find in them willing helpmates; and others for pleasure and to fill their houses with children." The system of polygamy and the longing for children which are referred to by Megasthenes are in conformity with the prescriptions of the *Dharmaśāstras* and the *Arthaśāstra*. Kauṭalya says[4] the giving in marriage of a girl for two cows is called the *Ārṣa* form of marriage, and this is what Megasthenes means by giving in exchange a yoke of oxen. The motives for marriage, such as securing helpmates, etc., is, in other words, an incorrect report of what he had heard about the eight accepted forms of marriage, of which four were popular. While

[1] J. J. Meyer, *Intro.*, p. 29.

[2] Stein, p. 64.

[3] Fg. 27.

[4] Bk. III, ch. 2. See Mookerjee, *Intro.*, p. xl.

the *prājāpatya,* and the *daiva,* aim at the higher ideal of the woman being the helpmate and life-partner in weal and woe, the *gāndharva* aims merely at the enjoyment of pleasure. As regards the longing for many children it is a fundamental principle of the ancient Hindus that the real aim of marriage is to secure offspring. With their belief of life after death, and the existence of awards and punishments in the other world as a consequence of actions in this world, they developed the idea of feeding the departed ancestors (*śrāddha*) and thus invoking their blessings and goodwill. It is only the son who could perform various religious ceremonials due to his ancestors without any grudge, and the idea was further developed that a man who had no issues would suffer eternal hell in spite of all his other good actions and pure conduct. The idea was that a sonless person must at least adopt a son who would be able to propitiate his spirit. Thus the religious element entered into the social institution and marriage became a sacrament on that account. Hence giving birth to a son came to be considered a sacred duty to the family and to the departed manes and ultimately to God. So Megasthenes must have been told of this complex principle, at once religious and biological, and he was not able to distinguish the significance attached to sons in the Hindu family.

It is amusing to find the remark of Megasthenes who says "since they have no slaves they have more need to have children around them to attend to their wants."[1] This is only an assumption of the Greek visitor but not a fact. It is not correct to state that there were no slaves in those days. Megasthenes

[1] Fg. I.

had apparently confused slaves and servants. He has taken servants to be slaves attributing the ideas of his own country. Every family could not afford to have servants, and absence of servants in certain families must have obviously driven Megasthenes to this conclusion, or his statement in this respect is incorrect as many others are. But what is more important is that we find coincidences between the two versions as regards the institution of marriage.[1]

12. *On writing*

Passing on to the question and practice of writing, Stein quotes Megasthenes who is of opinion that "there were no written laws in ancient India and that the people were ignorant of writing and that they trusted to memory in all the business of life."[2] These statements are again a distorted version of actual conditions obtaining in the land. Megasthenes must have been evidently told that the laws of the land were contained in the *smṛtis,* and the *smṛtis* were remembrances in the form of codes of Vedic injunctions which every judge was expected practically to carry in his head. The judicial officers were so well posted with the laws and customs of the land that they decided cases without reference to the codes of law and this fact must have induced Megasthenes to draw the conclusion that they had no written laws, and to make a further inference that they were ignorant of writing. Evidently Megasthenes did not care to enquire deeply into things he saw and heard. He had gathered a few facts at haphazard and he perhaps thought it worth his while to put them in black and white along with his own

[1] *Meg. und. Kauṭ.*, pp. 64-69.
[2] Fg. 27.

impressions. Most of them have unfortunately remained as impressions and have not carried us much farther. Thus far and no further is the impression which the *Indika* makes on us at present.

We had occasion to refer to the question of writing in India and tried to show how writing had been in existence centuries before Megasthenes came as the ambassador to the Indian Court. Prof. Stein, who has examined all the available Greek records, shows on the authority of Nearchos the existence of the custom of writing in B.C. fourth century.[1] And this fits in well with the *Kauṭalīya* which speaks of different kinds of written documents (*patra, śāsana*), art of writing (speech, style, and logic), as well as defects of writing, and the materials of writing.[2] In fact the whole chapter 10 is full of interesting materials as regards writing and its technique. The term *tāla* occurs in various places in different connections. In the chapter on royal writs the phrase *kālapatra* occurs. If we may venture a conjecture it may be *tālapatra,* and *k* for *t* could have been plausibly the mistake of the copyist. If we are to take it as *kāla,* then the word *patra* must evidently refer to *tālapatra* (palmyra leaves) as can be gathered from contemporary and earlier records.

Bühler speaks of leaves of *tāḍa-tāla* and *tāḍi-tāla* as writing materials of the Buddhists.[3] H. P. Śāstri also speaks of two kinds, narrow and broad, called *tala* and *teḍet.*[4] Megasthenes[5]

[1] *Meg. und. Kauṭ.,* p. 70.
[2] Bk. II, ch. 10.
[3] *Palaeography,* p. 89.
[4] *Mag. Lit.,* p. 63.
[5] Fg. 50.

and Arrian[1] refer to *tāla,* and even to-day in spite of the growing popularity of paper, orthodox pandits prefer to write in the palmyra leaves especially the writing of horoscopes. Tradition is so strong in India that even now when our boys are sent to school on the first day they are sent with a palmyra leaf with alphabets inscribed thereon. It therefore stands to reason that palmyra leaves were used as writing materials from earliest times known to literary history. If Megasthenes was not fully posted with the correct information at least we have the evidence of other Greek writers such as that of Nearchos, which falsifies the theory of Megasthenes and bears testimony to the statement of the *Kauṭalīya.*[2] These well-authenticated documents give the lie direct to the statement of Max Müller that the art of writing did not exist in India before the 4th century B.C.[3] Haraprasad Śāstri has drawn attention to an important data which may be adduced as a serious argument for the ancient character of the *Gṛhyasūtras.* In the list of the *saṃskāras* of the *Gṛhyasūtras* of old, the first initiation into the mystery of learning is not mentioned as a sacrament, while the *Arthaśāstra* mentions it definitely. Therefore some time after the composition of the *Gṛhyasūtras* and much earlier than the *Arthaśāstra* the art of writing must have been evolved. A pre-Buddhist work like the *Vāsiṣṭha Dharmasūtra* refers to written documents (*lekhya*). This art had advanced so much that bad writing was discouraged.[4]

1 VIII, 3.

2 Cf. Jolly, *Intro.*, p. 35. Keith, *Sans. Lit.*, p. 460.

3 *History of Sanskrit Literature.*

4 *Magadhan Literature,* pp. 61-62.

Let us take again other subjects and institutions which have been examined by Dr. Stein. Under the general heading,—the King, he discusses massage, bodyguard, daily work, justice, sacrifices, hunting, drink, income, army, kingly surroundings, name, and dynasty.[1] We shall now proceed to see how far both the *Arthaśāstra* and the *Indika* concur or demur in these respects.

(*a*) The massage of the body of the king seems to have been a familiar custom with the ancient kings. Arthaśāstras like the *Kauṭalīya* and the Purāṇas like the *Agni Purāṇa* mention this, among the daily routine of the Indian king. This fact is also recorded by Megasthenes. It is the duty of the *Samvāhaka*.[2] But Megasthenes has added that the king was being massaged when the court was in session. Either it was a fact or a simple case of imagination of the Greek writer. What is of importance to us is that both agree in the main particulars. Even women were engaged for this purpose as is referred to by both the authorities.[3]

(*b*) The *Arthaśāstra* speaks of a bodyguard of soldiers protecting the king. The statement that women armed with bows and arrows guarded the king in the palace is in correspondence with the *Kauṭalīya*.[4] Evidently Megasthenes refers to these details when he simply mentions that just in front of the palace the bodyguard and a portion of the army were quartered.[5]

[1] *Meg. und. Kauṭ.*, ch. V.

[2] Bk. I, ch. 21.

[3] See Fg. 27; *Ar. Śās.*, I, 12; I, 20; *Agni*, ch. 280; *Meg. und. Kauṭ.*, pp. 73-4.

[4] Bk. I, ch. 1.

[5] Fg. 27; Bk. I, ch. 20.

(*c*) With regard to the administration of justice, both the authorities do not mention the king as the administrator of justice. Both mention, however, judicial officers. But according to Megasthenes the king is present almost the whole day in the court.[1] This evidently refers to the engagement of the king in the court to decide cases of appeal.[2] This interpretation alone would be consistent with the statement of Megasthenes which definitely mentions a body of judges to administer justice and deliver judgment.[3] Curtius is perhaps right when he says[4] that the king's citadel was ever open to those who approached it. It could not be entirely an exaggerated statement, for the same is mentioned about Aśoka. It was expected of every righteous monarch to render justice without delay. Prof. Stein however contends that Curtius speaks of kings in general and not Candragupta in particular.[5] Whatever this may be there seems to have been a practice in Ancient India that the king was always accessible to the people. The *Arthaśāstra* prescribes thus: "When in the court he shall never cause his petitioners to wait at the door, for, when a king makes himself inaccessible to his people and entrusts his work to his immediate officers he may be sure to engender confusion in business and to cause thereby public disaffection, and make himself a prey to his enemies. He shall, therefore, personally attend to the business of gods and heretics, of Brahmans learned in

[1] Fg. 27.

[2] Bk. I, ch. 19.

[3] Fg. 32 and 33.

[4] VIII, 9.

[5] P. 81.

the Vedas, of cattle, of sacred places, of minors, of the aged, the afflicted and the helpless and of women. All this is in order (of enumeration) or according to the urgency or pressure of representations. All urgent calls he shall hear at once, but never put off; for when postponed they will prove too hard or impossible to accomplish."[1]

(*d*) According to Megasthenes the king goes out during sacrificial sessions.[2] Commenting on this passage Lassen is right when he maintains that this does not refer to the daily sacrifices but only to special sacrifices.[3] This is corroborated by the *Kauṭalīya*.[4] Here it is said that the king goes out of the palace on certain occasions—festivals, fairs, processions, or sacrificial sessions. The fact that Megasthenes has mentioned only the occasion of sacrifices shows that he must have personally witnessed the king attending an *yajña* outside the palace. Otto Stein thinks[5] that it refers to the daily sacrifices and contends that Megasthenes' statement is not provable. Megasthenes does not say expressly that the king goes out daily, and even if he has so expressed he must be in the wrong, for Vedic sacrifices could not be done in all the seasons of the year. Certain periods of the year are prohibited as inauspicious for the performance of sacrifices. Hence the learned scholar's view cannot be accepted in the light of the passage in the *Arthaśāstra*.

(*e*) The *Indika* reports that whenever the king set out for hunting, the roads were always blocked by

[1] Shāma Śāstri Trans., p. 40; Bk. I, ch. 19.
[2] Fg. 27 and 33.
[3] *Ind. Alt.*, II, p. 270.
[4] Bk. I, ch. 20.
[5] P. 83.

ropes and when the king was leaving the city, portions of streets reserved for the king were cleared of dangers and dangerous persons. He was also accompanied by women.[1] The phrase of Megasthenes "portions of streets reserved for the king" evidently means *rāja-mārga* or the royal road of Kauṭalya, the main street or streets of the capital city. Kauṭalya says that whenever the king went out of the city or came into it, the royal road was to be guarded on both sides by staff-bearers and was to be clear from armed persons, ascetics and the crippled. It is said that he was further policed by the representatives of the ten tribes.[2] The hunting forests were free from highway robbers, snakes, and enemies. In the chapter entitled *ātmarakṣitakam,* mention is made of the armed women appointed for the personal safety of the king.[3]

(*f*) Megasthenes reports that the Indians are not addicted to drinking.[4] Evidently Megasthenes moved with those members of the community who were bound by the law of the land to forsake alcoholic drinks and wine. This we see from the *Arthaśāstra* where there is a prohibition for the Brahmans. From the same work there is evidence to demonstrate that the other classes were not prohibited from taking these drinks, though some restrictions were placed on their use. Thus Megasthenes in this particular cannot be said to be correct.[5]

(*g*) Megasthenes speaks of the state ownership of land. In other words, the king was the owner of all

1 Fg. 27.
2 Bk. I, ch. 20.
3 Bk. I, ch. 21.
4 Fg. 27.
5 See, for more details, the chapter on *Sūrādhyakṣa,* Bk. II, 25.

the lands as well as the soil of the state.[1] This is to deny the existence of private property as an institution. That there was the king's property as distinguished from private holdings no one can deny. Kauṭalya deals largely with crown lands and their regulations. Kauṭalya also mentions private holdings which are apparently communal as can be gathered from the prescriptions. In all disputes about boundary marks and fields and gardens it is the elders of the village or even neighbourhood who decided them. The state could only appropriate holdings which have ceased to be enjoyed by any person.[2] This means that unclaimed property became state property.[3] In this connection attention may be drawn to the monograph of Bernhard Breloer, entitled *Kauṭalīya Studien I, Das Grundeigentum in Indien,* where he makes a comparative study of modern land revenue systems with those which obtained in the Maurya times as is evidenced by the Greek accounts and the *Arthaśāstra*.[4] Megasthenes says: "Besides the land tribute, they pay into the royal treasury a fourth part of the produce of the soil."[5] But Kauṭalya says that one-sixth of natural produce was to be paid to the king.[6] Other rates were one-third or one-fourth. This means that land revenue varied from one-sixth to one-third according to the seasons. Megasthenes was apparently not able to distinguish between rent and tax. It is possible that he was not aware of the legal conditions prevailing in the land. If what Megas-

[1] Fg. 1 and 33.

[2] Bk. III, ch. 9.

[3] See also Bk. III, ch. 8.

[4] Published by Kurt Schroeder, Bonn., 1927.

[5] Fg. 1.

[6] Bk. VII, ch. 1.

thenes said refers only to crown lands, then there is agreement between the *Indika* and the *Kauṭalīya.*[1]

(*h*) Under the head, army, we shall simply quote the conclusion of O. Stein. What Kauṭalya says agrees with Megasthenes that the king was staying in the Head-quarters, but at which time and on what occasion it cannot be said. That the king was directly taking part in the wars is admitted only in a restricted way. He went to the war but he did not take the personal leadership in the army, but it was entrusted to qualified men. His relation to the army was that of the highest War-master. He inspected the four divisions of the army, and a portion of the army served as his body-guard.[2]

(*i*) In four different places of the *Indika*[3] there are statements which definitely mention that the Indians do not know slavery. It has been pointed out how Megasthenes was wrong if servants were also slaves. Kauṭalya mentions a number of slaves with the prescription that an Ārya slave could regain his liberty by a compensation price.[4] There were both male and female slaves. In this particular Megasthenes' report is decidedly incorrect and if such portions of the report are not correct, one is tempted to ask, what amount of credit can be given to the other portions of the same report? During his brief sojourn, Megasthenes apparently took some notes at random and that in an indiscriminate manner. Therefore it is not right on our part to use such doubtful materials as authorities and build theories

1 *Meg. und Kauṭ.*, pp. 95-100; cp. *Glories of Magadha.* p. 60.

2 *Meg. und Kauṭ.*, pp. 106-7.

3 Fg. 1, 26, 27, 41.

4 Bk. II, ch. 13; Bk. II, ch. 27.

upon them unless they are corroborated by other evidences.[1]

(*j*) In Fg. 2 Megasthenes refers to the king of Indians, Sandrakottas.[2] Says S. Levi: "The identity recognised by William Jones of the Indian Chandragupta and the Sandrakottas of the historians of Alexander remains the cornerstone of all Indian chronology."[3] The contention of Otto Stein is that Kauṭalya does not mention either King Chandragupta or the name of his dynasty in his work. No doubt the name Candragupta does not occur. But it should be noted as a matter of profound significance that the term Narendra has been used and according to scholars Narendra is only a synonym for Candragupta.[4] There is again an indirect reference to the Maurya dynasty in the last verse.[5] Here it is said that the Nanda dynasty had been uprooted and the new dynasty has become *fait accompli.* Taking into consideration these two unmistakable references, though still indirect they are, we must credit the work with the worth which it deserves. The sum and substance of these different verses shows the hand of the minister of Candragupta and it will be a spurious argument to advance these views in deciding the authenticity of this all important treatise on ancient Indian Polity.

How is it, then, it has been asked, that Megasthenes has failed to mention such a far-famed minister

[1] *Meg. und Kauṭ.*, p. 115; cf. Jolly's Intr., pp. 38-9.

[2] Cp. Arrian V.

[3] *Journal of Dept. of Letters,* Cal. IX, p. 12. Cp. Rapson, *Ancient India,* pp. 20-21 (1916).

[4] Bk. II, ch. 10. See above pp. 86 and 303.

[5] Bk. XV, ch. 1. Cp. Keith, *Sans. Lit.,* p. 459.

Cāṇakya as tradition makes him out to be? The following reasons among others may be adduced in reply:—

(*i*) The head of the administration according to the prevalent conception of those times was always the king. The king being considered an all-important factor it would be meaningless and derogatory to glorify the minister however illustrious he might have been, and this, by a foreign minister to the court, would be out of place. (*ii*) There might have been an occasion when his name could have been mentioned. To testify to this we are not in possession of the complete *Indika*. To judge from the extant fragments it will be illogical and unreasonable. After all the name of the king is mentioned only once though other statements have been repeated oftentimes. (*iii*) Or it may be that the minister had gone out of office when Megasthenes visited the Court. For he came to India 20 years after the accession of the king. That Megasthenes had been to India several times before this has not been conclusively proved. And again granting that Cāṇakya was still in power when Megasthenes came, his name had become so much a commonplace one that Megasthenes did not think it worth his while to mention him. (*iv*) Or as has been surmised Kauṭalya was not living at the time of the visit. Thus probabilities can be answered by other possibilities also. Lastly, (*v*) as Keith suggests this argument cannot be stressed owing to our fragmentary knowledge of Megasthenes.[1]

In a long chapter (III) Otto Stein considers the question of castes and professions comparing Megasthe-

[1] *History of Sans. Literature*, p. 459.

nes and the *Kauṭalīya* and trying to find out marked differences which amount indeed to little. Megasthenes writes[1]: "The whole population of India is divided into seven castes of which the first is formed by the collective body of philosophers which in point of number is inferior to the other classes but in point of dignity pre-eminent over all. . . . . The second caste consists of husbandmen who appear to be far more numerous than the others . . . The third caste consists of the neatherds and shepherds and in general of all herdsmen who neither settle in towns nor in villages but live in tents. . . . The fourth caste consists of the artizans. . . . The fifth caste is the military. It is well organised and equipped for war, holds the second place in point of numbers, and gives itself up to idleness and amusement in the times of peace. . . . . The sixth caste consists of the councillors and assessors—of those who deliberate on public affairs."

Dr. Stein has examined the Greek terms occurring in different places for caste, and has come to the conclusion that the expression of Megasthenes could not be interpreted as caste.[2] Schwanbeck, however, has attempted to identify these seven divisions as caste divisions: (1) Philosophers, Brahmans; (2) Husbandmen, Vaiśyas; (3) Herdsmen, Niṣādas and other lower castes; (4) Artizans, Vaiśyas and Śūdras; (5) the Military, Kṣatriyas; (6) a mixed caste, overseers; (7) Councillors and assessors, Brahmans. Though this is an explanation in a way it is not very satisfactory. There is some truth in Pischel's remark that Megasthenes has

[1] Fg. 1. 40 and 41.

[2] *Op. cit.*, p. 120-21.

confounded castes and classes.[1] It is more reasonable to assume that Megasthenes has been told of the caste system and the chief regulations underlying the system.[2] He must have also learnt that the principle of division was at best a division of labour, castes being based on professions. As he has divided all the professions into seven kinds he has divided the wholy body of the people into seven classes. Evidently Megasthenes' classification was according to professions and not castes. As the professions were more or less hereditary, especially so at that time, Megasthenes could have easily taken the community of peoples following a certain profession to form a separate caste by itself. From all Greek accounts we gather that the class of philosophers was constituted by Brahmans and Śramanas.[3] The husbandmen were agricultural people who belonged to the Śūdra caste. According to Kauṭalya every village must have not less than 100 families and not more than 500 families of agricultural people of the Śūdra caste.[4] Again that the Śūdra caste was numerically strong is attested to in so many words by Kauṭalya.[5] There is further the prescription of the *Arthaśāstra* that the king shall protect agriculture from devastation of any sort. Such of those undesirables as would cause disturbance to the work of the villagers who are wedded to their fields were subject to severe punishment.[6] This is all in keeping with Megasthenes' account.[7] About

1 See p. 51 of B. Breoler, *K. Studien*, 1.
2 See Fg. 1, 41, especially last sentences.
3 See Strabo XV, p. 711-13.
4 Bk. II, ch. 1.
5 Bk. IX, ch. 2.
6 Bk. II, ch. 1.
7 Cp. Jolly, *Intro.*, pp. 37-38.

neatherds and shepherds the account of Megasthenes is proven from the *Arthaśāstra* almost throughout.[1] As regards hunters though Megasthenes is in agreement with Kauṭalya a discovery is made, *viz.*, Kauṭalya does not mention wandering hunters, those who live in tents.[2]

Of artisans Megasthenes says: "Of these some are armourers while others make the implements which husbandmen and others find useful in their different callings. This class is not only exempted from paying taxes, but even receives maintenance from the royal exchequer."[3] Evidently state employees are referred to here. According to the *Arthaśāstra* we find the state engaging itself in industries like weaving, in manufactures of arms and armour, where, besides free labourers, artisans were employed and paid for their services. One of the regulations laid down by Kauṭalya is that agricultural people should be supplied with the necessary implements by blacksmiths, carpenters, borers, rope-makers, snake-catchers, and similar workmen.[4] Kauṭalya speaks of both time and piece wages.[5] There is a definite ruling where it is said 'artisans shall be provided with wages and provision in proportion to the amount of work done. The menials were paid a monthly salary of $1\frac{1}{4}$ *paṇa*."[6] Excepting private workmen who undertook some industry after previously obtaining a licence to carry on that industry we do not

[1] Stein, *op. cit.*, p. 134; *Ar. Śās.*, Bk. II, ch. 24 and also ch. 29.

[2] P. 136.

[3] Fg. 1, 41.

[4] Bk. II, ch. 24.

[5] Bk. II, ch. 23.

[6] Bk. II, ch. 24.

come across passages where there is a definite injunction that these artisans in the state employ were taxed. If O. Stein means by his statement[1] that people other than those in the state employ, he is right. But that Megasthenes is not concerned with these but only with those in the state employ is evident from the circumstances in which his statement is made.[2]

The Greek writer has the following on warriors. "They have only military duties to perform. Some make their arms and others supply them with horses and they have still others to attend on them in camp, who take care of their horses, clean their arms, drive their elephants, prepare their chariots and act as their charioteers. As long as they are required to fight they fight and when peace returns they abandon themselves to enjoyment; the pay which they receive from the state being so liberal that they can with ease maintain themselves and others besides".[3] As regards military duties Kauṭalya gives it as the function of the Kṣatriyas.[4] That their pay was liberal is seen from the list contained in the *Arthaśāstra*. The chiefs of the military corporations, the chiefs of the elephants, horses, chariots, and of the infantry, each, got 8,000 *paṇas*. The superintendents of the infantry, cavalry, chariots, and elephants were paid 4,000 *paṇas* respectively. The chariot-driver, the physician of the army, and other non-military officials employed in training horses and other animals got 2,000 *paṇas* each. The pay of the trained soldier was 500 *paṇas*. This means

[1] *Steuern haben die Handwerker zu Zahlen,* p. 147.

[2] See also Bk. IV, ch. 1.

[3] Arrian, XII.

[4] Bk. I, ch. 3; cp. Bk. IX, ch. 2.

that the pay of a trained soldier exceeded four times that of an artisan. The arsenal department and the departments under the superintendents of horses and of elephants bear testimony to the fact that the state employed a large number of people to minister to the wants of the soldiers. All the necessary arms and armour, animals, and servants were supplied to the soldiers whenever they went out on a campaign. They were not allowed to have any arms without licence. The state regulated their keeping of arms and armour.

That the military men gave themselves up to idleness and amusement in times of peace is no exaggeration either of Arrian or Megasthenes for the matter of that.[1] It is obvious that Megasthenes is referring to the hereditary army which was dependent for its existence on the state. In times of peace the soldiers composing this constituent did not take to any other profession and earn their livelihood. War or no war they had their regular and fixed salary, and in times of peace they could lead a free life and enjoy life in their homes and family.[2] The only call during this period on their time was drill, for, without constant drilling the army might lose its efficiency. This is certainly not the case with the other kinds of armies—such as the hired, the corporation of soldiers, the army of an ally, and the army of wild tribes.[3] These were recruited if necessary, on the eve of certain engagements for the time being. When the work was over they were disbanded. They had perhaps to take to their old pro-

[1] Stein, p. 162.

[2] Bk. IX, ch. 2.

[3] *Ibid.*

fessions and earn their living. Megasthenes was not concerned with them. He knew of the Kṣatriya hereditary force and referred to it.

The Overseers who moved about the country and reported to the king or their immediate superiors must undoubtedly refer to the *Cāras* or intelligence officers to whom several sections are devoted by Kauṭalya.[1] To ensure efficiency the chief feature of ancient administrative practice was to let loose on officials of every department, special commissioners to watch their movements and proceedings. Their function was to see that the officials of the state did not lend themselves to temptations of any sort including corruption, miscarriage of justice, and disloyalty to the state. If the *Cāras* heard reliable information about a certain official abusing his power and position, then a report was made in secret. The Government took action not at once but only after it was confirmed by three independent sources.[2] Apparently members of this intelligence department must have been influential and powerful so as to attract the notice of a foreign ambassador. When he learnt about their status in the administration he referred to them by mistake as a caste engaged for that purpose. In fact members of all castes including the Niṣādhas (hunters) were appointed to this purpose and Megasthenes had misunderstood the true conditions in India. This is again another instance why we should not attach great value to these Greek accounts.

Again the councillors and the assessors are "those who deliberate on public affairs. It is the

[1] Bk. I, ch. 10-12.

[2] Bk. I, ch. 12.

smallest class looked at from their number but the most respected, on account of the high character and wisdom of its members; for, from their ranks the advisers of the king are taken, and the treasurers of the state and the arbiters who settle disputes. The generals of the army also, and the chief magistrates, usually belong to this class."[1] Megasthenes is again committing a mistake by confounding professions with classes. Evidently he refers to the different kinds of councillors and ministers who guided the ship of the state. The qualifications expected of these ministerial officers were more than what Megasthenes could say. "Native, born of high family, influential, well trained in arts, possessed of foresight, wise, of strong memory, bold, eloquent, skilful, intelligent, possessed of enthusiasm, dignity and endurance, pure in character, affable, firm in loyal devotion, endowed with excellent conduct, strength, health and bravery, free from procrastination and fickle-mindedness, affectionate and free from such qualities as excite hatred and enmity—these are the qualifications of a ministerial officer (*amātya sampat*)."[2] When such officers are put to the test and not found wanting, they were appointed as judges of civil and criminal courts, revenue collectors, chamberlains, prime ministers, in fact, as the head of every department in the state.[3] As regards the minister Kauṭalya recommends three or four for deliberative purposes but he holds that the number will depend on the circumstances of the case in question.[4] Thus Megasthenes is right in every detail except that he

[1] See also Arrian, XII.
[2] Bk. I, 9. Trans., p. 15.
[3] Bk. I, ch. 10.
[4] Bk. I, ch. 15.

entitles the system as a class or a caste. Otto Stein raises a question here[1] why Megasthenes has not mentioned officials in the country parts and surmises, perhaps rightly, that he had little or no knowledge of the conditions of the flat land and his osbervations were merely confined to the capital city of Pāṭaliputra.

In his endeavour to establish a thesis Dr. Stein has not left a stone unturned. The following minor differences are stated:—(*a*) Megasthenes says, "there are usages observed by the Indians which contribute to prevent the occurrence of famine among them."[2] The *Arthaśāstra* on the other hand gives details as to what one should do when famine occurred.[3] In the absence of details and from a general statement we cannot draw any inference. Perhaps Megasthenes might have meant 'to prevent the spread' instead of 'prevent the occurrence'. If we simply substitute 'spread' for 'occurrence' there is every agreement with Kauṭalya. (*b*) "The simplicity of their laws and their contracts is proved by the fact that they seldom go to law. They have no suits about pledges or deposits nor do they require either seals or witnesses but make their deposits and confide in each other."[4] From the *Arthaśāstra* we gather distinctly different conditions. The law has become territorial and even complex in character. Many a contract is mentioned with elaborate rules guiding every one of them.[5] Both courts, civil and criminal, are mentioned as well as the cases which come

[1] *Meg. und Kauṭ.*, p. 196.

[2] Fg. 1, 36.

[3] Stein, p. 204; *Ar. Śās.*, Bk. IV, ch. 3.

[4] Fg. 27; Strabo XV, p. 709-10.

[5] Bk. III, ch. 10, 11 and 13.

under the cognisance of such courts. Regulations about pledges and deposits and seals are elaborately laid down in chapters xi and xii of Book III. Witnesses, their payment, eligibility, and punishments, are also given in instructive detail.[1] One has to concede that this disagreement is distinct and clear. The one explanation that can be offered is that "in his anxiety to idealise the facts he has overdrawn the picture to such an absurd length that we could give no credit possibly to his other statement also."[2] Equally significant is the statement that while false witnesses suffered mutilation Kauṭalya has recommended only fines.[3] (*c*) Arrian writes: "The custom of the country prohibits intermarriage between the castes, for instance, the husbandman cannot take a wife from the artisan caste, nor the artisan a wife from the husbandman caste. Custom also prohibits any one from exercising two trades or from changing from one caste to another. One cannot, for instance, become a husbandman if he is a herdsman or become a herdsman if he is an artisan. It is permitted that the sophist only can be from any caste: for the life of the sophist is not an easy one, but the hardest of all."[4]

This was then the prevailing practice of social polity known in Indian literature as the *varṇāśrama dharma*. According to the regulations of caste a member of one caste cannot enter into marital relations with the members of other castes. It is also stated that members of the different communities were to follow their

[1] Bk. III, ch. 1 and 9.

[2] Stein, p. 205.

[3] Bk. III, ch. 11; cp. *Intro.*, p. 40, Jolly ed.

[4] XII.

own hereditary duties which are, in other words, the *svadharma* of the *Arthaśāstras* and the *Dharmaśāstras.* The *Arthaśāstra* clearly recognises the system of castes and orders and enforces strictly disciplinary rules for any departure from the ordained path. It was the caste that determined the profession. The son of the husbandman continued to be a husbandman and the son of the artisan continued to be an artisan. This is the *svadharma* or engaging oneself in his own *dharma,* without in any way interfering with the functions of others, thus ensuring continuity of employment and efficiency of labour. However much it has degenerated in recent times, the system avoided unhealthy competition in the earlier ages and was a safe insurance against unemployment. The Greek account simply elaborates the *svadharma* and *varṇadharma* of the Hindus. As for the last statement regarding the sophists there seems to be some confusion of ideas. Either it refers to the members of the Brahmana community who were legally allowed to marry woman members of the other three castes, or it refers to the system of asceticism which was embraced practically by all members of the four castes though restrictions were placed for its being adopted at will.[1]

(*d*) Megasthenes speaks of cities and countries where sovereignty was dissolved and democratic governments were set up.[2] Dr. Stein calls our attention to some more passages and has tried to show that these might refer to the forest tribes outside the pale of the state having their own organisations

[1] *Meg. und Kaut.*, p. 221-4.
[2] Fg. I, 32, 38, 50.

and leaders.[1] But it may also be held .to denote the republican states which, as is evident from the *Arthaśāstra,* continued to flourish side by side with the monarchical state. Kauṭalya deals with these institutions which are styled as the *saṅghasandhi,* the policy to be adopted by the king towards them.[2] Some of these democratic states mentioned in the extant work are the Lichchivikas, the Vrijikas, the Mallakas, the Madrakas, the Kukuras, the Kurus, the Pāñcalas and others. These, K. P. Jayaswal calls, king-consul republics, while the Kambojas, Surāṣṭras and others are styled as nation-in-arms republics.[3] This, then, is what the Greek accounts mean. Historians of Alexander's invasion to India refer to a number of free and autonomous states which, after Alexander's invasion and Candragupta's accession to the throne, were either merged in the imperial government or continued to maintain their prestige and power independently of the imperial rule. Kauṭalya has got a great regard for such constitutions as is evident from the following verse:—

kulasya vā bhavēt rājyam
kulasaṅgho hi durjayaḥ|

In speaking of the functions of the overseers Megasthenes definitely states that these overseers must report to the king, or if there is no king, to the magistrates. Thus the idea is clear that Megasthenes has found two forms of government prevailing at the same time—monarchical and republican.[4] That these references

[1] P. 232.

[2] Bk. XI, ch. 1.

[3] See the interesting chapter on the subject by Jayaswal, *Hindu Polity,* Pt. I, Ch. VII.

[4] Fg. I, 50.

are to forest tribes outside the pale of the state is a statement far-fetched and inconclusive in the face of such significant statements.

(*c*) With regard to the administration of public affairs,[1] Megasthenes says:—"Of the great officers of state some have charge of the market, others of the city, others of the soldiers. Some superintend the rivers, measure the land as is done in Egypt and inspect the sluices by which water is let out from the main canals into their branches so that every one may have an equal supply of it. The same persons have charge also of the huntsmen and are entrusted with the power of rewarding or punishing them according to their deserts. They collect the taxes and superintend the occupations connected with the land as those of the woodcutters, the carpenters, the blacksmiths, and the murers. They construct roads, and at every ten stadia set up a pillar to show the by-roads and distances." Let us now proceed to draw parallels for each of the above statements from the *Arthaśāstra.* The latter mentions superintendents of horses, elephants, chariots and infantry, besides the commander-in-chief. There is also the city superintendent. There are again superintendents of commerce, of forest produce, weights and measures, and tolls, etc., who are directly or indirectly connected with the market. There are other officials like lohādhyakṣa, lakṣaṇādhyakṣa, ākarādhyakṣa, or khanyādhyakṣa. What we can call the economic functions of the state are cryptly expressed by Kauṭalya. "He (the king) shall carry on mining operations and manufactures, exploit timber and elephant forests, offer facilities for

[1] Fg. 34.

cattle-breeding and commerce, construct roads for traffic both by land and water, and set up market-towns."[1]

It is further said that the king shall also construct reservoirs (*setu*) filled with water either perennial or drawn from some other source. Or he may provide with sites, roads, timber and other necessary things to those who construct reservoirs of their own accord.[2] *Setu* is translated 'reservoir' but it is a waterway by which water is regulated. Again the superintendent of rivers is the *nadīpāla* of Kauṭalya.[3] The question whether measurement of lands in general was in vogue is easily answered by a reference to the chapter entitled 'measurement of space and time'.[4] Here the following statements occur: 'One *hasta* used in measuring pasture lands and timber forests, one *kiṣku* used in measuring the camping grounds as well as forests and palaces, one *gārhaspatya dhanus* for measuring roads and fort walls, one *daṇḍa* for measuring *brahmadeya* lands.' Certainly officials must have been there to measure these various lands and places. It should be noted as a significant fact that Kauṭalya uses the terms '*rajjus*' and '*corarajjus*' translated as 'ropes' and 'ropes to bind thieves.'[5] But the translator has remarked in the footnote: "The precise meaning of the word is not known. The *Jātakas* or the Buddhist literature contain similar expressions, *rajjuka* or *rajjugrāhaka*, as the Aśokan inscriptions *lajuka* or *rajuka*."[6]

[1] Bk. II, ch. 16.

[2] Bk. II, ch. 1. Trans., p. 50.

[3] Bk. II, ch. 6.

[4] Bk. II, ch. 20.

[5] Bk. II, ch. 6, *see* above p. 216.

[6] Bühler, *Z.D.M.G.* (1893), pp. 466-71.

These denote the officials who were engaged in the measurement of the land. The *Arthaśāstra* which is a composition after the *Jātakas,* which according to Bühler, must be placed in the fifth and sixth centuries B.C., and which is pre-Aśokan, contains similar expressions, and these terms therefore must refer to the same officials engaged in measuring the land. This is further attested to by another fact of great importance. The term *'rajju'* is a measurement of space according to the *Kauṭalīya.* The table is as follows:—

10 daṇḍas = 1 rajju.
2 rajjus = 1 paridesa (sq. measure).
3 rajjus = 1 nivartana (a measurement for measuring square).[1]

We have there the expression definitely used by the author in the technical sense of the measurement of space. Hence the term *'rajjus'* must mean those officials engaged in the survey of lands by means of the *rajju* measurements. Some of these points have been raised by Otto Stein but his interpretation could not carry him further.[2] As regards the supervisor of hunters, of woodcutters, etc., it is reasonable to presume that the superintendent of pasture meadows (*vivītādhyakṣa*) was in charge.[3] Again he was the superintendent of passports.[4] With the help of hunters he was to secure safety to country-parts and protect timber and elephant forests, keep roads in good repair and assist the mercantile people. In addition to these functions they were expected to

[1] Bk. II, ch. 20.

[2] P. 236.

[3] See Mookerjee, *Intro.*, p. xxxvii.

[4] Bk. II. ch. 34.

levy taxes and collect them on behalf of the state. Or there might have been separate revenue officials under the direction and control of the *samāhartā* and Megasthenes has not been fully informed of the duties of each and every official complicated as the machinery was.[1]

(*f*) With regard to the officials of the city,[2] says Megasthenes:—"Those who have charge of the city are divided into six bodies of five each. The members of the first look after everything relating to the industrial arts. Those of the second attend to the entertainment of foreigners. To those they assign lodgings and they keep watch over their modes of life by means of those persons whom they give to them for assistants. They escort them on the way when they leave the country or in the event of their dying, forward their property to their relatives. They take care of them when they are sick and if they die, bury them."[3]

The *Arthaśāstra* does not mention anything of administration by committees though it is reasonable to suppose that such institutions existed.[4] Parallel passages have been traced and examined already in connection with the administration of the city.[5]

(*g*) On military officials Megasthenes writes:"Next to the city magistrates there is a third governing body which directs military affairs. This also consists of six divisions with five members each. One division is appointed to co-operate with the admiral of the fleet,

1See also Stein, p. 242.
2 See Keith, *Sans. Lit.*, p. 460.
3 Fg. 34; Diodor, II.
4 Smith, p. 127; *Ind. Ant.*, 1905, p. 200.
5 See above p. 228.

another with the superintendent of the bullock trains which are used for transporting engines of war, food for the soldiers, provender for the cattle, and other military requisites. They supply servants who beat the drum, and others who carry gongs, grooms also for the horses, and mechanists and their assistants. To the sound of the gong they send out foragers to bring in grass and by a system of rewards and punishments ensure the work being done with despatch and safety."[1] In the *Arthaśāstra* again there is no mention of a kollegium to carry on military affairs. Either it was the imagination of Megasthenes or more probably something like it was in practice. It is to be admitted that there is no express mention of a commander of fleet but it is reasonable to presume that the *nāvādhyakṣa* was the officer-in-charge of fleet as well as other vessels devoted to commercial and other uses. Among the ships mentioned, men-of-war also figure,—vessels bound for the enemies' country. Evidently it signifies the existence of a navy. The fact that Kauṭalya does not give details of the navy shows that land-engagements were more common than sea-fights which were perhaps few and far between.[2]

The commissariat as such there is again no definite mention. But the work of the commissariat is definitely mentioned when Kauṭalya says that the work of free labourers consists in the examination of camps, roads, bridges, wells and rivers; carrying the machines, weapons, armours, instruments, and provisions; carrying away the men that are knocked down along with

[1] Fg. 34.

[2] Bk. II ch. 28. Cf. Jolly, *Intro.*, p. 37.

their weapons and armours.[1] Hunters reconnoitred forests and when the enemy was in sight they hid themselves under trees or mountains and blew their conch shells and beat their drums.[2] The *praśāsta* may perhaps answer to the superintendent of bullock trains of Megasthenes. With his followers including carpenters and free labourers he marched in front of the army clearing the road and digging wells for water. In the camp were the king, the priest, the hunters with hounds and with trumpets, the spies and the sentinels, changing their watches in turn.[3] The army marched through places where grass, fuel, and water were available. In some places the army was made to carry foodstuffs. In the centre were the women of the harem.[4] Thus Megasthenes' statements agree in the main with those of the *Arthaśāstra*.

Megasthenes continues: "The third division has charge of the foot-soldiers, the fourth of the horses, the fifth of the war-chariots, and the sixth of the elephants. There are royal stables for the horses and elephants and also a royal magazine for the arms, because the soldier has to return his arms to the magazine and his horse and elephants to the stables. They use the elephants without bridles. That chariots are drawn on the march by oxen but the horses are led along by a halter, that their legs may not be galled and inflamed nor their spirits damped by drawing chariots."[5]

Corresponding to these are the chiefs of elephants, horses, chariots, and of infantry as well as the superin-

[1] Bk. X, ch. 4; see also above p. 189.
[2] Bk. II, ch. 34.
[3] Bk. X, ch. 1.
[4] Bk. X, ch. 2.
[5] Fg. 34.

tendents of infantry, of cavalry, of chariots, and of elephants.[1] The chariot-driver, the trainer of horses, and those who train other animals are also mentioned among the government servants.[2] In exact parallel to Megasthenes' statements are mentioned in the *Arthaśāstra* the stables of horses and of elephants with fuller details.[3] There is also the mention of a separate arsenal department where arms and armour were manufactured, and from where soldiers were supplied with arms on the eve of an impending expedition. Thus there is coincidence of institutions of vital importance. Whether elephants had bridles, or horses were led by a halter are insignificant details which are not worth comparison. It is no argument of Prof. Jolly to say that this correspondence possesses no chronological value as these practices were prevalent at all times in India.[4] We are not aware of texts more ancient than the *Arthaśāstra* which contain any details of regulations of stables for different animals, their architecture, foodstuffs, medicine for the animals, etc.

(*h*) The subject of the last chapter[5] of Otto Stein's thesis is religion and philosophy. According to Megasthenes philosophers who live on the mountains are worshippers of Dionysos.[6] He distinguishes two kinds among them: (1) Brachmanes who are best esteemed

[1] Bk. II, ch. 33.

[2] Bk. V, ch. 3.

[3] Bk. II, ch. 30-31.

[4] Intro., p. 38.

[5] Ch. VIII, p. 277.

[6] Fg. 41 (58).

for consistency in their opinions, and (2) Sarmanes most of whom were physicians, diviners, and sorcerers.[1] Arrian speaks of sophists who held the supreme place of dignity and honour by performing sacrifices to gods on behalf of the state. They are sages, some of whom go about naked, living upon roots and fruits.[2] The word *sarmanes* is one of some significance. Schwanbeck has shown with ability that the word *sarmanes* corresponds to the Sanskrit *śramaṇa* which means an ascetic.[3] H. H. Wilson in his gloss opined that the term might refer to the Buddhists. But Lassen is perhaps nearer the truth when he takes the term to be Brahman ascetics.[4] Elphinstone is also of the same opinion and remarks that "the habits of the physicians seem to correspond with those of Brahmans of the fourth stage". As we have already said it is indeed remarkable that the religion of the Buddha was not expressly noticed by the Greek authorities though it has existed long before Alexander.[5] It has been shown elsewhere[6] that there is nothing remarkable about this because the early history of Buddhism in India was quite different from its later history. The actual teachings of the Buddha did not tend to revolutionise ideas, social or religious as some scholars would have us believe. In one place we have some philosophers following the precepts of 'Boutta' identified with the Buddha.[7] Some take *Śramaṇas* from this to be Jains. Whatever view

[1] Fg. 59, 60.

[2] XI.

[3] Stein, p. 289.

[4] *Ind. Alt.*, II, 70 (2nd Ed.).

[5] See above p. 269.

[6] See *J.B.H.S.*, Vol. II, p. 1.

[7] Fg. 43.

may be taken, weighty arguments are adduced in favour of the theory that older forms of Hinduism flourished when Alexander or Megasthenes visited India.[1] This fits in with that in the *Arthaśāstra* where again there is no notice of the Buddhists but where on the other hand an elevated place is given to the Vedas and the *Dharmaśāstras* as well as the *śrotriya* Brahmanas.[2] Brahmanical rituals and sacrifices are mentioned elaborately and the king is said to take part in them. Festivals and festivities are mentioned as taking place at the commencement of the rainy season. Among the *śrotriyas* were sages and ascetics of different kinds. Some were shaven while others had matted hair. There were some who observed vows of silence and hence were called *munis*. Otto Stein is probably right when he says that the statement of silence alluded to as a punishment for those who professed to predict the future by Megasthenes is a misunderstanding or a misinterpretation.[3]

A point is again raised how it was that Megasthenes had not stated the three kinds of priests, ṛtvik, ācārya, and purohita of whom the last holds a high position even in political administration. We agree with Prof. Stein who remarks that according to Megasthenes the king was more in the camp than in the palace and the purohita was also in the camp.[4] To conclude, Megasthenes' picture of the religious life of the period is insufficient, inaccurate, and far from being trustworthy.

[1] See Colebrooke, *Essays*, Vol. II, p. 179 ff.

[2] Bk. II, ch. 1 and 12.

[3] *op. cit.* P. 285.

[4] P. 290.

Bereft of mythological, geographical, and legendary details, the useful portion of Megasthenes' report is very meagre and its authority cannot be taken as absolute.[1] Considered calmly and impartially Dr. Stein must himself admit that the differences between Kauṭalya and Megasthenes are not fundamental but are only noticed in minor and trifling details which might well escape an enlightened author on Ancient Indian Polity as too insignificant to mention.[2] So far as the important institutions which functioned as organs of the administration of land went, there is plenty of evidence in point of agreement which cannot be, by any stretch of imagination, discarded. In our opinion to build a theory on such a doubtful authority like the *Indika* of Megasthenes or the Greek accounts for the matter of of that, is not worth the while. Further there are so many remarkable coincidences while there are not very many appreciable differences. It is hardly necessary to compare the much misunderstood report coloured by fables and myths with a work containing solid facts attested to uniformly by tradition.[3]

---

[1] *Meg. und Kauṭ.*, p. 297.

[2] *Contra,* see Keith, *Sans. Lit.*, p. 460.

[3] See also *Kauṭalīya Studien,* I, p. 47.

BOOKS CONSULTED

1. Original Sources

Atharvaveda Saṁhitā (H.O.S.).

Aitareya Brāhmaṇa. (Bibliotheca Indika, Sanskrit Series No. 1, Asiatic Society of Bengal.) Translated by M. Haug and also by A. B. Keith, in H. O. Series.

Agni Purāṇa. Translated by M. N. Dutt.

Abhidhānacintāmaṇi of Hemacandra.

Amara Kośa. (Trivandrum Sanskrit Series.)

Āpastamba Dharma Sūtra. (Bombay Sanskrit Series, S. B. E., Vol. II.)

Alberuni India by Sachau. (Trūbner Or. Series.)

Ancient India. (Megasthenes and Arrian.) Translated by McCrindle.

Ancient India as described in Classical Literature. Translated by McCrindle.

Ancient India as described by Ktesias and Knidian. Translated by McCrindle.

Ancient India—its invasion by Alexander. Translated by McCrindle.

Āryasūra *Jātakamāla.*

Āryasūra *Laṅkāvatārasūtra.*

Ancient India. Rapson.

Ayarāṅga sutta. Edited by Jacobi. (P.T.S.)

Anguttara Nikāya. (P.T.S.).

Ahanānūru. (Tamil Classic.)

Bāna, *Kādambari.* (Bombay.)

Bhāsa—*Pratijñayaugandharāyaṇa.* (Trivandrum Series.)

Bodhāyana Dharma Sūtra. (Mysore Oriental Series.)

Bharatanāṭya Śāstra. (Kāvyamālā Series.)

Bhagavadgītā. (Vani Vilas Edition). Translation S.B.E., Vol. XIV.

Bhartṛhari's Vākyapadīya. (Benares San. Series, 1887.)

Bhāgavatapurāṇa. (Kumbakonam Edition.)

Bṛhaddevata. Edited by A. A. Macdonell.

Bṛhadāraṇyaka Upaniṣad. (Ānandāsrama Sanskrit Series, Vol. XV.)

Brahmāṇḍa Purāṇa.

Buddhagoṣa's Samantapadasika.

Buddhist Records of the Western World. Translated by S. Beal.

Corpus Inscriptionum Indicarum, Vol. I. (Aśoka.) Edited by Hultzsch, 1925.

Corpus Inscriptionum Indicarum, Vol. III. Edited by Fleet.

Cāṇakya Rājanītiśāstram. (Calcutta Oriental Series.)

Chāndogya Upaniṣad. (Ānandāsrama Sanskrit Series, XIV.)

Divyāvadāna. Edited by Cowell.

Dīpavaṁśa.

Dhammapada.

Daṇḍi—*Daśakumāracaritram*. (Bombay.)

Epigraphia Indica.

Epigraphia Carnatica.

Epigraphist's Reports. (Madras.)

Gotrapravaranibandha kadamba. (Mysore Oriental Series.)

Harṣacarita of Bāṇa. (Nirṇayasāgar Press.) Translated by E. B. Cowell and F. W. Thomas.

Hemacandra's Pariśiṣṭaparvan (Bib. Indica.)

Itivuttaka. (New York Ed.).

Jātakas. (Vols. I to VI.) Translated by E. B. Cowell.

Jaina Sūtras. Edited by Jacobi. S.B.E. XXII and XLV.

Jīmūtavāhana—*Vyavahāra-mayūka*, (1912).

Kalpasūtra. Edited by Jacobi.

Kāmandaka Nītisāra. (Trivandrum Sanskrit Series.)

Kāmasūtra of Vātsyāyana (Nirṇayasāgar Press).

Kauṭalya Arthaśāstra. (1) Edited by R. Shāma Śāstri (Mysore Sanskrit Series). (2) Dr. Jolly and Schmidt (Punjab Sanskrit Series). (3) T. Gaṇapati Sastri (Trivandrum Sanskrit Series). (4) Translated by R. Shāma Śāstri. (5) Translated into German by J. J. Meyer. (6) Bhaṭṭasvāmin's Commentary J.B.O.R.S.

Kumāralāṭa's Kalpanāmaṇḍitīka. Edited by H. Lūders (Leipzig, 1926), Vol. XI.

Mahābhārata. (Kumbakonam edition.) Translated by P. C. Roy and M. N. Dutt.

Maṇimekalai. (Tamil Classic.) Edited by Pandit V. Śwāminatha Aiyar.

Mudrārākṣasa. (Nirnayasagar Press.)

Mahāvaṁśa. Translated by Wm. Geiger (also, Sacred Books of Ceylon, Vol. I.)

Matsya Purāṇa. (Ānandāsrama Sanskrit Series.)

Mānavadharma Śāstra. (Nirnayasagar Press.) Translation S.B.E., Vol. XXV.

Mṛcchakaṭika. (Bombay Sanskrit Series.)

Nānārthārṇava Saṁkṣepa.

Nītivākyāmṛta of Somadeva. (Kāvyamālā Series, Bombay.)

Pāṇinī Vyākaraṇa.

Liṅgānuśāsanam.

Patañjali, Mahābhāṣya. Edited by Kielhorn.

Puṟanānūru. (Tamil Classic.) Edited by Pandit V. Swāminātha Aiyar.

Pañcatantra. Edited by Hertel and F. Edgerton.

Pratijñayaugandharāyaṇa of Bhāsa. (Trivandrum Sanskrit Series.)

Rāmāyaṇa. (Kumbakonam Edition.)

Raghuvaṁśa of Kālidāsa. (Bombay Sanskrit Series.)

Rājataraṅgini of Kalhana. (Bombay Sanskrit Series.) Translated by M. A. Stein, 2 Vols.

Ṛgveda Saṁhitā. (Edited by Max Müller.) Translated by H. H. Wilson.

Śukranītisāra. (Edited by Oppert) Translated by B. K. Sarkar.
Śilappadikāram. Edited by V. Swāminātha Aiyar.
Śabda Kalpadruma (Calcutta).
Śivatatvaratnākara (Madras).
Śakuntalā of Kālidāsa. (Nirnayasagar Press.)
Tantrākhyāyika. (Har. Or. Series.)
Tāranātha, Geschichte des Buddhismus. Edited by Schiefner (1869).
Upādhyāya nirapekṣa tīka. (Bibl. Ind., New Series No. 511.)
Vinaya Piṭakam S.B.E. Edited by Oldenberg.
Vāyupurāṇam. (Ānandāśrama Sanskrit Series.)
Viṣṇu Purāṇa. Translated by H. H. Wilson.
Yājñavalkya Smṛti. (Nirṇaya Sāgar Press) Bombay.
Do. with Viśvarūpa's commentary (Trivandrum Sanskrit Series.)
Vaijayanti. Edited by Oppert (Madras 1893).
Vājasaneyi Prātiśākhya.
Vedāṅga Jyotiṣa.
Yāska's Nirukta. (Bibl. Indica.)
Watter's Yuan Chwang.

2. Journals, etc.

Archaeological Survey of India, Reports.
Memoirs of Archaeological Survey of India.
Mysore Archaeological Reports.
Hyderabad Archaeological Reports.
Annals of Bhandarkar Research Institute, Poona.
Asiatic Researches, Bengal.
Journal of the Bombay Historical Society.
Journal of the Bihar and Orissa Society, Patna.
Journal of Indian History, Madras.
Journal of the Royal Asiatic Society, London.
Journal of the Royal Asiatic Society, Bengal.
Journal of the American Oriental Society.

Journal of Oriental Research, Madras.

Indian Antiquary, Bombay.

Indian Historical Quarterly, Calcutta.

Zeitschrift der Deutschen Morgenlandischen Gesellschaft.

Zeitschrift Für Indologie und Iranstik.

Vienna Oriental Journal.

Journal of the Czecho-Slovakia Oriental Institute, Prague.

Quarterly Journal of the Mythic Society, Bangalore.

Journal of the Department of Letters, Calcutta.

Modern Review, Calcutta.

3. Modern Works

Aiyangar, K. V. Rangaswamy, *Some Aspects of Ancient Polity* (*Madras University*, 1916).

Aiyangar, S. Krishnaswami, *Beginnings of South Indian History* (1918).

Aiyangar, S. Krishnaswami, *Sources of Vijayanagar History* (1919).

Aiyangar, P. T. Srinivasa, *History of the Tamils.*

Aiyangar, M. Raghava, *Ceran Śeṅguṭṭuvan.*

Banerjea, P.N., *Public Administration in Ancient India.*

Bandopadhyaya, N. C., *Kautilya*, Vol. I.

Bandopadhyaya, N. C., *Development of Hindu Polity and Political Theories* (Cal. 1927).

Bandopadhyaya, N.C., *Economic Life and Progress in Ancient India* (Cal. 1925).

Barnett, L. D., *Antiquities of India.*

Beni Prasad, *State in Ancient India.*

Bevan, E. R., *The House of Seleucus* (1902, London).

Bhandarkar, D. R., *Carmichael Lectures* (1918).

Bhandarkar and Majumdar Śāstri, *Inscriptions of Aśoka* (1920, Cal.).

Breloer, Bernhard, *Kauṭalīya Studien, I and II* (Bonn., 1928).

Bühler, G., *Indische Palaeographie.*

Burnouf, *Lotus De la Bonne Loi*, (Paris, 1925).

Burgess, *Political Science and Constitutional Law,* Vols. 1 and 2.

Cambridge History of India, Vol. I. Edited by E. J. Rapson, 1922.

Cambridge History of India, Vol. III.

Chakladar, *Social Life in Ancient India,* (Cal., 1929).

Childer's *Pāli Dictionary.*

Colebrooke, H. T., *Miscellaneous Essays,* 2 Vols., (1872).

Cunningham, A., *Coins of Ancient India.*

Cunningham, A., *Ancient Geography of India.*

Cunningham, A., *Inscriptions of Aśoka.*

Dey, N. L., *Geographical Dictionary* (Cal. Or. Series).

Dikshitar, V. R. R., *Hindu Administrative Institutions* (Madras University, 1929).

Dikshitar, V. R. R., *Studies in Tamil Literature and History* (London, 1930).

Dutt, Sukumar, *Early Buddhist Monachism.*

Encyclopaedia Britannica, 11th edition.

Farquhar, J. N., *Outlines of the Religions Literature of India* (Oxford).

Fick, R., *Social Organisation in North-East India.* Translated by S. K. Maitra (Calcutta University).

Freeman, *Historical Essays.*

Gaṇapati Śāstri, T., *Bhāsa's Plays* (a criticism).

Gour, Hari Singh, *The Spirit of Buddhism.*

Goshal, U. N., *Hindu Revenue System* (Calcutta University, 1929).

Gilchrist, *Principles of Political Science,* (3rd Ed.).

Hardy, Edmund, *Konig Aśoka* (Mains, 1911).

Havell, E. B., *History of Aryan Rule in India.*

Hildebrandt, A., *Uber das Kauṭalīya Studien.*

Hœrnle, A. F. R. and Stark, *History of India,* 4th edition, 1909.

Hœrnle, A. F. R. *Uvasaga Dasio.*

Jacobi, *Das Rāmāyaṇa Geschichte und inhalt* (Bonn., 1893).

Jayaswal, K. P., *Hindu Polity.*

Joshi, H. C., *Economiques et Politiques dans l'Inde ancienne.*

Keith, A. B., *History of Sanskrit Literature.*

Keith, A. B., *Religion and Philosophy of the Vedas and the Upaniṣads.*

Kern, *Manual of Indian Buddhism.*

Kirfel, Willibald, *Das Purāṇa Pañcalakṣaṇa* (Bonn., 1927).

Lassen, C., *Indische Alterthumskunde,* 4 Vols., revised edition.

Law, Narendranath, (1) *Studies in Ancient Hindu Polity* (Longmans). (2) *Aspects of Ancient Indian Polity.* (3) *Interstate Relations in Ancient India,* (Cal. Or. Ser., 1920). (4) *Studies in Indian History and Culture.*

Law, B. C., *Buddhist Studies,* (Calcutta, 1931).

Losch, Hans, *Die Yājñavalkyasmṛti* (*Harrossowitz: Leipzig,* 1927).

Maine, Sir Henry, *Ancient Law* (George Routledge & Sons, London).

Meyer, J. J., *Uber das Wesen der Altindischen Rechtsschriften* (Leipzig).

Monahan, *Early History of Bengal* (Oxford, 1925).

Mookerjee, R. K., *Aśoka.*

Moraes, G. M., *Kadamba Kula* (Bombay).

Macdonell, A. A., *History of Sanskrit Literature,* (2) *India's Past* (Oxford, 1927).

Maxmüller, *History of Ancient Sanskrit Literature.*

Majumdar, R. C., *Corporate Life in Ancient India.*

Macphail, J. M., *Aśoka.*

Marshall, Sir John, *Mohanjo-dāro and the Indus Civilisation* (1931, London).

Nāg Kālidās, *Les Theories Diplomatiques in Ancien Indien.* Translated by V. R. R. Dikshitar.

Oldenberg, H., *Buddha.*

Pargiter, F. C., *Purāṇa Text of the Dynastics of the Kali Age* (Oxford).

Pargiter, F. C., *Ancient Indian Historical Tradition,* (Oxford).

Pillai, Swāmikannu, *Indian Chronology.*

Pradhan, *Chronology of Ancient India,* (Calcutta).

Proceedings of the Second Oriental Conference, (Calcutta).

Proceedings of the Third Oriental Conference, (Madras).

Proceedings of the Fifth Oriental Conference, (Lahore).

Poussin, Vallee, *L'Inde Aux Temps des Mauryas* (1930).

Pran Nath, *A Study in the Economic Condition of Ancient India.*

Rayachaudri, H. C., *Political History of India,* (Revised Edition, 1932).

Ramavatara Sarma, *Piyadasi Inscriptions, Text and Translation* (Patna).

Rockhill, *Life of the Buddha.*

Rice, Lewis, *Mysore and Coorg from Inscriptions.*

Roy, P. C., *History of Hindu Chemistry.*

Rhys Davids, T. W., *Buddhist India,* (Story of the Nations Series).

Rhys Davids, Mrs., *Buddhism* (Home University Library Series).

Samaddar, *Glories of Magadha.*

Śāstri, Haraprasad, *Magadhan Literature.*

Scott, F. H., *Routes in the Peninsula of India,* (Madras, 1853).

Senart, *Les Inscriptions de Piyadasi,* (1881).

Shah, C. J., *Jainism in North India,* (Longmans, 1932).

Sir Ashutosh, *Memorial Volume,* (Patna).

Smith, V. A., *Early History of India* (4th Edition).
Oxford History of India.
Aśoka. (Rulers of India Series).

Sorensen, *Index to the Mahābhārata.*

Stein Otto, *Megasthenes und Kauṭilya* (1921).

Strong, C. F., *Modern Political Constitutions* (1930, London).

Thomas, *Early Faith of Aśoka.*

Vedic Index, Macdonell and Keith, 2 Vols.

Viśvanātha, S. V., *International Relations in Ancient India.*

Waddell, L. A., (1) *The Discovery of the Exact Site of Aśoka's Classic Capital.* (2) *Report on the Excavations at Pāṭaliputra* (1903 Ed., Calcutta).

Weber, *History of Sanskrit Literature.*

Indische Studien.

Winternitz, M., (1) *Some Problems in Indian Literature.* (2) *History of Indian Literature.*

Woolner, *Asoka Text and Glossary.*

INDEX.

A

N

T

U

V